MASTERING
THE ART of
SUCCESS

Published by CelebrityPress®, Orlando, FL.

CelebrityPress® is a registered trademark.

Printed in the United States of America.

ISBN: 978-0-9983690-4-4
LCCN: 2017937036

This publication is designed to provide accurate and authoritative information with regard to the subject matter covered. It is sold with the understanding that the publisher is not engaged in rendering legal, accounting, or other professional advice. If legal advice or other expert assistance is required, the services of a competent professional should be sought. The opinions expressed by the authors in this book are not endorsed by CelebrityPress® and are the sole responsibility of the author rendering the opinion.

Most CelebrityPress® titles are available at special quantity discounts for bulk purchases for sales promotions, premiums, fundraising, and educational use. Special versions or book excerpts can also be created to fit specific needs.

For more information, please write:
CelebrityPress®
520 N. Orlando Ave, #2
Winter Park, FL 32789
or call 1.877.261.4930

Visit us online at: www.CelebrityPressPublishing.com

MASTERING

THE ART of
SUCCESS

CelebrityPress®
Winter Park, Florida

CONTENTS

CHAPTER 1

MASTERING THE ART OF SUCCESS

BY JACK CANFIELD

It's often been said that success is a team sport. It's not just *what* you know, it's also *who* you know. And while you may be able to create tremendous success on your own, traveling the path of success with others makes the journey more enjoyable. Plus, the added accountability will propel you to success faster (and further) than you originally envisioned.

In my career, success in any undertaking has come down to not just *who I know*—but also *who I have on my team.* Along the way, I've learned a number of success principles that can now help *you* build your own network of influencers, mentors and experts—and develop a support team of people who can help you succeed.

BUILD YOUR PERSONAL NETWORK OF INFLUENCERS AND EXPERTS BY DEVELOPING GENUINE RELATIONSHIPS

One of the most important skills for success in today's world, especially for entrepreneurs and business owners, is networking. Jim Bunch, the creator of the Ultimate Game of Life, once stated, "Your network will determine your net worth." In my life, this has proven to be true. The more time I have spent consciously building and nurturing my network of advisers, colleagues, clients, students and fans, the more successful I have become.

Businesses and careers are built on relationships, and relationships form when people meet and interact with each other over time in an authentic and caring way. As I'm sure you're aware, statistics confirm over and over that people prefer to do business with people they know, respect and trust.

Effective networking, therefore, is all about developing relationships.

Your goal for networking

In developing your own personal network, your job is to seek out people who know what you don't—and who can help you connect where you can't. Initially, your goal shouldn't be to make a sale, but instead to seek advice, connections, recommendations and insights. To the extent that you can provide something in return, do so. But remember that developing genuine relationships that you can call upon at any time—for years into the future, potentially—takes time and consideration. It requires careful thought and a mindfulness for others.

My good friend Ivan Misner, founder of the international networking phenomenon BNI Worldwide, explains that good networking is a combination of three things: visibility, credibility and profitability.

Visibility is you and another individual becoming aware of each other. The individual—who may be a source of information, referrals to people who can help you or even a potential customer—may learn about you through your public relations, social media or advertising efforts—or through someone you both know. Soon, you might become personally acquainted and communicate on a first-name basis. That's visibility.

Credibility means you take the next step and become reliable and worthy of the other person's confidence. You begin to form expectations of each other and those expectations are fulfilled. Credibility increases when appointments are kept, promises are acted upon, facts are verified, and services are rendered. The old saying, *Results speak louder than words*, is true. Credibility also comes from third parties. Will someone they know vouch for you? Are you honest? Is your project or business legitimate? Are you effective? Are you someone who can be counted on in a crunch? If you are, your credibility will grow—as will important and beneficial relationships.

Profitability is what comes from mature relationships (business or personal) that are mutually rewarding and where both people gain something from the connection. This stage may be reached quickly—such as when an urgent need arises—or it may take years. Most likely, it's somewhere in between. Of course, much depends on the quality of your interaction with each other—but most especially on the desire of both parties to move the relationship forward.*

My closest and most productive network

Of course, profiting from relationships isn't limited to making money from a new customer or getting a referral. It may come in the form of a connection to someone who can help you launch a new initiative or otherwise grow your business. It may include access to a mentor or a professional adviser or a contact in another industry who can help you expand your market. It might be the ability to delegate more of your workload, gain substantial free time for your hobby or personal interests—or spend more quality time with your family.

My closest and most productive network has included my business partner Patty Aubery, and my *Success Principles* coauthor Janet Switzer—two women who've not only been close friends and colleagues for 25 years, but who have also developed a robust and influential network from which I've benefitted. By combining their own contact list with people I know, we've generated millions of dollars in business, accumulated a million Facebook fans, and produced millions of customers, clients and students who follow *The Success Principles*. Our combined contact lists are filled with hundreds of key individuals who can help out with advice, direction, a name, an idea, resources, marketing assistance and more. At any time, we can ask each other, *Who do we know who can help with this new initiative?* —confident that we can get our needs and wants addressed within days. That's the real "profitability" of a network.

FORM A MASTERMIND GROUP TO KEEP YOU FOCUSED, ENTHUSIASTIC AND INNOVATIVE

One of the most powerful tools for success ever identified is a process

---

* You can read more of Ivan's strategies at: www.TheSuccessPrinciples.com/resources. Scroll down to Principle 44 and click the link you find there.

called *masterminding*. We all know that two heads are better than one when it comes to solving a problem or creating a result. So, imagine having a permanent group of five to six people who meet regularly for the purpose of problem-solving, brainstorming, networking, encouraging and motivating each other.

Napoleon Hill first wrote about mastermind groups in 1937 in his classic book *Think and Grow Rich*. All the world's richest industrialists—from the early 20th Century to today's modern icons of business—have harnessed the power of the mastermind group. In fact, it's the one concept achievers reference most when they credit any one thing with helping them become successful.

Millions have discovered that a mastermind group can focus special energy on your efforts—in the form of knowledge, new ideas, introductions, a vast array of resources, and, most important, spiritual energy. It's this spiritual aspect that Napoleon Hill wrote about extensively. He said that if we are in tune with the mastermind—that is, God, Source, the universal power, Infinite Intelligence—we have significantly more positive energy available to us, a power that can be focused on our success.

How a mastermind group works

A mastermind group is made up of people who come together on a regular basis—weekly, biweekly, or monthly—to share ideas, thoughts, information, feedback, contacts, and resources. By getting the perspective, knowledge, experience, and resources of others in the group, not only can you greatly expand your own limited view of the world, you can also advance your own goals and projects more quickly.

A mastermind group can be composed of people from your own industry or profession—or people from different walks of life. It can focus on business issues, personal issues or both. But for a mastermind group to be powerfully effective, people must be comfortable enough with each other to tell the truth. Some of the most valuable feedback I have ever received has come from members of my mastermind group confronting me about overcommitting, selling my services too cheaply, focusing on the trivial, not delegating enough, thinking too small, and playing it safe.

If you're not in a mastermind group already, I recommend that you form one (or join one) as soon as possible.*

Mastermind groups nurture new ideas and initiatives

In 2010, Jill Douka of Athens, Greece left my *Breakthrough to Success* training with the commitment to be part of a mastermind group with five other attendees from different countries. When the economic downturn in Greece began affecting her local network, Jill looked forward to meeting with her global mastermind group on Skype and Google Hangouts—spending an hour every other week using words other than *default, unemployment* and *debt.*

Before long, Jill learned through her mastermind group about TED talks and gave her first international speech in Chennai, India. On the plane trip home, an idea took shape in her mind: what if instead of just one TED talk, Jill created positive-focused, interactive events—then made videos of them available on YouTube so people around the world could benefit?

While civil unrest and economic problems in Greece made Jill hesitant to discuss her idea with colleagues in Athens, her mastermind group was enthusiastic. With their constant encouragement and support, Jill held the first one-day workshop in Athens to a jam-packed audience of 500 attendees and 300 livestream participants—all supported by 70 volunteers and 57 corporate sponsors. The feedback was tremendous. The following November, Sergio Sedas—another of my graduates— produced the second such event in Mexico—with more than 4,000 people participating in interactive solution-focused workshops given by presenters from the United States, Mexico, Canada, and Bermuda.

What could a mastermind group do for you?

FIND A MENTOR AND FOLLOW THEIR ADVICE

Another key strategy that successful people use is to constantly seek out experts in their field for advice, direction and information. The truth is

---

* You'll find a complete kit for assembling a mastermind group and conducting meetings at www.TheSuccessPrinciples.com/resources. Scroll down to Principle 46 and click on the link you find there.

there are *countless* people who've triumphed over the specific hardship you're facing—or who have succeeded in your specific area of endeavor. Why not take advantage of all that wisdom and experience by finding a mentor who has already been down the road you want to travel?

All you have to do is ask.

It's easier than you think

While it may seem daunting at first to contact successful people and ask for ongoing advice and assistance, it's easier than you think to enlist the mentorship of those who are far ahead of you in the areas in which you'd like to succeed.

What mentors do more than anything, says famed speaker and bestselling author Les Brown, is help you see possibilities. In other words, mentors help you overcome "possibility blindness" both by acting as a role model for you and by conveying a certain level of expectation as they communicate with you.

When Les started his speaking career in the early 1980s, he sent a cassette tape of his earliest keynote speech to the late Dr. Norman Vincent Peale, the world-renowned speaker and publisher of *Guideposts* magazine. That cassette tape led to a long and fruitful relationship for Les, as Dr. Peale not only took Les under his wing and counseled him on his speaking style, but also quietly opened doors and helped Les get important speaking engagements.

Perhaps like Les, you just need someone to open doors for you. Or perhaps you need a referral to a technical expert who can help you build a new service for your company. Maybe you simply need validation that the path you're pursuing is the right one. A mentor can help you with all of these things, but you need to be prepared to ask for specific advice.

Do your homework

One of the easiest ways to research the names and backgrounds of people who have been successful in your field is to read industry magazines, search the Internet, ask trade association executive directors, attend trade shows and conventions, call fellow entrepreneurs, or approach others who operate in your industry or profession.

Look for mentors who have the kind of well-rounded experience you need to tackle your goal. When you start seeing a pattern of the same few people being recommended, you know you've identified your short list of possible mentors.

The Success Principles coauthor Janet Switzer regularly mentors people on how to grow their small business. When Lisa Miller of CRA Management Group called Janet, she was just about to sign away a large percentage of her revenues to someone she thought would help her develop a new area of her business. Janet showed Lisa how to instantly accomplish the same goal without outside parties and even helped her land new business from existing clients, accelerating Lisa's company growth plan by four months and earning her hundreds of thousands of extra dollars.

To contact possible mentors like Janet and ensure a successful conversation once you do, make a list of specific points you'd like to cover in your first conversation, such as why you'd like them to mentor you and what kind of help you might be looking for. Be brief, but be confident, too.

The truth is that successful people like to share what they have learned with others. It's a human trait to want to pass on wisdom. Not everyone will take the time to mentor you, but many will if asked. You simply need to make a list of the people you would like to have as your mentor and ask them to devote a few minutes a month to you.

Some will say no, but some will say yes. Keep asking people until you get a positive response.

Follow their advice and return the favor

Mentors don't like to have their time wasted. So when you seek out their advice, follow it. Study their methods, ask your questions, make sure you understand the process—then, as much as is humanly possible, follow your mentor's suggestions. Try them on and see how they work for you. You can always adjust and improve upon them as you go along.

Be prepared to give your mentors something in return, too—even if it's something simple such as keeping them updated on industry information or calling with new opportunities that might benefit them. Look for ways to give back to your mentors. Help others, too. What a great reward to any mentor—to eventually have their former protégé out in the world mentoring others!

BUILD A POWERFUL TEAM THAT LETS YOU FOCUS ON YOUR CORE GENIUS

Every high achiever has a powerful team of key staff members, consultants, vendors, and helpers who do the bulk of the work while he or she is free to create new sources of income and new opportunities for success. The world's greatest philanthropists, athletes, entertainers, professionals, and others also have people who manage projects and handle everyday tasks—enabling them to do more for others, hone their craft, practice their sport and so on.

To help you clarify what you should be spending your time on and what you should be delegating to others, I recommend an exercise called *The Total Focus Process*. The goal is to find the top one, two or three activities that best use your core genius, bring you the most money, and produce the greatest level of enjoyment.

1. *Start by listing those activities that occupy your time,* whether they're business-related, personal or volunteer work. List even small tasks like returning phone calls, filing or photocopying.
2. *Choose from this list those one, two or three things* you're particularly brilliant at, your special talents—those unique things very few other people can do as well as you. Also choose from this list the three activities that generate *the most income* for you or your company. Any activities that you are brilliant at and that generate the most income for you or your company are activities you'll want to focus on.
3. *Finally, create a plan for delegating remaining activities to others.* Delegating takes time and training, but over time you can off-load the nonessential tasks on your list until you are doing less of the ones with little payoff—and more of what you're really good at. That is how you create a brilliant career.

Seek out key "staff" members and advisors

If you're a business owner or career professional, start training key people to take over the tasks you identified above. If you're a one-person business, start looking for a dynamic number-two person who could handle your projects, book your sales transactions, and completely take over other tasks while you concentrate on what you do best. If philanthropic pursuits or community projects are your "business," there are volunteers you can "hire" to help you—including college interns, who may work solely for class credit.

And if you are a stay-at-home parent, your most valuable "staff" will be your house cleaner, your babysitter and other people who can help you get away for time by yourself or with your spouse. A part-time helper can do grocery shopping, get your car washed, pick up the kids or pick up the dry cleaning—all for a modest wage. If you're a single parent, these folks are even more important to your successful future.

In addition to business and personal helpers, high achievers typically have a powerful team of *professional* advisors to turn to for support. Today's world is a complicated place. Professional advisors—such as your banker, your lawyers, a high-net-worth certified public accountant, your investment counselor, your doctor, nutritionist, personal trainer, and the leader of your religious organization—can walk you through challenges and opportunities, saving you time, effort and usually money. If you run a business, these advisors are essential.

BUILD A COMMUNITY AND PASS ON YOUR LEGACY

To truly master the art of success, you also need to pursue one more critical activity: building a community of followers who can join you in expanding your work, fulfilling your vision and—most importantly—securing your legacy.

Virtually all great thinkers of our age have managed to pass down their wisdom and life's work once they can no longer be active. Today, that "act of succession" is easier than ever.

The Internet and social media makes it possible

Today, social media has hit the tipping point where we're now seeing millions of followers convert into fellow devotees, passionate advocates, enthusiastic buyers, and committed partners for social change. Building a community of followers for your work or philanthropic pursuit guarantees there will be a network of people to join you in virtually any venture you want to pursue.

The key is to attract followers who will stay engaged with you and your message—then pass on your information to their own friends, colleagues and fans. To reach that goal, you'll want to maintain an ongoing presence on the most popular social media sites including Facebook, LinkedIn and Twitter.

While you can spend time writing your own posts and articles, then master the technology needed to "boost" your social media activity, I recommend you check out Social5Marketing.com, a done-for-you service that provides a team of world-class writers from top publications with smart online marketers to write, post and even run advertising for you on the major social-media platforms. Best of all, your online activity is scheduled, managed, executed and tracked for less than you'd pay your teenager. Whether you use this service (which also writes your blog, does email marketing and helps generate prospective buyers for your business or cause), you'll want to establish a personal brand, build your online presence, and pursue community building as an activity to ultimately support your success.

About Jack

Known as America's #1 Success Coach, Jack Canfield is the CEO of the Canfield Training Group in Santa Barbara, CA, which trains and coaches entrepreneurs, corporate leaders, managers, sales professionals and the general public in how to accelerate the achievement of their personal, professional and financial goals.

Jack Canfield is best known as the coauthor of the #1 New York Times bestselling *Chicken Soup for the Soul®* book series, which has sold more than 500 million books in 47 languages, including 11 New York Times #1 bestsellers. As the CEO of Chicken Soup for the Soul Enterprises he helped grow the Chicken Soup for the Soul® brand into a virtual empire of books, children's books, audios, videos, CDs, classroom materials, a syndicated column and a television show, as well as a vigorous program of licensed products that includes everything from clothing and board games to nutraceuticals and a successful line of Chicken Soup for the Pet Lover's Soul® cat and dog foods.

His other books include *The Success Principles™: How to Get from Where You Are to Where You Want to Be* (recently revised as the 10th Anniversary Edition), *The Success Principles for Teens, The Aladdin Factor, Dare to Win, Heart at Work, The Power of Focus: How to Hit Your Personal, Financial and Business Goals with Absolute Certainty, You've Got to Read This Book, Tapping into Ultimate Success, Jack Canfield's Key to Living the Law of Attraction,* and his recent novel—*The Golden Motorcycle Gang: A Story of Transformation.*

Jack is a dynamic speaker and was recently inducted into the National Speakers Association's Speakers Hall of Fame. He has appeared on more than 1000 radio and television shows including Oprah, Montel, Larry King Live, the Today Show, Fox and Friends, and two hour-long PBS Specials devoted exclusively to his work. Jack is also a featured teacher in 12 movies including *The Secret, The Meta-Secret, The Truth, The Keeper of the Keys, Tapping into the Source,* and *The Tapping Solution.*

Jack has personally helped hundreds of thousands of people on six different continents become multi-millionaires, business leaders, best-selling authors, leading sales professionals, successful entrepreneurs, and world-class athletes while at the same time creating balanced, fulfilling and healthy lives.

His corporate clients have included Virgin Records, SONY Pictures, Daimler-Chrysler, Federal Express, GE, Johnson & Johnson, Merrill Lynch, Campbell's Soup, Re/Max, The Million Dollar Forum, The Million Dollar Roundtable, The Entrepreneur Organization, The Young Presidents Organization, the Executive Committee, and the World Business Council.

He is the founder of the Transformational Leadership Council and a member of Evolutionary Leaders, two groups devoted to helping create a world that works for everyone.

Jack is a graduate of Harvard, earned his M.Ed. from the University of Massachusetts and has received three honorary doctorates in psychology and public service. He is married, has three children, two step-children and a grandson.

For more information, visit:
- www.JackCanfield.com

CHAPTER 2

SHAKING YOUR SNOW GLOBE: THREE NECESSITIES FOR MAKING A SUCCESSFUL CHANGE

BY NICOLE NASON

Fear of change is officially known as metathesiophobia. It is defined as a persistent, irrational fear of a different future. However, most people who say they are "afraid of change" do not mean it clinically; that is, they are not literally terrified of anything other than status quo in their lives.

Instead, people who proclaim themselves "afraid of change" usually mean they are afraid to take a chance and only find failure. It is far easier to never try, than to try and not succeed. One can read a biography of a successful change agent like Thomas Alva Edison and feel amazement at his persistence. Social media is replete with posts of Edison's famous quote, "I have not failed. I've just found 10,000 ways that didn't work." While inspiring, however, the concept of eventual, wait-for-it, one fine day, hang-in-there buddy, success is not comforting enough to people who are contemplating changing their lives. This is especially true when change could impact current and former spouses, children, and friends dramatically. The hesitation lies not in the fear of the change, but rather in the fear that the change will not be successful. So fear of failure overtakes desire for change.

My teenage daughter collects snow globes. Periodically, I make her dust them off and turn them over and back again. Move the snow around, I encourage her, it will change the look and the feel of the souvenirs. The landmarks inside won't move and won't disappear. The snow globes are MEANT to be shaken. They were designed to be changed. I believe this concept applies to people.

Living in Washington, DC and working on Capitol Hill with all of the Members of Congress was a life dream I never thought I would fulfill. My father was a police officer and my mother taught elementary school, so the closest we ever got to politics was showing up to vote every few years. But I pursued it aggressively. I left the Eastern shore of Long Island and deliberately chose a college located right in the Northwest corner Washington, DC. Using connections and friendships made during my four years on campus, I scored an internship with a congresswoman in the U.S. House of Representatives. After three years away for law school, I made a beeline back, working for free every day at a prestigious congressional committee until I passed the Maryland State bar. I was offered a precious attorney's slot on the Committee on the Judiciary and my career was launched.

By the time I was forty, I had worked for several highly-regarded Members of Congress, run the U.S. Customs Service government affairs office, and been confirmed by the U.S. Senate to lead government relations at the Department of Transportation. At the pinnacle of my long-desired career in government, I was again confirmed by the U.S. Senate as the youngest-ever Administrator of the National Highway Traffic Safety Administration. I ran America's road and vehicle safety programs, testified frequently before Congress, and travelled the world giving speeches and negotiating with foreign dignitaries. A primary responsibility was to promote national vehicle safety efforts, and I appeared routinely on local and national news shows. On behalf of the federal government, I signed a landmark agreement with China to combat the dangers posed by defective auto parts. I spoke at the United Nations in Geneva, Switzerland, regarding harmonization of world motor vehicle regulations. I won awards from the government, and was described in a *USA Today* profile as, "an accomplished political strategist who uses good humor and charm."

Then I quit.

I walked away from my hard-earned reputation and distanced myself, both literally and emotionally, from the relationships I had developed over fifteen years. I spent the next five years training in Connecticut in several forms of Japanese martial arts. I turned my snow globe upside down and shook it violently.

My husband had been hired by General Electric, and his new position necessitated a move to Connecticut. I planned on working as a consultant in D.C., and I set up shop as The Nason Group. I filled out the required paperwork and registered myself at the Office of the Clerk at the U.S. Congress. I found my first clients, and set about making a travel plan for regular visits to DC.

In the days leading up to the move, I focused on the critical issues: finding a place to live, registering for children's schools, selecting a pediatrician and other doctors. I also wanted to get my two oldest daughters signed up for town activities. I hoped that, by plunging them into local community programs, I would help them make friends more quickly. On the first month in my new town, I walked into a karate dojo to get the girls registered for class.

The sensei of the program was a Japanese-trained expert who had lived in Hokkaido, Japan, for nearly a decade honing his craft. He was fluent in Japanese, and used only the traditional names for his forms and movements. I quizzed him about his experience, and was so impressed I found myself uttering the words, "teach me."

I had never been interested in martial arts in my life before this moment. I never took a class as a child, and no one in my family practiced or trained in any style. Yet something told me this was an opportunity I might never get back. I have no logical explanation, but I listened to my inner voice say, "try something new." I shut down my nascent business, and threw myself into training.

I took private classes several days a week, and eventually became proficient enough to assist teaching other students. It took four-and-a-half years of one-on-one training, but I finally earned my black belt. I was the only adult in the program to ever start training as an adult, and complete all the way to black belt. Shortly thereafter, I put my Japanese certificate in a frame, and flew to Hokkaido, Japan, with my sensei to meet his "family" and gain some inspiration.

After our trip, we created a program we named Project Koe. Koe is the Japanese word for voice. We focused on empowering women, not exhausting them. The fitness workouts were all built around real Japanese movements, kicks, strikes, and blocks. I developed kickboxing routines, ballet bar exercises, and body bar workouts (modeled after weapons class) with included elements of empowerment. I taught the program in facilities at Fortune 100 corporations, and offered free instruction to all-girls high schools located in NYC. My TedxTalk entitled, "Finding your Inner Kiai," about finding inner power helped me get selected as the morning wellness instructor for TedWomen2016.

People who have successfully changed make it sound easy. Inspiring quotes from world leaders and public figures are everywhere on the Web. In shaking my own snow globe, I have realized three necessities to successful change.

1. The first necessity requires only mental effort, which is in some ways the easiest, yet many people stumble at this first step. The only way to allow for change – big or small – is to focus on the positive outcome exclusively. If you imagine the failure, you'll never start. Yes, the fear is rational, and fear can only be overcome by assuming success. It is repeated everywhere by inspirational speakers, but I know it personally to be truth. You must believe you will succeed, even during the initial mistakes and problems. For example, our original program was called Project Kiai, but we had trouble with our trademark lawyers. We didn't dwell on the disappointment, we simply worked the problem using the highly-stylized logo we had already developed. Project Koe was born out of this roadblock, and it turned out to be a better name and fit for our vision. Your success will not look like exactly what you expected, but it will be there, in bright, bold colors, if you focus only on achieving a positive outcome.

2. The second necessity is to ask for help. Do not wait until you are in trouble to ask for assistance. I didn't know anyone who had a black belt except my sensei, but I knew a hundred people who worked in marketing, business, advertising, and media. I sought everyone's counsel, drank in all of the various commentaries and critiques, and saved the final decisions for the Project Koe team. It seems

counterintuitive, but it only helps to hear contrasting opinions. It will sharpen your own thought processes and guide your decision-making. As an example, we changed our motto after a public relations expert causally made a suggestion over coffee one day. I hand out blank comment cards to my class participants every few months, just in case someone has a suggestion or improvement. Good ideas can come from anyone, so ask everyone who is willing to help with what they think.

3. The third necessity is to formulate a long-term plan. Having a long-term plan helped steer our precious time and resources in the first few months, and it guides us as we strive to expand. We made decisions that seemed boring and uncreative in our first weeks, but we saw our long-term success and worked our way backwards. For example, we filed all necessary paperwork with state and local governments, and hired lawyers to help us review teaching and hiring requirements. While others strongly encouraged us to jump on social media and start filming our movements, we established our vision and developed our logo first. We discussed in detail what we wanted to achieve. After months of interviewing film producers, we created instead our own studio, and saved thousands of dollars by having professional camera equipment and lighting available to us anytime. Upon a recommendation from a friend, I even hired an experienced freelance television producer for assistance. Months later, we used his company to film our first DVD. We continue to take small steps, and follow a long-term plan.

Proof of successful change is everywhere. Martha Stewart was a model, who turned to Wall Street and worked as a stockbroker, and then reimagined herself as a gourmet cook and lifestyle creator. Vera Wang was a figure skater before she became a household name in the fashion industry. Spanx founder Sara Blakely sold door-to-door fax machines before she became a billionaire with her invention of footless pantyhose. Long before she was a comedienne and an original panel member on ABC's *The View*, Joy Behar taught high school English. Tim and Nina Zagat were practicing corporate lawyers when they founded the restaurant review guide, *Zagat*.

The strongest case possible that can be made for shaking your personal snow globe comes from people who have gone back to their original work. You name the field, it will be there when you return. The worlds of finance, business, education, science, travel, etc., etc., including politics, are not going to disappear anytime soon. If the thought of a landing pad comforts you, know that your professional field will not go up in smoke in your absence.

Do you like John Glenn the astronaut or John Glenn the politician? John Glenn himself chose both, and he returned to space in 1988 while still serving as a Senator from Ohio. He became the oldest person ever to fly in space as a crew member aboard the Discovery. Michael Bloomberg returned to his position as CEO of his eponymous company after he spent three consecutive terms as the Mayor of New York City. For me, I am certain that I will return to politics one day soon. I love the field, and I don't believe I need to choose only one passion in my life. When the time feels right, I will shake my snow globe again, and let the flakes fall where they may. I hope you will shake yours as well.

About Nicole

After a successful career as an attorney and senior government official in Washington, DC, Nicole Nason founded Project Koe, a fitness and empowerment program that incorporates elements of traditional Japanese martial arts. She developed Project Koe after taking a five-year hiatus from government to train intensively in karate, aikido, and bo and jo jitsu. Nicole earned a black belt in karate in 2014, and promptly travelled to Hokkaido, Japan, with her sensei, to gain inspiration for the creation of her fitness and empowerment program. She is an ACE-certified group fitness instructor, and often travels to corporate conferences as both a speaker and wellness instructor.

Prior to founding Project Koe, Nicole held two positions in government requiring Senate confirmation, including Administrator of the National Highway Traffic Safety Administration. As the Nation's chief vehicle safety regulator, she frequently testified before Congress and appeared on local and national news programs. As Administrator, Nicole updated the national child seat use ratings system, and initiated the first comprehensive revision of the New Car Assessment Program (5-star safety) in the agency's history.

Her international work included a speech at the United Nations in Geneva, Switzerland, to press for global harmonization of vehicle safety testing, which resulted in the adoption of two UN Global Technical Regulations. She also signed the agency's first-ever bilateral agreement with the Chinese government, to combat the dangers posed by defective auto parts. A *USA Today* profile called her "an accomplished political strategist who uses good humor and charm."

Previously, Nicole served as the Assistant Secretary of Government Affairs at the U.S. Department of Transportation. Prior to her work at the Department of Transportation, she was the Assistant Commissioner of Government Affairs at the U.S. Customs Service. She also worked previously as an attorney for the Committee on the Judiciary in the U.S. House of Representatives.

Nicole graduated from American University in 1992, and received her Law Degree from Case Western Reserve University in 1995. She lives in Connecticut with her husband David and their three children, ages 9-16. She recently completed two new fitness DVD's, "Battle Cry Kickboxing" and "Battle Cry Body Bar." Her TedxTalk, "Finding Your Kiai," can be found on YouTube and at: www.projectkoe.com

CHAPTER 3

FINDING SUCCESS THROUGH THE TOUGH TIMES

BY ROLAND THOMPSON

When I consider my personal road to success, I reflect on the people and events that brought me to where I am and try to visualize how others can benefit from my experiences. My parents divorced when I was 5. I lived with my mom until I was a teenager, then my brothers and I lived with my dad. I graduated high school in 1969, joined the Navy and did three tours in Vietnam. I married at age 21, between my second and third tour. Then I came home in December 1973 and saw my one-month-old son for the first time. After the Navy, I worked full time, went to school full time on the GI Bill, had three more kids with our fifth on the way. In 1981, I had earned two AA degrees and a Bachelor's degree in Accounting and took an awesome management position on the other side of the state – where I moved my pregnant wife and four children. At the age of 29, I was on the road to success.

In June of that year, my fifth child was born. A month later, my oldest son drowned, six months later, my father committed suicide. The following two years, my grandparents passed away, my wife and I divorced – she and our children moved back to the other side of the state – I had to resign from my "awesome job," and my brother-in-law was murdered. Yogurt had really hit the fan in my life.

Soon after these events, I heard a speaker at church tell the "Chinese Farmer" story: In an ancient Chinese farming community, people lived on whatever they could produce for the year. One day a farmer's son left the gate to the corral open, and their only horse ran off into the hills. The neighbors were very sympathetic. They told him it was terrible to have such bad luck: for he could not plow his fields. He replied, "Good Luck. Bad Luck. We'll see." A few days later, his horse came back with four wild horses following it. His shocked neighbors told him what good luck he had: he could sell the horses and be wealthy. His reply, "Good Luck. Bad Luck. We'll see." Then his son broke his leg while training one of the wild horses. The neighbors commented on his bad luck again; he would have to do all the chores alone and care for his son. He simply replied, "Good Luck. Bad Luck. We'll see." A Chinese army came through, conscripting young men who would probably never return. They rejected the farmer's son because he was lame. The neighbors again marveled at his so called "Good Luck." He still wisely refrained, "Good Luck. Bad Luck. We'll see."

Since then, whenever "yogurt hits the fan" in my life, instead of dwelling on the setbacks, I look for the good that will come of it, which it always does. A few of the best things in my life came out of the life events that I was hit with. I met my current wife and found the Financial Planning Industry. I also became closer to my children, because I valued my relationships more after losing so many family members in a short period. I also discovered my life's purpose and try to keep this my daily focus.

AVOIDING THE UNLIVED LIFE

I heard that 50 people age 95 and older, were surveyed on what they would do differently if they could live life over again. I was surprised when I learned the number one response was they wished they had taken more risks in life. They felt they had missed some great opportunities because of fear. I like the acronym I learned from Mark Victor Hansen:

FEAR is Fantasized Experiences Appearing Real.

I try to teach my children a simple concept I learned from Jack Canfield: the answer is always 'No' if you don't "Ask." I knew that my son grasped this concept when in March of 2004 the guest speaker at our annual Chamber of Commerce meeting was the CEO of the Seattle Seahawks. I suggested to the Chamber that it would be nice if someone sang the National Anthem at this meeting. They agreed and I volunteered my son, a high school senior. When the speaker was finished, he asked the audience if they had any questions about the Seahawks' coming season. When I looked over, my son had his hand up. I was nervous about what he was going to ask. He said, "Don't worry, I won't embarrass you."

When he was picked, he stood and asked, "What would it take for me to sing the National Anthem at a Seahawk game?" In a TV interview after the meeting they asked my son why he asked that question. He casually said, "The answer was no if I didn't ask." Nothing will ever touch my feeling as a dad standing on Quest Field at a Bronco-Seahawk game while my son sang the National Anthem in front of over 50,000 people. Many people don't ask because of fear, and miss out on opportunities for success. Ralph Waldo Emerson said, "Do the things you Fear, and the Death of Fear is certain."

The number two response from the survey was: they would "smell the roses" more along the way. After many years as a Financial Planner, I look at life a whole lot differently now. I have helped numerous people plan for their dream retirement – and some never made it due to health or other unforeseen issues. I've concluded that waiting to live our dreams until we retire is not the way to go.

Prior to the Industrial Revolution, people worked until they could not physically or mentally work anymore. In 1935, life expectancy for U.S. males was 58, and a social insurance program was created (Social Security). This fund was available to persons 65 years old and intended to help widows and people through the incapacitated years of life. This "insurance" pools funds from everyone participating in it, to help those that need it. Today, thanks to advances in health care, life expectancy is around 80, yet the "retirement age" has been lowered to 62! Incongruously, by law, I cannot delay "claiming" my benefits beyond age 70, yet I calculate I will have received all that I and my employers have paid into the pool in just four years. Am I the only one that sees a big problem here? My slogan is: "I will run until I can run no more, as long as I can run, I will run."

Today I am blessed with over 30 grandchildren. I try to devote my life to helping these children discover their life's dreams and passion. For me, this is the epitome of success. I may not be able to connect with all of them individually, but I am not going to just "retire" and sit by a pool sipping lemonade until I die, or wondering who all these kids are and why they keep calling me grandpa.

The number three response to the survey was they wished they could leave some sort of legacy. I am writing this as part of my legacy, to inspire others to live life without regrets. I feel that if everyone was focused on leaving a legacy, it would help our country get back on track and make it a better place then we found it. I like to define my "Leaving a Legacy" as "Because I walked this planet, a lot of people's lives are much better because I was here."

This is going to be very unpopular among some of my fellow boomers who view retirement as the "reward" for their "success" in a career of hard work – that they would finally live just for themselves. A "do more than just invest" attitude may sound especially strange coming from a financial advisor. Today I look at our country and see that it is very divided politically, socially, economically, etc. We also have a greater disparity between two generations than ever before. The Boomer Generation has lived most of their lives without the technology we have today by figuring out life's problems without the help of Google.

Millennials have never known life without current technology. I love to share the story with an audience of Millennials of my "old days," a life before today's technological abundance. We did not have television until I was five, we had to walk a couple of hundred feet to an outhouse on the edge of the woods to use the bathroom, and we bathed outdoors in a big tub in water that was hand pumped from a well, then heated in a big pot on the wood stove by my mother. My young audience especially found it humorous when I explained that the stove was not made of wood – which would be dangerous – but burned wood.

Time magazine ran an article titled "Millennials: The Me Me Me Generation." When I offer my opinion to other Baby Boomers that we need to help them find direction before we "check out" of this world, they just say, "We can't help them. They don't listen to us." Rightly so – they don't need us to tell them anything; they have all the information they need at their fingertips. What they lack is our generation's wisdom and experience to use it. This younger generation is getting the short end of the stick. One of my favorite mentors has been Steven Covey the author of *The 7 Habits of Highly Effective People*. His Habit 5 (where

I still need the most work) would really help facilitate communication between Boomers and Millennials. It is: seek first to understand, then to be understood.

When a Boomer commits to making that "final impact" during his last years of life, he could pick a Millennial to invest his time in. Seeking to understand instead of telling, should be their goal. Lecturing, name calling and accusations never help. We need to encourage creativity and not condemn. My intellectual level will never be high enough to justify calling anyone I walk the earth with, "Stupid." I have not lived their life experiences, so how can I judge?

I was a speaker to a group of older gentlemen and asked what they thought of the young people of today and their piercings and tattoos? One man answered, "It's disgusting how they mark up their bodies." I replied, "Do you think those tattoos fell off after you said that?" I challenged them, the next time they see a young person with a tattoo, to acknowledge it. Tell them it is interesting and ask, "What's the story behind it?" Observe how they brighten up, and then actually listen to the story. Most of the time it is a symbol of an event in their lives. Judging instead of listening causes a sad loss of the opportunity for true connection.

I was reflecting on the proverb, "Give a man a fish and you feed him for a day. Teach a man to fish and you feed him for a lifetime." The problem with the disparity between the two generations is that we cannot truly teach them if they don't listen. I feel the solution is to "fish" with *them*. Seek to understand and ask them what their dreams or passions are, then support them in *their* dreams and let them know we have their backs.

I also learned from Steven Covey, if you want to learn something, teach it. If you are a Boomer working with a Millennial this can be very effective. Have them teach you. After all, it's their dream or passion. I used this concept in encouraging my son in his career. He has taught me so much about the music business and has grown to be one of the best in the music world (no bias there). My experience in the Accounting and Financial Planning industry and his not being afraid of taking risks in life and business, have formed a perfect partnership. I cannot explain the fulfillment in life I have in using this method.

Instead of waiting to die in "retirement," maybe we should dedicate the rest of our lives to using the knowledge and wisdom we have earned to positively impact those we will be leaving behind.

We all have one of two mindsets: either a "poverty" mindset or a "prosperity" mindset. A person with a prosperity mindset knows there is "enough" for everyone and is willing to help others achieve. Someone with a poverty mindset fears that there isn't enough for "everyone" so they focus on getting more for themselves. A prosperity mindset is mandatory to being truly successful in life. One practice that helps me keep a prosperity mindset, is to give thanks every morning for everything I have as though when I wake up tomorrow, I will only have those things for which I expressed gratitude today.

I am surprised almost every day how blessed I am! To reinforce this attitude, I like to internalize that there are over seven billion people walking on this planet and not one person has anymore right to walk on it then anyone else. No one is better than me and I am not better than anyone else. Do you like to hang around with negative and complaining people? Are you that person? You have very little control over what other people think, only what and how you think. I have found that a person's self-esteem, attitude and mindset really affects those around them, as well as themselves. I define self-esteem as "how you view other people viewing you." If you spend your days trying to build other's self-esteem, your own self-esteem rises in direct proportion.

Meaningful success cannot be attained without involving others. Giving and receiving coaching, mentoring, and networking are essential. Much is recorded on how one individual inspired the heroes of our country. Teaching these concepts has helped me find success in my life. If I can help just one person achieve their life's dream, all my effort was worth it.

Baby boomers, look around you and see how you are accepted by the millennials you interact with. How are you treating them? Do you constantly criticize them and what they are doing? Incorporating these concepts in your life is a win-win solution to our country's problems. Our country is too divided to fix it "top down", it needs to be fixed "bottom up" – the way it was created 250 years ago. Now go out and share this with others. Remember, if you want to learn something, teach it. You master this, you master success.

About Roland

Roland L. Thompson, CFP® has been called "One of the Nation's top Financial Advisors to Baby Boomers." His book, *Now That I Am Retiring, What Do I Do with My Money?* has helped many people gain basic financial planning knowledge before they pull the trigger and retire. The book is a very easy and a fun read for just about anyone wanting basic knowledge in the financial world.

After graduating from High School in 1969, Roland joined and served four years in the United States Navy with three tours in Vietnam. Roland attended Green River College where he received two Associate of Arts degrees. He earned his Bachelor of Science degree in Accounting from Central Washington University while working fulltime as a Manager for a non-profit organization. He then worked with MetLife over a 17-year period as a Life Insurance Agent, a Branch Manager, a Financial Planner and a General Manager before starting his career as a Fee-Only Financial Advisor with his own firm. Roland received his Chartered Financial Consultant (ChFC®) designation from the American College in Bryn Mawr, Pa. He also received his CFP® (Certified Financial Planner Practitioner) designation from the CFP Board of Standards.

Roland is the past president of his local Estate Planning Council and past president of the local National Association of Insurance and Financial Advisors (NAIFA). He has served as a board member for many associations in his area and has been awarded "Ambassador of the Year" twice from the Regional Chamber of Commerce. Roland was a member of the National Speakers Association and spent a lot of his time doing the thing he really loves, which is Public Speaking. He is a frequent speaker at the local College and loves to lecture on overcoming fear to go after dreams and the art of Networking, using humor and some of his interesting life stories.

Currently, he is president of ALP (Achieving Life's Purpose) Financial Planning Inc. where he works with Baby Boomers in helping them make an impact in their final years. His philosophy is that Financial planning does not need to be complex and confusing, just simple. He also is a partner with his son in the entertainment industry, where they both own SoulFound Entertainment, LLC, which is the parent company of Rainmaker Recording Studios – one of the top recording studios in the Northwest. His biggest treat is going on tour with his son's band, *Night Argent.*

Roland's lifelong passion is to make a positive impact on the nation by connecting the Baby Boomer's wisdom and experience with the Millennial generation.

Roland and his wife, Teri, have 35 grandchildren and 2 great-grandchildren, they also care for 6 medically-fragile foster children at their home in Pasco, Washington.

If you are interested in having Roland speak at your next event, he can be contacted at his office in Kennewick, Washington via phone or email:

- 509-591-0100 office
- Roland@ALPFP.com
- WWW.ALPFP.com

CHAPTER 4

TRUSTING YOUR INTUITION: THE REAL KEY TO SUCCESS

BY TOM STONE

How it began. . .

I was living in a house set back from the road about 100 yards, in the small town of Fairfield, Iowa. Through the oval glass in my front door, I could see who was there. It was dinner-time on December 7, 1993. The doorbell rang. It was someone I didn't recognize. I got up to greet the stranger. As I started to open the door he pulled a .44 caliber handgun out from behind his back.

"Oh God! He's got a gun." I yelled out to my wife. I could see my 9-year-old daughter in her room just a short ways away. I yelled at her to stay in her room as I tried to slam and lock the door. But the stranger stepped over and shot through the oval glass. The bullet hit me in the chest on the right side. I reeled back from the impact. "I'm hit!" I yelled. I tried to get away by stumbling into another room that was close by and I fell to the floor.

Then I yelled to my wife as loud as I could to call the police, thinking that perhaps that might discourage the stranger from coming into the house. I was shocked and terrified. I could hear the tempered glass in the door cracking as it granulated. All the stranger would have had to do was to tap it with his gun and it would have fallen inwards. Then he could reach in and unlock the door and finish me off and kill my family. These were the terrifying thoughts I had as I also yelled to my wife in a somewhat softer voice to also call an ambulance. Waiting in this terrified state, I was gradually relieved to find that he didn't come into the house. He must have felt that he had done whatever it was he wanted to do and turned and walked or ran away.

Fortunately, I had enough presence of mind to put pressure on the bullet hole wound. I found out later that I had kept myself from bleeding to death by doing that. The ambulance finally came and took me to the local hospital in the small town of Fairfield, Iowa, population about 10,000. The hospital wasn't big enough to handle this kind of emergency, so the University of Iowa hospital sent a helicopter to pick me up.

I had a big abdominal surgery because the x-ray showed the bullet lodged behind my 5th lumbar vertebra. It had taken a strange path through my body just missing major nerves and arteries. The bullet was lodged in the 5th lumbar bone right next to my spinal cord in such a way that they couldn't get it out from the top without a lot of risk, so they left it in and sewed me up. I have a big scar from my solar plexus to my pelvis.

The assistant surgeon came by to check on me after a few days of recovery and he said to me, "Tom, you know you are really rather lucky." I said, "What? I just got shot in the chest, what do you mean lucky?" He replied, "Well, if you are going to get shot in the chest at close range with a .44, one in 100,000 people would survive it and 1 in a million would escape with as little damage as you have." He was right!

As the scar tissue was forming around the bullet, it started to create a lot of pain. So, I went back for a second surgery a few months later and they managed to remove the bullet by going in from my low back.

So, although there was plenty of physical healing to do from the two surgeries, the biggest healing that I desperately needed was from the trauma of the whole experience. I was grateful that I hadn't died, but I had all of the typical PTSD symptoms, nightmares, flashbacks, startle response, anxiety... I didn't know that it was called Post Traumatic Stress Disorder, but I certainly had it.

Psychologists' view is that people don't recover from this kind of trauma. They have to learn how to live with it. But I had an intuitive sense that there must be something missing from this picture. So, I decided to follow my intuition and see if I could find some way to really cure my trauma symptoms.

It took a few years to find it, but I was very fortunate to discover an amazingly simple insight that was the key to actually being able to completely cure my PTSD. Unheard of! But I did it. No more nightmares. No more startle response. No more anxiety. All the PTSD symptoms were completely gone!

The simple insight was that when we are little, we all get emotionally overwhelmed many times. Nobody likes it. And everyone rapidly learns to suppress painful emotions like traumas and hurt feelings in an attempt to not have to experience painful emotional overwhelm.

I had another intuition… what if I did the opposite of that. So, I decided to give it a try. I could still easily remember the terror of the event when I thought of it. So, I got up my courage and allowed myself to feel the sensation of the terror, in fact I allowed myself to notice the strongest part of the sensation, right in the middle of it.

The first thing I noticed was that it didn't kill me to do that. Yes, it was intense, but it was possible. The intensity level of the sensation seemed to stay, more or less, the same for a while but after some time it gradually started to become less intense. So, I tried bringing my awareness even closer to the remaining intensity of the feeling. That made it seem stronger again. But eventually it started softening again.

Now I was encouraged. I continued to get closer to it as it continued to soften and eventually it softened so much that I couldn't find it any more. I thought of the event and to my amazement and delight I couldn't sense any terror. I decided I'd wait until the next morning to see if the effect lasted. When I woke up the next day I thought of the event again and didn't feel any terror. I also immediately realized that I hadn't had a single nightmare that night for the first time since the shooting.

Now I knew that I was on to something. So, I started to share this discovery with friends and family, and I rapidly learned that it was highly effective for resolving all kinds of emotional problems. You didn't have to have severe trauma to benefit from it. I started to give seminars and one-on-one sessions helping people resolve all kinds of problems. It was amazingly fast and effective. It evolved into a system that I now call Inner Greatness Optimizing (IGO). I'm currently using IGO to launch a network of Inner Greatness Centers around the world with the first 12 centers just opened in China in 2016.

THE SECRET TO SUCCESS: INTUITION

I didn't realize it at the time but what I had done is what other successful people do more consistently than the general population. They follow their intuition.

I've asked thousands of people at my seminars if they have the experience of having an intuitive idea, and then – NOT following it and later really regretting that they didn't. Everybody says - yes.

Here's what successful people say:

- *Often you have to rely on intuition.* ~ Bill Gates

- *Follow your instincts. That's where true wisdom manifests itself.* ~ Oprah Winfrey

- *The only real valuable thing is intuition.* ~ Albert Einstein

- *I've never been led astray by these intuitive insights and they've helped me guide my actions, create prosperous business and personal relationships, and avoid costly mistakes.* ~ Jack Canfield

- *Have the courage to follow your heart and intuition. They somehow already know what you truly want to become. Everything else is secondary.* ~ Steve Jobs

Although successful people follow their intuition, they don't necessarily know how to show others how to do that. That's because the barriers to following your intuition are deeply conditioned habits that have not been well understood… until now.

Because I did manage to follow my intuition, I discovered new techniques for getting rid of PTSD and emotional pain. This led to the creation of IGO. And IGO can be used to eliminate the real barriers to trusting and acting on your intuition much more consistently. I'm going to show you exactly how to do that.

TWO WAYS TO IMPROVE ACTING ON YOUR INTUITION

I discovered that there are two main ways to greatly improve your ability to follow your heart and intuition and thereby be much more successful:

1. Eliminate the fear that blocks you from trusting your intuition
2. Remove the root causes of clouded thinking and poor decisions

#1 – Getting rid of the Fear of Punishment

I discovered that the fear of punishment is the primary inner barrier to following your intuition. When we are little we do things to explore the world around us. Some of these things might not be acceptable to our parents. For example, if we paint a picture all over our bedroom wall we might think it's great, but our parents may not agree. We might get punished for our innocent acts of intuitive creativity. It doesn't take many punishments before you start to hesitate to act on the next intuitive impulse.

The fear of punishment is an unresolved stress. It's still inside of you. And now when you get an intuitive idea this old unresolved stress gets activated, triggering the fear of punishment. Whether you are aware of the fear or not, it gets in the way of trusting your intuition.

The solution is called the IN Technique. It's what I discovered for curing my PTSD. The IN technique starts with allowing yourself to feel the energy of this fear. The LOCATE Technique on the website will show you how to simply tell the body to show you the energy of that fear. The body will show you a tight knot or ball of energy inside somewhere. You then just notice the strongest area of the energy field of this sensation.

You can use the tinyurl in the bio to access the Inner Guidance App and guide yourself through the LOCATE Technique and the IN Technique to thoroughly resolve the fear of punishment. The app is a series of audio instructions that you access by clicking on a large button on the screen that you can keep clicking even with your eyes closed.

At first, the level of intensity of the energy field may stay the same for a while. But as you just continue to notice it, gradually it will start to soften. When it does, bring your awareness closer to it. Continue to focus right into the center of the strongest part of the remaining energy and it will soften again. Each time the energy gets softer, get closer to it until there's nothing left.

You'll also find instructions for getting rid of other kinds of emotional problems like depression, anxiety, resentments, stress, grief, heartbreak, etc. Just join the site as a free member and you'll have access to all of this. It's also available on your smart phone.

Once you resolve the fear of punishment you'll find that it will be much easier to trust and act on your intuition. You'll find that you have more awareness of when you have an intuitive thought and you'll be more able to take action on it.

#2 – How to remove the real root causes of clouded thinking and poor decisions

There are two types of not-useful emotions. Some emotions are useful, but most of them are not. Here's a chart about the types of emotions. Fortunately, there are only two categories of "not-useful emotions." However, you do have lots of entries in each category.

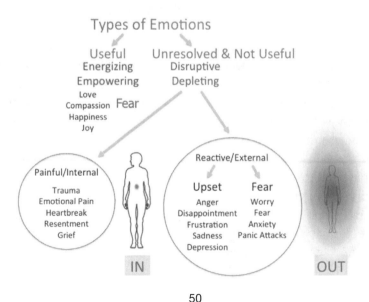

There is an IGO Technique for resolving each of the two types of disruptive emotions:

1. The IN Technique for the Painful/Internal ones
2. The OUT Technique for the Reactive/External ones

Everyone learns to suppress their feelings when they are very little to try to avoid the awful experience of being emotionally overwhelmed. You certainly will have many accumulated unresolved disruptive emotions. These two kinds of disruptive emotions cause all kinds of thoughts that cloud your thinking and cause you to make poor decisions. Think about times that you have made a decision out of fear or anger. You usually regret such decisions later, but you tend to do it anyway.

The OUT Technique starts by noticing that the energy of a reactive emotion radiates out into the space around you. It creates a kind of cloud or aura of energy that surrounds and engulfs you. The way out of it is to let your awareness move out into the space around you further and further until you find the outer edge of the cloud of energy. You then simply notice the quietness out beyond the edge of the energy field and it starts to fade away. You can also now see the story you made up in your mind that you are reacting to. Once you are out of the energy cloud of the reaction, you can simply stop giving the story energy and both the story and the energy disappear.

What's needed is to use the IN and OUT Techniques to clean up your inner emotional landscape. You've been accumulating disruptive emotions all your life. But when you clean them out you will have much less "mind-clutter" and you'll be able to more clearly distinguish your intuitive thoughts from your emotionally-based thoughts. This will allow you to much more consistently recognize, trust and follow your intuition.

My wish for you is that you will take these first steps in eliminating your fear and clouded thinking and start to move powerfully toward the level of success that you want and deserve that's latent inside of you.

About Tom

Tom Stone is an internationally-acclaimed speaker and seminar presenter, as well as an inventor, writer and entrepreneur. He has spent much of his life developing the most efficient and effective techniques for solving problems using principles and techniques from biophysics and consciousness.

Tom is the pioneer of the new emerging field of **Inner Greatness Optimizing** (IGO) in which he has made a number of unique discoveries, including a set of profound insights into the nature of human conditioning, which he calls the 12 Causes of Human Problems. This unique body of work provides the tools for eliminating the barriers and blocks that weigh people down, infringe on potential, and keep people from having the success they truly want. Tom's techniques have led to remarkably effective solutions to many of the seemingly intractable problems that plague modern society such as anxiety, depression, ADD/ADHD and PTSD.

Here's a tinyurl to a website where you can guide yourself through the IGO Techniques and fully remove the barriers that have been blocking your intuition. To check it out, visit: http://tinyurl.com/zn8s3xn

Tom has written twelve books including *The Power of How, Vaporize Your Anxiety* and *Vaporize Your Fear of Rejection*. He also stars in the movie *The Keeper of the Keys* with Jack Canfield, John Gray and Marci Shimoff.

I am truly grateful to Tom for his help in my life, and I am certain that this pioneering work will help many others in a profound way. ~ Jack Canfield, Co-creator of the *Chicken Soup for the Soul* series.

Tom Stone is nothing short of a genius. He is an expert in the area of dynamics, and he has the cleanest energy of ANYONE I've ever met, bar none. ~ Thomas Leonard, Founder of CoachVille, International Coach Federation and Coach Industry Pioneer.

Currently, Tom is developing a growing network of Inner Greatness Centers in China and the U.S.A. with more opening soon in different countries.

For more information or to book a speaking engagement with Tom, contact him at:

- Info@innergreatnessglobal.com
- www.innergreatnessglobal.com

CHAPTER 5

THE ART OF AUTHENTICITY: USING STORYSELLING™ TO PROJECT YOUR PERSONA

BY NICK NANTON & JW DICKS

It's very possible that none of us today would still remember the comic genius of Richard Pryor – if he hadn't had the guts to change up his act. That's because that comic genius was carefully concealed for so long. In 1970, after he had a few years of stand-up under his belt, he achieved a limited level of fame as a cookie-cutter imitation of Bill Cosby. He did family-friendly mainstream material that was silly and fun and, because of his talent, he found himself getting bookings on national talk shows such as Merv Griffin's and on network variety shows such as Ed Sullivan's. He came of age when, as he described it, "…America wanted their black comedians colorless,"[1] so he emulated the stand-ups who wore suits, delivered relatable jokes clearly and professionally, and rarely rocked the boat with his content.

But then, he was performing a gig at the Aladdin Hotel in Las Vegas and realized he couldn't do it anymore. He wasn't being himself on stage and he was tired of pretending to be someone else. So, in the middle of his act, he simply walked out – and went into seclusion to figure out what to do next. In his words, "…my days of pretending to be as slick and colorless as Cosby were numbered."[2]

He disappeared for over half a year. He cleared his head and filled it

---

1. Jason Bailey, Richard Pryor: American Id, The Critical Press, November, 2015
2. Bailey

with the stuff of real life. He hung out in neighborhood bars and barber shops, listening to people talk, and created new characters and routines, which he tried out at hip clubs in the San Francisco area. He hosted his own local radio show and fine-tuned his new voice. And then, finally he returned to Los Angeles with a new stage act that rattled audiences with its honesty and its hilarity. The story he put out to his public finally matched up with his own authentic story – and that linkage propelled him into superstardom.

The result? He's currently listed as number one in Comedy Central's survey of the greatest stand-up comics of all time. The first-ever Kennedy Center Mark Twain Prize for American Humor was presented to him in 1998. And Jerry Seinfeld himself has labelled him, "The Picasso of our profession."[3]

Presence is one thing – Richard Pryor already had that working for him. What wasn't working for him was his *StorySelling*™ – the primary core of what he built his comedy around. By pursuing an inauthentic copycat style, his comedy approach didn't resonate with who he really was. As a result, he didn't stand out from his peers and he himself became increasingly dissatisfied with his work. Once he finally began to construct his act around his genuine experience and true-life observations, however, he not only unleashed his true genius, but he also made himself into a unique performer that no one else could copy. That in turn led to massive success in records, TV, and movies – making Pryor a true MediaMaster (our term for a thought leader who is able to leverage all media opportunities available).

Now – what about *your* StorySelling™? How do you craft and position your own personal messaging so you can make the greatest impact with it? Those are good questions – and in this chapter, we're going to answer them for you!

YOUR STORY – YOUR MESSAGE

Every successful MediaMaster's message grows organically out of their *story*—it's the combination of who you are as a person and what value you offer to your audience that creates the magnetic attraction you're

---

3. Bruce Morton, *"Those We Lost,"* CNN, December 21, 2005

looking for.

Creating powerful stories is incredibly important to marketing success, which is why, a few years ago, we wrote a whole book on the subject: *StorySelling*™. Obviously, we won't have the space for a book's worth of StorySelling™ lessons in this chapter, but what we are going to do is focus specifically on the four most important elements of a MediaMaster's messaging. How you "mix and match" these four in your particular story is going to depend on how strong you are in each area – but having aspects of all four make for an unbeatable combination, in our opinion.

Make no mistake about it, you want to have the most powerful story in place when you take your first steps towards becoming a MediaMaster. On today's Information Superhighway, there are millions of different marketing "vehicles" constantly traveling, all trying to get attention – but most end up getting lost in the endless traffic. If you're going to join in that never-ending stream, you're going to have to find a way to get everyone's attention. But there's a simple way to do that. After all, how does the driver of a car get people to look at them?

That's right – they hit the horn and make a very loud BEEP.

Coincidentally, our four elements of a MediaMaster's Message add up to that inescapable BEEP…just look below and you'll see for yourself.

The Four Elements of a MediaMaster's Message

- **B**ackground
- **E**xperience
- **E**xpertise
- **P**romise

Yes – it all adds up to BEEP, which could be the sound of your own MediaMaster success. Let's examine each component of BEEP - and discover how each of them helps you create the most breakthrough messaging possible.

Element #1: Background

In America, we're fond of saying that it doesn't matter where you come from, you can still experience massive success. Well, when it comes to MediaMasters, where you come from can actually *help* you succeed! For example, the late, great Zig Ziglar was the tenth of a dozen children whose father died when he was very young. But his tough origins acted as a personal testimony to reassure his audience – if he could overcome those kinds of odds, his audiences could do the same.

Now, if you're currently hanging your head in shame because you had a perfectly normal upbringing with middle-class parents who loved you and supported you – well, we feel for you, but take heart! Today's MediaMaster doesn't have to spring from the most brutal of upbringings. Instead, they only need to identify that special "Aha!" moment that inspired the motivation for what they're delivering as a MediaMaster.

Case in point: Tim Ferriss, the MediaMaster Supreme who has made an industry out of telling the world how to get things done in only 4 hours.

Ferriss was raised in New York's famous playground for the rich, the Hamptons. But he wasn't a lazy rich kid; instead, he got himself accepted at Princeton despite his mediocre grades (he thinks his essay got him in the door),

It worked: In 1995 he arrived at Princeton, graduated four years later, and then took a sales job. On the side, he also built up his own internet business, a nutrition supplements company. By 2004, he was making over $40k a month with that business – when, suddenly, his girlfriend dumped him because he was working around the clock. "Because I did not know what to do with myself," is how he explained his mental shutdown. "My identity and my activities had been so solely occupied by business for so long..."[4] In turn, that motivated him to find a way to have a successful business – but not allow his entire life to be consumed by something that left him feeling empty and drained at the end of every day.

That journey provided the spark that resulted in his huge bestseller, *The 4-Hour Workweek*, whose very title, of course, delivered a hugely attractive message to a country filled with workaholics. And Ferriss's own personal story validated the premise of the book – because if he could do it, then just maybe the reader could too!

4. Stephanie Rosenbloom, "The World According to Tim Ferriss," *The New York Times*, March 25, 2011

In the 21st Century, things have changed. You don't need a "Rags to Riches" story to capture the imaginations of a crowd; you just need the personal story that inspires your ultimate message, as Ferriss did.

Element #2: Experience

Experience differs from background in that it refers to your life accomplishments in terms of business or your area of expertise. For example, Ferriss had the *experience* crafting a new business that didn't tie him up all day and all night. Since he was actually able to do it for himself, he had the credibility to make others believe it was possible for them.

The main point to remember with experience is that if you're promising that something almost magical is possible to your audience, *it's best if you've proved you can do it yourself.* People only trust a huge outcome if they can see for themselves that others have experienced it. Testimonials, of course, can provide the same type of validation, but it's so much more powerful if you've done it yourself.

Element #3: Expertise

Are you great at what you do?

It's an important question to ask – because no matter what it is, that level of expertise could launch you into the MediaMaster all-star team.

You probably have heard of Gary Vaynerchuk—he's been profiled in *The New York Times*, network news shows and he's appeared on national talk shows. He's described on the internet as an "entrepreneur, investor, author, public speaker, and internet personality." But he only became all that because he was gifted at reviewing wine – even before he was old enough to legally drink it!

His parents owned a brick-and-mortar store, Shoppers' Discount Liquor, located in Central New Jersey. Gary grew up working in the place and trained himself in wine-tasting as a teenager (he says he spit the wine out after tasting, so he didn't actually ingest it). As a result, he began doing his own unconventional wine reviews and recommendations for his customers and he began increasing the store traffic and sales because people sought out his maverick advice. He then began recording a video wine blog, called Winelibrary TV in 2006 and started gaining close to a 100,000 views on a daily basis, because of his relatable in-your-face, tell-it-like-it-is attitude. In 2011, however, he gave up the wine reviews and pivoted to being a social media expert coach – and took along his massive following for the ride. Remarkably, it all worked for him.

Now, not everyone can pull this kind of transition off – but his unique expertise, as well as his authentic delivery, definitely laid the groundwork for his ongoing and incredibly successful career as a MediaMaster. If you can draw everyone's attention with an amazing skill or talent that relates to their everyday lives, consider making it an integral part of your StorySelling™!

Element #4: Promise

The promise is, of course, the motivating factor that draws your crowd, which is why it's perhaps the most essential element in the MediaMaster messaging mix. You have to promise something dramatic and yet credible, something transformative but easily mastered, something that seems difficult (if not impossible) but that you can demonstrate (mostly through the other three Elements) is achievable.

The 4-Hour Workweek is, of course, a prime modern example of this kind of promise. A couple of others are *The 7 Habits of Highly Effective People* (a book that subtly promises to make the reader a highly effective person in easy steps) and *The Purpose-Driven Life* by Rick Warren (also subtle – promises to give meaning to the reader's life indirectly). Even Gary Vaynerchuk's *Crush It!* promised to help his followers enjoy the same kind of social media success he experienced with his relatable, reliable wine reviews. In all cases, the promise offers the possibility of improving people's lives in a measurable manner – through ways that can be financial, spiritual or personal development in nature.

Background, Experience, Expertise and Promise. When you have strength in all four of these areas, you have the ingredients to create an incredibly strong StorySelling™ narrative, because you combine the authenticity of who you are and what you're all about with a marketing perspective specifically designed to attract your audience.

Action Guide: Sharpening Your StorySelling™

Of course, with any recipe, it's not enough to know what the ingredients are – you also have to know how to put them together – so we're about to take you through some Action Steps to help you better define your BEEP.

- **Action Step #1: Define Your "Promise"**

Yes, we're going to work backwards here. That's because you're going to want to emphasize various aspects of the other three elements to back up this one. It's kind of like coming up with the end of your story first, so you know where you're going when you write the rest of it.

A note here: Developing your promise may be something of a work-in-progress. You'll want to test and fine tune it as you go along, until you find something that has the right attraction to your target audience. So, don't get too attached to it until you're sure it's right.

Oh, yeah – and who is your target audience, by the way? This is another important aspect to your promise – who are you making it to? If you're a successful dentist who wants to begin a business as a coach to other dentists, for example, you don't have to think very hard – you want a promise that will appeal to other dentists. But you may want to narrow that down even further. Are you interested in helping unsuccessful dentists become successful? Or dentists that are doing well but maybe could do a whole lot better? The right promise has to match up with the right audience (and we'll go more in-depth on this topic in a couple of chapters), so have a sense of who you're going after with your initial MediaMaster launch.

Here are a few other attributes of a promise that make it more magnetic:

- **Uniqueness** – It should be a promise that differs from your competition (best case scenario is, it's so unique, there IS no competition!). That can be a difficult task in this crowded marketing landscape, but it's a goal worth shooting for.
- **Excitement** – It should also be a promise that your audience will be genuinely pumped up about – because it will help them with a difficult objective they'd love to reach and will improve their lives.

- **Achievability** – Yes, it should address a difficult objective, but it should be an objective that can be accomplished. You can't promise the moon, unless, like our friend Peter Diamandis, you're working on a practical way to get there!
- **Simplicity** – Finally, your promise should be easy to sum up in a quick sentence (and without qualifiers). Think of the titles of the MediaMaster-authored books we've already shared – they're all just a few words and contain their promises in full.

When you get to the point that you're personally happy with your promise, test it out with a few members of your potential audience. They'll be quick to let you know if it works for them or not.

- **Action Step #2: Tailor Your Background, Experience and Expertise to Your Promise**

Once you have your promise in place, think about what aspects of your background, experience and expertise positions you as the person to deliver on that promise. And that means you must be selective in what you choose to share about yourself in relation to your promise, because, as interesting as it might be, in all of the rarest of circumstances nobody is really looking to hear your entire life story, just the parts that matter and relate to doing business with you. But, when told correctly, with the right elements of your personal life and business experience strung together, the result is nothing short of pure magic.

If you're going to represent your promise, there must be something about you that validates your ability to help others. Ideally, of course, **you've fulfilled the promise for yourself**, as people like Tim Ferriss, Gary Vaynerchuk and Tony Robbins did before they became MediaMasters. The second most optimal situation is that **you've helped *others* fulfill your promise for themselves**, through coaching or a system you developed and tested successfully.

It's also important to **identify your "Aha!" moment**, if you have one – that moment when you realized you can make this promise work for yourself or for others. Hopefully, there's some significant drama or emotion attached to this moment that adds to the power of your storytelling.

It's also great to **relate the promise back to yourself** in a compelling and believable way. If you're proposing a new diet and/or exercise program that delivers massive health benefits, talk about a relative that may have suffered because they didn't keep themselves in shape (or yourself for that matter, if you've had that experience) – and maybe how they turned their lives around if that was the case.

Finally, identify **proof of your expertise** in this area – and, again, this can be through another life story of how you shook up the establishment with your knowledge or showed up another so-called "expert." Use a little humor and humility when doing this, so you don't come across as obnoxious or a big talker that people might distrust, especially if you aren't yet a known commodity.

- **Action Step #3: Create Your Story**

Next, review what you came up with in Action Step #2 – and distill it down to the highest of high points. Feel free to throw everything else out (but don't literally throw it all out – there will be ways to use other material down the line). Again, this isn't about relating your entire biography – this is about creating the most compelling and *concise* StorySelling™ possible. That means no more than a minute or two. And in that time, you want to deliver a story that's:

- **Realistic** – In other words, try to avoid UFOs. Yes, some truth is stranger than fiction, but if it sounds too strange, maybe reconsider or at least tone it down. You want to be as believable as possible.
- **Logical** – Your story elements should connect to each other in a meaningful manner and consistently build to a strong finish.
- **Relatable** – Your audience has to be able to identify with your story, which means you should use "You" often, as in "You can imagine," "You have probably gone through this," etc. Make the listener an active participant in the storytelling.
- **Justifiable** – Your story should not only build to your promise, but also justify you being able to fulfill that promise. Almost every aspect of your story should be in some way a validation of your ability to deliver on your promise, so that when you arrive at that promise at the end, the audience is nodding, and not shaking their heads in bewilderment.

Once you have your story down, practice saying it out loud – and record yourself doing so. Look for weak points, places where you can change the wording and make it more expressive or powerful, and ask others you trust for input on content and delivery.

And finally, make sure it really seems to spring from who you are. Hopefully, this process has helped you plug into your authentic self and that self is heavily represented in your story. Because, as we learned from Richard Pryor's example at the beginning of this chapter, that authentic self is how you make your real impact.

About Nick

An Emmy Award-Winning Director and Producer, Nick Nanton, Esq., produces media and branded content for top thought leaders and media personalities around the world. Recognized as a leading expert on branding and storytelling, Nick has authored more than two dozen Best-Selling books (including *The Wall Street Journal* Best-Seller, *StorySelling*™) and produced and directed more than 40 documentaries, earning 5 Emmy Awards and 14 nominations. Nick speaks to audiences internationally on the topics of branding, entertainment, media, business and storytelling at major universities and events.

As the CEO of DNA Media, Nick oversees a portfolio of companies including: The Dicks + Nanton Agency (an international agency with more than 3000 clients in 36 countries), Dicks + Nanton Productions, Ambitious.com, CelebrityPress, DNA Films®, DNA Pulse, and DNA Capital Ventures. Nick is an award-winning director, producer and songwriter who has worked on everything from large-scale events to television shows with the likes of Steve Forbes, Ivanka Trump, Sir Richard Branson, Rudy Ruettiger (inspiration for the Hollywood blockbuster, *"Rudy"*), Jack Canfield (*The Secret*, creator of the *Chicken Soup for the Soul* Series), Brian Tracy, Michael E. Gerber, Tom Hopkins, Dan Kennedy and many more.

Nick has been seen in *USA Today, The Wall Street Journal, Newsweek, BusinessWeek, Inc. Magazine, The New York Times, Entrepreneur® Magazine, Forbes,* and *FastCompany.* He has appeared on ABC, NBC, CBS, and FOX television affiliates across the country as well as on CNN, FOX News, CNBC, and MSNBC from coast to coast.

Nick is a member of the Florida Bar, a voting member of The National Academy of Recording Arts & Sciences (Home to The GRAMMYs), a member of The National Academy of Television Arts & Sciences (Home to the EMMYs), Co-founder of The National Academy of Best-Selling Authors®, and serves on the Innovation Board of the XPRIZE Foundation, a non-profit organization dedicated to bringing about "radical breakthroughs for the benefit of humanity" through incentivized competition – best known for its Ansari XPRIZE which incentivized the first private space flight and was the catalyst for Richard Branson's Virgin Galactic. Nick also enjoys serving as an Elder at Orangewood Church, working with Young Life, Downtown Credo Orlando Entrepreneurs International and rooting for the Florida Gators with his wife Kristina and their three children, Brock, Bowen and Addison.

Learn more at:

- www.NickNanton.com
- www.CelebrityBrandingAgency.com

About Jack

JW Dicks, Esq., is a *Wall Street Journal* Best-Selling Author®, Emmy Award-Winning Producer, publisher, board member, and co-founder of organizations such as The National Academy of Best-Selling Authors®, and The National Association of Experts, Writers and Speakers®.

JW is the CEO of DNAgency and is a strategic business development consultant to both domestic and international clients. He has been quoted on business and financial topics in national media such as *USA Today, The Wall Street Journal, Newsweek, Forbes, CNBC.com,* and *Fortune Magazine Small Business.*

Considered a thought leader and curator of information, JW has more than forty-three published business and legal books to his credit and has co-authored with legends like Jack Canfield, Brian Tracy, Tom Hopkins, Dr. Nido Qubein, Dr. Ivan Misner, Dan Kennedy, and Mari Smith. He is the Editor and Publisher of *ThoughtLeader®* Magazine.

JW is called the "Expert to the Experts" and has appeared on business television shows airing on ABC, NBC, CBS, and FOX affiliates around the country and co-produces and syndicates a line of franchised business television show such as *Success Today, Wall Street Today, Hollywood Live,* and *Profiles of Success.* He has received an Emmy® Award as Executive Producer of the film, *Mi Casa Hogar.*

JW and his wife of forty-three years, Linda, have two daughters, three granddaughters, and two Yorkies. He is a sixth-generation Floridian and splits his time between his home in Orlando and his beach house on Florida's west coast.

CHAPTER 6

INCREASING SALES WITHOUT EVER SELLING
—BE THE GIRAFFE !

BY CHRIS JARVIS, MBA, CFP®

"Sales" is the fuel that powers a business. When sales are up, the office is a fun place for everyone. Investors are happy. Managers are hands-off and flexible. Employees feel appreciated, are free to do their jobs without much supervision, and are well compensated. When sales are down, things look very different. Previously passive owners start to take an interest in daily operations. Micromanagement becomes the new culture. Raises and bonuses are on hold. People are tense, fearing their jobs are in jeopardy.

Given that 'sales' have such a direct impact on every employee, why does the negative stereotype of a "salesperson" and "selling" in general persist in our culture?

The simple answer is that we don't trust salespeople! It's not that salespeople get paid commissions. The issue is that we don't believe that salespeople put our needs ahead of their own financial interest. As a result, many people think that the only thing worse than having to deal with a salesperson is being CALLED a salesperson.

This leaves professionals in a precarious position. By professionals, I mean highly trained people including accountants, attorneys, architects, investment advisors, insurance agents, and physicians. Professionals can be more broadly described as individuals who could financially benefit from a client, customer or patient choosing to consult or work with them or their companies. The precarious position is that professionals have a duty to their clients, customers and patients. Often, there is a very valuable piece of advice that they need to hear and act upon. However, the professionals often worry that a strongly-worded suggestion may come across as self-serving ("sales-y"). The key question is, "How do you help your clients and prospects see the wisdom of your advice without coming across as a 'salesperson' in the process?"

In this chapter, I will share my selling secrets that have successfully worked for over two decades. My strategy works when your buyers are intelligent or well-informed consumers. My system works especially well for intelligent professionals and highly technical experts whose stomachs turn at the thought of the sales mantra, "A-B-C. Always Be Closing," (*Glengarry Glen Ross*). If you truly want to help your clients do the right thing, but refuse to resort to high-pressure sales tactics, then this chapter will provide the missing piece to your sales puzzle.

Who am I? I am a mathematician by education and an actuary by training. I have been called a bean counter, math geek and quant jock. Though all of those labels may be true, you are probably more interested in what I've done: I have earned more than one million dollars in annual life insurance commission income multiple times. I have earned sales recognition awards from five different insurance companies and wholesale organizations. I have even been the top salesperson (out of 22,000 licensed and appointed agents) at a mutual insurance company. And, before you lump me in with other successful salespeople who may or may not be of the highest moral character, you should be aware that I accomplished this feat while selling insurance part-time. Until last year, when I sold my company, my full-time job was running a multi-million-dollar risk management consulting firm.

According to the Bureau of Labor Statistics, the average life insurance agent earns $50,000 per year, and the average income for a more seasoned financial advisor with a life insurance agent's license is closer to $105,000 per year. What allows one person to earn 10-20 times the average income in his field... while working part time?

The good news is that I have a three-part system that any professional or firm can successfully implement at little or no cost. The better news is that Jack Canfield and Nick Nanton have convinced me to share my secret with you in *Mastering the Art of Success*. The best news is what the secret is NOT.

The secret does not involve miraculously turning everyone in the organization into an expert closer. There is no magic pixie dust that you can sprinkle to make someone a more effective rainmaker. This chapter will offer neither motivational speeches nor sales incentives ideas to build or recruit the best salespeople in the world. I know that there is no way to inspire your current staff to make a thousand cold calls or to schedule two hundred appointments. I know that you can't hire away the best salespeople in your industry without overpaying them, so I won't waste your time focusing on adding costly staff. I will not suggest spending a single dollar on direct marketing, online advertisements, expensive sales or contact management systems, or on an inflatable gorilla. For decades, sales training has focused on the salesperson and the products or services being sold. In this chapter, I am going to concentrate on three ways to increase sales by focusing on things that are not typically associated with "sales."

> *When you change the way you look at things,*
> *the things you look at change.*
> ~ Wayne Dyer

My highly effective system is the result of behavior we refer to as "Being the Giraffe." Why a giraffe? Giraffes obviously have very long necks. This unique characteristic gives the giraffe an elevated perspective – allowing it to see things other animals can't. The neck also allows the giraffe to reach things other animals cannot. Wouldn't you like to see a better path to reaching your sales goals?

We started by reviewing our intake forms from clients. We ask prospects to share the characteristics of their most valuable and least favorite professional advisors. By discussing both the positive and negative of their past experiences, we can better understand what works well, and more importantly, what doesn't work well for those prospects in an advisor-client relationship.

We then did a review of our most successful clients. This is indeed an impressive group, including: multiple billionaires, $100 million healthcare operations, family offices, Big Four accounting firms, multinational law firms, and franchisors with thousands of locations. We found that the most successful clients reached those levels by seizing an opportunity others didn't. Some purchased real estate in undeveloped areas while others created entirely new markets for services. A few overhauled processes for manufacturing and distribution. They saw a better path, stuck their necks out (figuratively and financially), and ultimately reached levels of financial success only one in ten thousand Americans ever will.

You can reach similar levels of success if you embrace the "Be the Giraffe" mantra. Dare to be different and increase your sales with a three-part system:

1. Give Away Your Secrets
2. Turn Prospects into Partners
3. Leverage Your Limitations

How much easier would business be if you didn't waste time (or money) worrying about protecting trade secrets, convincing potential clients of your motives, or trying to cover up for inefficiencies?

In this chapter, you will learn how each one of these secrets significantly increased my income and the income of my partners. Then, you will learn how the combination of all three secrets helped me make more than $1 million in two different businesses in the same year!

1. Give Away Your Secrets

Knowledge is Power.
~ Francis Bacon

While earning my MBA from The Anderson School at UCLA in the mid to late 1990s, I entered the business plan competition for a physician-focused financial services firm based on education-based marketing. Though I made it to the finals, I did not win. The judges said, "Your business model is based on a flawed premise – you believe you will be able to reach physicians. They have tons of people knocking on their doors every day. You'll never reach them. It's an implausible concept." Twelve years later, I had written 10 books for doctors, published more than 100 articles, and held more than 100 seminars. Most importantly, fifteen thousand (15,000) physicians had called or emailed me directly asking for assistance.

You might find it interesting that everything I shared in my educational materials was nonproprietary. Attorneys, accountants, insurance agents or investment advisors could legally handle every idea I shared. If millions of professionals want to work with doctors and those same advisors can implement my ideas, why did so many doctors contact me instead of working with local people? Like most success stories, it was a combination of good strategy and blind luck.

I knew smart people would rather research financial strategies and products than lean on a salesperson's advice. What I didn't foresee was the internet changing education and research forever. People started looking for everything online. Those advisors who already had a library of content were uniquely prepared to educate their future clients. While other companies were using one-on-one sales interactions to generate prospects, we could publish articles that would generate hundreds, if not thousands, of book orders or newsletter registrations. People would read our materials, self-diagnose, and then make decisions about working with us before we ever met them.

2. **Turn Prospects into Partners**

If you want to go fast, go alone.
If you want to go far, go together.
~ African proverb

Our customers' concerns about the financial services industry are consistent with those expressed in other polls. The biggest one is "conflict of interest." How can a client trust a recommendation from an advisor when the advisor is being paid for selling that product? Our answer is to disclose commissions.

When you disclose commissions to clients who purchase insurance products, you eliminate the uncertainty of your motivation. There has been strong resistance from the insurance industry to allow this disclosure to be mandatory. Maybe insurance agents feel they are being paid too much? Personally, I would urge the industry to reconsider its position. It looks like the industry is trying to hide something. As an anecdote, I recently shared the impact of a strategy involving life insurance to a client. The client's family would benefit by $10,000,000 and I would earn $400,000. When I told the client, the response was "Good for you!" This strategy eliminates the appearance of impropriety.

Additionally, we have worked with corporate clients to create their own insurance companies. When corporations are large enough (having $10,000,000 or more of gross revenues), they are likely to have some risk that is not adequately covered by commercial insurance. This could be litigation risk, regulatory or legislative risk, cyber risk, or product or service warranties. By creating and managing insurance companies for our clients, we align our goals. When the risk management measures are effective, we both make money. This is very different from a traditional model where commissions are based on premiums – and the broker actually makes more when the clients pay higher premiums. By partnering with your best clients, your retention rate is higher and you receive an endless stream of referrals from your happy customers.

3. <u>Leverage Your Limitations</u>

Strive not to be a Success, but rather to be of value.
~ Albert Einstein

Another common complaint from wealthy clients is the "Yes" phenomenon. Clients get frustrated when an advisor says he can do something, then either doesn't do it or spends a lot of time (and money) learning how to do it. Clients are willing to accept people saying "no" to requests. They don't expect advisors to know how to do everything.

A mentor of mine, Hank Frazee, once taught me a valuable lesson. He encouraged me to spend a great deal of time with "other" advisors, learning what they do well. He taught me to ask questions like:

- What is the most profitable transaction (service) you offer?
- What types of clients are most difficult for you?
- What is your ideal client and why is that so?
- What is your favorite type of problem to solve?
- Who is your most valuable referral source, and why?

We try to connect with these professionals annually for another reason. Our goal is to make 100 referrals to other advisors each year. We refer our clients to service providers, clients to other clients, and professionals to other professionals. It is not important for us to be paid for these introductions. What is important is that we show our clients and strategic partners that we are interested in their continued success.

Before you dismiss this practice as wasteful, consider that we have received *handwritten* thank you notes for recommending advisors. On the other hand, we have never received a 'thank you' note for successfully handling a multimillion dollar transaction. People really appreciate your thoughtfulness, especially when there is no financial incentive for doing so.

Though it may be hard to put a price on good karma, consider this one example. In 2014, I sent two clients to an attorney at a national firm. Total billings were approximately $100,000. Both clients mentioned this introduction in their holiday cards. By 2017, we had earned more than $2,000,000 from their referrals.

Summary: More Sales, Less Selling

Help others achieve their dreams and you will achieve yours.
~ Les Brown

In this chapter, you learned that there is a better path to success. By changing your focus from sales to education, you become valuable. By focusing on the needs of your clients, rather than on your products or services, you build trust. By going out of your way to help others in your field and in your community, you show that you care.

Rather than looking at customer service and the supply chain as threats to your profitability, you see these valuable interactions as invaluable opportunities to show them who you are and what is important to you.

When your potential customers and colleagues see you as valuable, trustworthy and caring, you will never have to sell anything ever again. Elevate your perspective. See a better path.

Be the Giraffe!

About Chris

Chris Jarvis is an applied mathematician and former actuary. He has spent 25 years solving complex financial problems for multinational corporations, professional service firms, entrepreneurs, and family offices. This experience helped Chris discover the solution to successfully working with high net worth and highly-educated clients.

Chris is the author of twelve books, including *Wealth Secrets of the Affluent* and *Wealth Protection: Build and Preserve Your Financial Fortress* (both by John Wiley), *The Physician's Money Manual* and *Managing Risk: A Guide for Physicians and Practices*. Post Hill Press will publish his next book, *Six Secrets to Leveraging Success: A Guide for Entrepreneurs, Family Offices and Their Trusted Advisors*, in the fall of 2017.

In addition, Chris has been quoted in *The Wall Street Journal* and the *Los Angeles Business Journal* and appeared on Bloomberg Television's *Personal Finance*. Chris has over 100 articles in publication in various professional periodicals, including *California CPA* and *Physician's Money Digest*.

As a facilitator and public speaker, Chris has delivered over 100 continuing education seminars to doctors and hospitals. A partial list includes: American Association of Neurological Surgeons (AANS), International College of Surgeons (ICS), American College of Mohs Surgeons, American Association of Physicians of Indian Origin (AAPI), American Society of Plastic Surgeons (ASPS) and dozens of educational programs to Tenet Healthcare and Kaiser Permanente hospitals.

Chris acts as an advisor and consultant on healthcare industry trends. He has presented to the American Association of Medical Society Executives (AAMSE) and National CPA Health Care Advisors Association.

Chris is widely acknowledged as a subject matter expert and thought leader in the insurance industry. During his actuarial career, he created two captive insurance companies for one of the world's largest automobile manufacturers. He has provided risk management, captive consulting, risk pooling and insurance brokerage services to more than 250 businesses and insurance companies nationwide.

Chris has won sales honors from multiple companies and has qualified for Million Dollar Round Table's Top of the Table numerous times. Chris has delivered sales, marketing and motivational seminars to national insurance companies and brokerage organizations.

Chris focused on entrepreneurial studies and finance while earning his MBA from The Anderson School at UCLA – where he was awarded the Young President's Organization's (YPO) Ken Kennedy Fellowship for his entrepreneurial achievement. He has spent over five years as a member of Vistage International's Chief Executive Group.

He graduated from the Honors Program at the University of Rhode Island with a B.S. in applied mathematics — where he was awarded the Order of Omega *Man of the Year* award for his philanthropic and community service.

Chris proudly serves on the Board of Directors for Angel City Sports in Los Angeles, California and Arsenal Insurance Management in Montgomery, Alabama. Chris also holds a seat on the Board of Governors for the Sigma Phi Epsilon Educational Foundation.

Chris currently lives in Southlake, Texas with his wife Heather and their three children, Chloe, Kierstin and Tyler.

Chris can be reached at:
- Email: cjarvis@JarvisTower.com
- By phone: 817-442-6006
- www.linkedin.com/in/chrisjarvis

CHAPTER 7

PURSUIT OF PURPOSE

BY ZANDER FRYER

What is Purpose? And why is it so important?

I always ask my clients, "If you don't know where you want to go, how are you ever going to get there?" If you aren't clear on your purpose, how can you ever expect to live the life you want to live?

This was the single biggest issue I had preventing me from getting where I wanted to be, for years.

Imagine driving across the country from L.A. to the East coast. Most of us know our general direction; you know you need to go to East. What happens when you're half way across the country and you hit a fork in the road? One road reads "New York" and the other "Miami." You wonder 'where do I go'? You don't know what to do. And instead of just picking a direction you worry that if you choose New York and you hate it, then you might not have time to go to Miami after. So, you sit there... in Albuquerque, New Mexico. Definitely not the destination you expected, was it? That's what happens when you aren't clear about where you want to be.

One thing is certain; you cannot have success without purpose. I learned that the hard way.

When I was in high school I was a math and science nerd, so the question, *'what are you going to do with your life?'* was actually pretty easy for me. I was going to be an engineer.

I graduated high school and went to UCLA for electrical engineering, but let's be honest, I didn't give a s**t about quadratic equations. While at school I had my first run in with true purpose. I didn't know it at the time, but it's clear now. I had always wanted to serve my country, so in order to pay for my tuition, I joined Air Force ROTC.

While in ROTC, I thrived. I rose in the ranks quickly to be one of the leaders of my detachment. During Air Force Field Training – the Air Force's boot camp for future commissioning officers – I graduated at the top of my class with the Top Gun award.

That was what mattered to me: leading others, inspiring and empowering others to be more, to do more with their lives. I had found it. I knew how to bring purpose and meaning into my life. I was going to be a leader in the military.

Until, I wasn't.

Do you know what failure looks like? It looks like a breathalyzer reading '0.09% BAC'. Four months after my twenty first birthday, I made the decision to drive home after drinks with a couple friends I hadn't seen in a while and that was it. I ruined my entire life's vision in one evening: my dreams, my aspirations, my purpose, all gone. So, I did what any lost twenty-one-year-old kid would have done. I picked myself up, and I joined the corporate world. I *needed* a career and I had developed some amazing skills while in the Air Force to help me succeed in any endeavor.

I spent the next five years as a systems architect for a prestigious tech organization. I designed multi-million dollar networks for some of the biggest media, web, and service provider companies in the world. And I was good at what I did. In return they paid me a multi-six-figure income.

I was constantly getting promoted, receiving awards, and getting raises. I was happy. At least on the outside I was. Outwardly I had the appearance of success – I had money, good relationships, flexibility to travel – but I wasn't really happy. I was living someone else's dream and confused about what I really wanted. I was stuck in Albuquerque with no idea where to go next.

With every accomplishment came sharp peaks of joy, but they were shortly followed by a dull, unsatisfied hunger for more. I wanted to be successful, but clearly, I did not know what success meant to me or better yet, "why" I wanted it.

In May of 2016 I had a conversation with a mentor of mine, who travels the world as a public speaker in the health and wellness space. That conversation would change my life. He asked me: "Zander, what would you do if you couldn't fail?"

"That's easy. I would lead and inspire people as a full-time job. I have no idea what that means, but I know that is what I love to do. It's been the only piece really missing in my life, since I left the Air Force and every time I dig deep to clarify what I really want, it's the first thing to come up."

"That's amazing. So, what's holding you back from doing that?"

"Well I'm very successful in my career right now and I have a lot of potential here. I don't want to stop that momentum." I could feel my own hesitance as I answered that one.

"Just because you're good at something does that mean you should do it? Just because there is a path for you, does that mean you should follow it? Zander, do you know the difference between you and me?" he asked.

"Uh, you make a s**t ton more money than I do?" I responded sarcastically.

And in a very calm, confident tone he connected with the knockout blow, "Zander, you're dreaming your dream and I'm living mine. You're the only thing holding you back."

Wow! What a kick to the nuts. That just took my ego from an 11 down to about a 3. If you ever want to be humbled, have your mentor tell you that all of your 'success' is a self-imposed façade to mask your own fear.

I learned a very important lesson that day. It's near impossible to let go of something GOOD to go for something GREAT. But the second you admit the truth about where you really are and make the decision about where you really want to be, there is no stopping you.

That was the conversation that set my life back on track. I had learned my purpose and passion years before, but I had been hiding from the truth, because the truth was terrifying. The last time I went for my passion, it ended in disaster. But, the moment I made the decision to follow my passion again and *get clear why I was really here*, was the moment I truly started being successful. My destination was Miami and I wasn't going to take any more detours.

That next week I put in my two-weeks' notice with nothing but a dream, a purpose, and the knowledge that I was truly living my mission. Within two months I had found a form to fit my function. I got certified as a success coach and took on my first handful of clients. Two months after that I had spoken in front of hundreds at events and group workshops. And within five months of quitting I was offered the opportunity to co-author a book with one of the greatest of all time.

In less than half a year, I was able to go from empty, lost, and longing, to living the life I was meant to live. When your life is aligned with your passions and purpose, success just flows.

Consequently, we can never be truly successful until we focus inward and are honest about what we really want, not what others want from us, no matter how terrifying the answer is.

I spent years in an amazing company, working with amazing people, doing amazing things, being paid an amazing income. And as a kid in my mid-twenties, the only direction was up. But that's not success. Money, titles, luxuries mean nothing if it's not what you truly want.

I may have found purpose from an early age, but providing clarity and understanding around that purpose took years of intentional work. The reality in finding clarity of purpose is like putting together a puzzle. Each life experience you have, book you read, workshop you attend and conversation with a mentor or coach gives you another piece to that puzzle. As you collect pieces, you gain a little more clarity in the picture.

Most of us wander through life expecting to find these puzzle pieces in the bushes or lying on our desk at work, without actively searching for them.

How's that working so far? Would you be surprised if I said that process can be expedited through focused action? I have worked with dozens of clients on this and you can gain unusual clarity in just a few short hours of intentional introspection.

So rather than spending the next several years on sabbatical diving through trash cans in Thailand for puzzle pieces, let's front-load the process and paint a clearer picture today.

Below are two of the exercises I work through with every one of my clients to help them gain clarity:

1) FOLLOW YOUR JOY

We are all born with an inner guidance system that points us toward the direction we should be living our lives. That GPS is our joy. Unfortunately, many of us find it hard to follow joy. It is either clouded by social and culturally-imposed views of what we should want in our lives or hidden behind the fear of doing something uncomfortable and different. This exercise helps you flush out what really brings you joy and get in touch with that inner GPS.

First, start by thinking of the last time you really lost track of time: a time when you were so present, so at peace, you completely melted into the moment. Was it with family? Climbing the peaks of Mt. Fuji? On a beach, just relaxing? Whatever it was, close your eyes and bring that image back to you, just for a moment and really feel it.

Now, with a pen and paper, let's start a simple (but revealing) exercise to learn how to follow your joy. It starts as a list of 20 things that you love to do. For example:

1. I love to spend time with friends and family.
2. I love to read a good book.
3. I love to dance.
4. I love to drink good tequila (don't judge me).

The list itself is not all that important, but once you get to 20 you can go back through and decipher themes and commonalities. Comb the list again and, for each answer, now ask yourself, "Why do I love to do this?" and write that down.

Now look through that list of 'whys' and you will be able to find three to five 'themes' in your life of things you love to do. You love to connect with people. You love to be creative. You love to learn and grow. You love building and creating things. You love to help others. You love being part of nature.

You'll be surprised how deep this simple process can take you and how useful it can be when making future career and life decisions. When you come to a fork in the road you can ask yourself, which path takes me towards having more of what I love to do, in my life?

Oftentimes that path is the one that goes against the social norms we are sold every day, but trust that you are the only person that knows what's best for you and follow your joy.

2) LIFE PURPOSE EXERCISE:

This one will be a bit different and uncomfortable for some people, but it's amazingly powerful, and depending on your level of openness can lead to clarifying a life purpose in less than an hour.

First, you need to find a quiet place where you can get away from distractions for a bit. This could be the office on a weekend, or a favorite spot out in nature somewhere. Whatever it is, it just needs to be somewhere you won't be distracted.

Now, turn off your phone and take out either a journal or your laptop and open up a word doc. Start by just asking yourself, "What is my true life-purpose?" Now write down your answer. It may be a few words, or it may be a sentence or two. Whatever it is, write it down.

Now cross out that answer and ask yourself again, "What is my true life-purpose?" and answer it.

Now do it again, and again, and again. The repetition in this exercise causes you to calm your nervous system and intellectual mind and dig deep into the subconscious where the emotional intelligence of your own being will begin to show through.

Continue this process of asking what your life purpose is, and writing down your answer until you have an answer that literally moves you to such great emotions you can't continue. You will feel radiant, full, and may be brought to tears. Your life purpose is not about the intellectual, "What should I do with my life?" but rather the deepest emotional sense of what do I *really* want.

This may take 20 minutes, it may take an hour, it may take longer. If you believe you don't have a life purpose it will take a while, because you first need to work through your own limiting beliefs before getting to the really good stuff. I know, because I was one of those people.

I started by writing "I have no life purpose" and it took me about 15 minutes just to break past this idea. After an hour, I had bits and pieces of my purpose show up – which were major breakthroughs for me. By the end of the second hour, I was on the verge of tears and couldn't get up from my seat I was so swollen with emotions.

That's what you are looking for!

Now, back to your road trip from L.A to the East Coast. You've clarified that you really want to go to Miami. What happens when you hit that fork in the road and have to choose between New York and Miami? You take the Miami route! What happens when you hit another fork and have to choose between Charlotte, NC and Miami? You take the Miami route!

Let's do this one more time. Split between D.C. and Miami? ... MIAMI!

Makes life a lot easier, doesn't it?

Once you have clarified your life purpose and what you really find joy in - your passions - life becomes simple. You open your eyes and the path that aligns with your purpose and allows you to bring more passion into your life is the path you follow.

NOW IT'S TIME TO ACT!

About Zander

Zander is a certified Success Coach, ThoughtLeader, and Speaker who specializes in transformational work. He currently focuses on helping entrepreneurs, consultants, and coaches escape the monotony of a "9 to 5" and build six-figure businesses around their passion.

His mission is to inspire and empower others to find their success and passion in life. For those that are ready, the promise is not happiness; the promise is *mastery.*

Clients that work with him find his authenticity, passion, and playfulness magnetic. His energy on stage can lift a room and his depth of knowledge is second to none, but his ability to connect and care for those that he applies these principles to is what makes him *unique.*

To find out more, please visit: zanderfryer.com or reach out to him at: zander@zanderfryer.com

- Website: zanderfryer.com
- Email: zander@zanderfryer.com
- Facebook: facebook.com/zanderfryer
- Instagram: @zander.fryer

CHAPTER 8

THE "PBR!"
—THE PICK BUSINESS RETREAT!

BY DR. ROBERT M. PICK

Great things in business are never done by one person.
They're done by a team of people.
~ Steve Jobs

Be so good they can't ignore you.
~ Steve Martin

The Pick Business Retreat, or "PBR!" as it's affectionately called by most, is one of the most powerful secrets to creating the business, or in the case of healthcare individuals, the practice, of your dreams. In this chapter, I will tell you my story and how I could have failed, but instead won and kept winning, building my dream business. This business sees robust yearly growth, features a great team environment, and outpaces the competition using the principles of the business S-curve. If you incorporate PBR!s – and yes, they will involve hard work and time – you too can achieve greatness. The PBR!, more than any other action, will help your business climb to heights you never thought possible. But most importantly, I want you to avoid the mistakes that I made.

Let's first define a PBR! PBRs! take place biannually, away from the business, and removed from outside influences, distractions, or intrusions. I recommend that for the first year, you keep PBRs! to one-day, biannual events. After the first year, most businesses discover that the retreats become two-day biannual events. The PBR! affords you and your team the ability to get back on track, refocus, re-energize, brainstorm, develop strategies and protocols. Furthermore, these retreats are where you are the CEO of your business and where you act, think, and function like a Fortune 100 company. It's most importantly where you develop the skills and protocols to "be so good they can't ignore you!"

WHERE I BEGAN

About 20 years ago, I decided my business partnership (I began as a dental specialist) was no longer working for me. I bought out my partner only to realize that I was on my own with no business management knowledge or skills. It was either sink or swim, and I was in very deep waters. There is an old saying that goes, imitate those who are successful and then do it better. After contacting successful colleagues, I made one of the most important decisions of my career. I hired an amazing business management consultant, consistent with my goals and vision. After several years of intensive immersion, learning business principles and systems, absorbing key performance indicators (KPIs), getting my overhead under control, and developing the beginnings of a great team in a great team environment, we were off and running.

What was at the heart of this accomplishment? I became the CEO of my practice or business if you will, rather than the dentist in my office. Through reading books on business and practice management, and observing successful businesses, I discovered the business retreat was an invaluable tool. So I invented the PBR!, a solution for the business entrepreneur wanting to achieve at a high level.

DOING YOUR HOMEWORK

To be successful with a PBR!, business entrepreneurs need to branch out beyond the usual industry journals. They must read a plethora of motivational and business magazines, such as *Success, Harvard Business Review, Fortune, Fast Company,* and *Entrepreneur* to name a few. You will discover management and motivational principles in these pages. You will assign articles from these magazines to your employees to read as a part of the PBR! Each employee then reports on an article at different points during the retreat. As time goes on, relative articles from trade journals will also be reported on.

Each person at the retreat receives a binder containing these articles. In the coverslip of that binder is an 8.5x11" glossy sheet of paper bearing the business' name and logo, along with the name and date of the retreat. Most importantly, in the middle of that sheet is a color picture of each attendee along with their name and job title. Inside the binder are copies of all the articles relative to the retreat that were read not only by the attendee but by the rest of the team as well – all of which will be reported on. An agenda for the retreat appears in the front.

At the beginning of the day, each person is given a lightbulb. It's to be used when somebody has a great idea that cannot wait. They raise up their lightbulb, the meeting stops, and they present their idea. It should be used sparingly, but when done correctly, the lightbulb is a great motivator and makes each person feel like an important part of your team.

In addition to articles, PBR! attendees view assigned videos. Two examples are: "Daily Habits of Successful People – It's all About Routine" and "3 Words That Can Change Your Life Forever," by Brian Tracy.

SETTING UP AND GETTING STARTED

Arrive at the retreat ahead of all other personnel and participants. Greet all team members by name as they enter and welcome them to a motivating, life-changing PBR! day.

To motivate the team and spark some excitement, begin the day with a raffle. Have several raffles throughout the day to be deployed during lulls.

Here's an example. Let's say your business or practice has eight employees. You take a card and envelope and place a $25 Starbucks gift card inside along with a motivational note. On the outside of the envelope, a number from 1 to 10. Let's say the number is seven. You simply go around the room until someone guesses the number 7. They win the card and the motivational note inside. As guidance, the note can say something like, "Hey-hey! Well you and only you chose the number 7 making you the winner of the first of four surprise Rhonda Smith's Raffles, throughout the day. Enjoy the Starbucks and let's have an amazing day!" Modify to your liking.

Now that you are ready to get started there are a number of essential elements that are necessary to cover in your PBR! The scope of this chapter will not allow me to elaborate on all of these points, but I will cover the most necessary aspects of the PBR! and will make the others available to you as well.

Each PBR! needs to cover each of the following topics:

- YEAR IN REVIEW
- DEPARTMENTAL REVIEW
- SWOT and STEW
- UNIQUE SELLING PROPOSITION (USP)
- MISSION, VISION, AND CULTURE
- STARTING WITH WHY
- GOAL SETTING
- JUMPING THE S-CURVE
- SOCIAL MEDIA
- LOOKING AHEAD
- WORKING LUNCHES
- BUILDING BETTER TEAMS
- RECOGNIZING HARD WORK

Now, here are five core elements to success of your PBR!

I. YEAR IN REVIEW

During all PBRs!, there are certain repeating agenda items. One of the most important that will almost always lead off the day is the "Year in Review." This is when you look at the previous year's numbers, (scrutinizing production versus collection if you are a healthcare practice), for each of the 12 months. Now look at the current year, doing the same for each of the 12 months. This allows everyone on the team to see the numbers. It also provides insights regarding trends, such as months that consistently underperform or outperform. These numbers help you determine protocols, procedures and marketing that will boost poor performing months into robust months. Furthermore, take the strongest-performing months and make them even better.

Remember, you must be fiscally responsible and get your overhead under control. Think of it this way: There is gross production, which is the top line and the cost of doing business, which is the bottom line. What lies between the line is profit. Remember, it's always easier to raise the top line (unless your business overhead is out of control). Too many businesses spend too much time trying to control a small percentage of overhead. Yes, overhead must be controlled and fall within the KPIs for your specific business or practice, but you will achieve much greater success and make much more money by raising the top line.

As a quick note, I know there are some business and practice owners who are leery of showing employees the numbers. First, if the team does not see the numbers, there is no way they can help you. Second, if you don't think they have a pretty good idea of what the business produces and what you take home, I can assure you that they do. Besides, people like to be associated with success.

II. SWOT and STEW

Two more items on the repeating agenda at each PBR! are the business SWOT (Strengths, Weaknesses, Opportunities and Threats) and the business STEW (Satisfy the customer, Team, Extra mile, and the Wow factor). The SWOT analysis is a tool to help your business take stock of the internal factors (strengths and the weaknesses), and the external factors, (opportunities and threats) that affect your business. As an example, you conduct a round robin in which you ask each team member for business strengths. An assigned team member writes them down. Brainstorming occurs. Each idea is discussed, then prioritized in accordance with all four components of the SWOT. The goal is to capture as many ideas as possible.

Most organizations understand the SWOT analysis but very rarely go through it with their team members on a regular basis. In each category (Strengths, Weaknesses, Opportunities and Threats) you want to go around the room in a round-robin fashion gleaning as much information from each other as possible.

Repeat this process for the business STEW. The STEW helps separate the men from the boys and the women from the girls:

- S stands for Satisfy the customer. Repeat the round-robin, listing everything pertaining to the customer service issue. You have likely heard it before, but customer service needs to be at the Ritz-Carlton level. People talk about this type of service to their friends and it's something that will lead to five-star reviews online and an increase in business.
- T is for team. What's your business doing to create a great team and great team environment, both of which are stronger than your competition.
- E is for the extra mile. Again, what are you, your team and your business doing to go the extra mile?
- W stands for the "Wow factor!" The wow factor is self-explanatory. Make it part of your daily routine and watch your customers say, "Wow!"

Once you have transitioned into your role of business CEO, something that will improve your own performance is to have your team do a personal SWOT on you. It should not be done right away, but after several years. This allows you to build a comfortable rapport with your team first. In order for the self-SWOT to be effective, you must be able to take criticism. Sometimes that criticism may seem unfair or unfounded. However, you must sit back and listen. If at any time the team feels you are being defensive, they will potentially shut down, and you will have lost a golden moment that takes time to recapture. If the team realizes you can take the criticism, they will be honest and tell you how they feel about your strengths, weaknesses, opportunities and threats.

The first time I heard all of my weaknesses, I wanted to argue and fight back. But use this to your advantage. Take those weaknesses and make them strengths. You will become a better CEO, the practice or business will perform better, and your team will be impressed. I do a personal SWOT now once per year with my team. I carry the weaknesses sheet with me, and I look at it daily. I make those weaknesses my strengths.

III. MISSION, VISION, AND CULTURE

Also developed at your first PBR! are your business' Mission, Vision and Culture Statements. These are a must. Without them, the team does not know where they are going. These statements further help your business focus on what's essential. They should be visible to all.

The mission statement defines the present state or purpose of your business and answers three questions about why the business exists:
- What does the business do?
- Who does it do it for?
- How does the business do what it does?

The vision statement describes what that business wants to achieve over time. The culture statement defines a specific set of values specific to your business.

At each subsequent retreat, you will revisit the statements by refining them. Hopefully, over time, parts of the vision will become your mission. At that point, you really have begun to establish a successful business. Every employee should also know the mission and vision cold.

IV. GOAL SETTING

Goals are also set at every PBR! Goals are established and often never achieved. But for now, here are some quick tips on effective goal-setting:

1. Write down the goal. It must be clear and detailed.
2. Set a deadline.
3. Establish a method to achieve the goal. This is why most goals are never obtained. The method of achievement is never realized.
4. Identify those on your team that will be needed to achieve it.
5. Make a plan and create a series of steps from beginning to completion in achieving this goal.

V. RECOGNIZING HARD WORK

The PBR! is also a great opportunity to give awards and recognitions. A few examples include employee of the year, a most improved team member, or recognition for going above and beyond the call of duty. These awards will build teamwork and enhance employee performance. The awards themselves can either be plaques or trophies. Regardless, all should bear the employee's name, your name, and your company logo.

FINAL THOUGHTS

Retreats such as the PBR! pay off. These outings once seemed to be only a part of Fortune 500 corporate culture. But in today's competitive environment, can you afford not to start yours? I guarantee that you and your team will leave a PBR! charged, motivated, and ready to be "so good that you cannot be ignored!" This will lead to an increase in your business' and team's ability to perform, all leading to an increase in gross production. This gives the business owner and team the freedom, both professionally and economically, that they desire.

At the end of the day, and especially as you begin to be more profitable, have a grand prize raffle for something like a television. Use the numbered thank-you card mentioned earlier. But finally, and most importantly, send everyone home with a book that will motivate them. At my last "PBR!" I gave my entire team a copy of David Bach's "The Automatic Millionaire." On the inside of the front cover, I write a personal note to each employee and sign my name. You should do the same.

About Dr. Bob

Dr. Bob Pick is a popular business and practice management consultant, coach, author, and lecturer known for his high energy, fast moving, motivational, highly educational and entertaining programs. His audience always goes home with great information that can be used immediately for business and/or practice enhancement and reward! Bob is the CEO of The Pick Group, who takes their client's businesses or practices to new heights and beyond and makes them unstoppable! He will transform you from the business operator or clinician, to the CEO of your business or practice.

The Pick Group is committed to excellence and dedicated to business and/or practice entrepreneurs.

Dr. Pick began life as a dental specialist in the field of Periodontics and Implants. All his dental and dental specialty degrees are from Northwestern University. Bob has been involved with the Jack Welch Business Institute of Strayer University.

Over time and as the 21st Century rolled in, Bob realized the importance of business, business systems, having a great team and great team environment, and the importance of communication and relationships. Couple that with system operations, social media, building your brand, mission, vision, culture, goal setting and attainment, and you have a business or practice that is happy, healthy, and wealthy! Bob's business and practice consulting are centered on ethics and doing things the right way! All of the above allows for phenomenal business or practice growth, all obtainable by The Pick Group.

Dr. Pick is the recipient of numerous national and international fellowships, honors, and awards and most impressively won the 2014 Northwestern University Merit Award for outstanding achievement in a profession – the highest award given by the University! He is further the author or co-author of numerous books, chapters and articles.

Bob has frequently been featured in the media including: *Good Morning America, Fortune, Self, The Wall Street Journal, Glamour, McCall's, MORE, Popular Mechanics, Cosmopolitan, New York Times, Lear's, Chicago Tribune, Chicago Sun Times, L.A. Times*, CBS, NBC, ABC, CNN, Fox News, *Ladies Home Journal, Lifetime TV, Men's Health*, and even *The National Enquirer!*

In his spare time, Bob is a commercially-rated pilot, an avid guitar player and guitar collector, model railroader and a collector and restorer of Classic Corvettes.

If you would like to learn how you too can grow your practice and/or business, you can connect with Dr. Bob Pick at:

- drpick@thepickgroup.com
- www.thepickgroup.com
- www.facebook.com/thepickgroup

CHAPTER 9

UNLEASH YOUR COMPANY'S INNOVATIONAL POTENTIAL™

BY STEVEN L. BLUE

From Dumb Metal to Neural Networks

I am a business transformation expert. I take sleepy little rust-belt companies and turn them into global behemoths. In fact, I have never failed to triple the returns in everything I have touched. And one thing I have learned in over 40 years of doing this is that every company – without exception – is a gold mine. All you have to do is find the hidden treasure that lies beneath.

This hidden treasure might be in the form of restructuring how you go to market. It might be in the form of creating what I call a *Cirque du Soleil*™ culture – a team that is totally committed to performing on the edge of their abilities and sworn to do better tomorrow than they did today. Or it might be in the form of a never-ending blizzard of killer products. Products that destroy the competition and delight the customers. Products that blaze new trails and return huge profits to the shareholders.

But many companies are stuck in the wasteland of commodities. The dog-eat-dog world where everyone races to the bottom. Or they waste time and money on new products that never get out of the starting gate. And if they do, the returns are uncertain and paltry.

I can show you how any company can move from the underbelly of also-rans to the elite world of mega earnings. This can be done in a variety of ways, but my favorite 'go-to' method is in unleashing a company's Innovational Potential™. This is a battle-tested method that has proven time and again its astounding potential. So astounding in fact, that it transformed my company, Miller Ingenuity, from a supplier of dumb metal and plastic products to a high technology company that designs and delivers life-safety systems utilizing radar, LIDAR, and image recognition processing via neural networks.

But to transform a company from dumb metal to neural networks is a huge and complicated endeavor. It carries huge risk if done incorrectly. But it carries huge reward if done successfully – as was the case with Miller Ingenuity.

Unlocking a company's Innovational Potential™ is a key element of what I call Disruptional Transformation™. To truly become a market leader and obtain superior profits, it is essential to disrupt the market. And to disrupt the market, it is necessary to disrupt the company. Disrupting any company is very difficult. This is particularly true in rust-belt, old line, middle market companies in so-called mature industries. Even in some industries that are not so mature. The order of the day is disrupt or be disrupted. A perfect example of this axiom is what happened to Blockbuster. It was totally disrupted by Netflix. And who is gunning to disrupt Netflix? Amazon, the ultimate disrupter.

But disrupting the market requires "disruptional thinking." And disruptional thinking is not a random act. And it's not a natural act. It won't "just happen." You need to force it to happen. Disruptional thinking comes from using a methodology of unleashing creativity-or Innovational Potential™. And then doing it again and again. Over and over. And while every company has massive potential to innovate, most don't. And why is this? In my experience, it always boils down to one or more of four reasons:

1.) Lack of belief. Most people don't believe they are inherently creative and therefore don't act that way. Hence many companies don't believe they have the "right stuff" to innovate. So therefore, they don't even try.

2.) Lack of methodology. There is a methodology to ignite ideas and unleash creativity in any organization. But many people believe creativity and innovation is some mystical beast that only appears in the minds of the Einsteins in the world.

3.) Lack of resources. Some companies try to employ creative methodologies but don't provide the resources for them to take root. They don't view "this creative stuff" as the real work. They believe that if there is any time left over after "the real work" (there never is), then the creative stuff can begin.

4.) Lack of focus and commitment. Unleashing Innovational Potential™ takes laser-like focus and steely determination, straight from the top, to see it through no matter what. Read the last sentence again. Are you prepared to dismiss good people if they can't or won't go along with the Innovational Potential™ program? Are you prepared to go toe-to-toe and nose-to-nose with your Board if they want to shut it down? Starting down the Innovational Potential™ road is not for the faint of heart.

There are eight steps to unleashing your company's Innovational Potential™:

1. As the CEO, you must put a stake in the ground that no matter what, you are going to devote the time and resources to unlocking the company's Innovational Potential™. Gather the troops together and lay out your plan and your vision. Tell people why this needs to be done (here's a hint: survival), which is a pretty safe assumption for most companies. Be very clear that this is not an optional program. Full participation is mandatory. That will scare lots of people, which is why you talk about steps 2 and 3.

2. Hire a creativity consultant to conduct a company-wide survey to measure the current Innovational Potential™. You might be surprised to learn the company is more creative than you think. Your people may learn they are more creative than they think they are. In fact, study after study debunks the popular myth that all creative people are born that way. You either have it or you don't. Not so. Creativity can be learned and taught at any age.

With survey results in hand, you now know what you need to go to work on. And you know what you don't need to work on. Feed the survey results back to employees. And tell them what now needs to be done. And that is, everyone in the company will be trained in the principles and practices of creativity and innovation. This starts with basic brainstorming techniques and gets more sophisticated as time moves on. But brainstorming is where you start. You can't implement an idea you never had. Brainstorming gives you the raw material. The idea is to get good at generating new ideas all the time. Expect 99% of all brainstorming ideas to go nowhere. But the 1% that does is fabulous.

3. Provide the time for people to brainstorm and unlock their Innovational Potential™. At Miller Ingenuity, we allow for and expect people to spend 20% of their time innovating. And we hire more people than we need for production so they can achieve this. These days, our employees decide what problems or opportunities to brainstorm about and they decide where and when they will do it – all without a "boss" telling them what to work on.

4. Provide the space and the environment to unlock Innovational Potential™. I built an innovation space in the middle of the factory a number of years ago. Our employees named it "Creation Station." I call it a Google-like campus in the middle of a factory. It is a high-tech space designed and built to foster innovation, creativity, and collaboration. From the room darkening windows to electronic whiteboards, to cushy lounge chairs and a ping-pong table, the room is wired for innovation. Our employees are not only allowed, but encouraged, to go into brainstorming mode in the Creation Station any time they want. At any one time, on any day of the week, you will see our employees there, just "working on stuff." And does the "stuff" they work on pay off? It does.

From a million small improvements and ideas to lots of major ones, the payback came very quickly. But it took a leap of faith to build the space. It was a significant capital investment with a difficult to quantify return. You see, most CEOs won't bat an eyelash at spending $500K for a CNC machine. Why? Because they view it as an income-producing asset. And it is. But so is my Creation Station. Here is a key difference between the two. The CNC machine has a finite useful life and therefore finite production of income. And then it needs to be replaced. My Creation Station has an infinite useful life of income production.

5. Now comes the really hard part. Asking people to be creative may sound like an appealing idea to most people, but it's not. There are several reasons for this.

   a. Some people who don't believe they can be creative never will be, no matter how much training you give them. Innovation is an all-hands exercise and those that can't contribute have to go. Just that simple.

   b. Many people, especially in factories, have been trained to "check their brains at the door." For many people, that is a happy place. No accountability. All they have to think about is their bowling score. Most people like this can't or don't want to reengage their minds. Try and convince them of the merits of participating in the program. But don't try too long. Remember participation is mandatory and if anyone is allowed to be "not mandatory" it dilutes the whole effort. And if you can't convince them? They have to go. It's just that simple. Dismissing people that aren't participating will send a strong signal to the organization that you mean business. And when the health and happiness people tell you that you can't terminate people who don't participate, kick them out of your office. Of course, you can as long as you set the new expectations and give them reasonable time to comply. In union situations, it gets a bit more complicated depending upon the terms of the agreement.

6. In the beginning of this sea-change, people will be afraid their ideas are no good, or that they don't have any ideas. Tell people you will give them lots of help in this area. I hired the ex-Chief Creativity Officer from the QVC network to teach brainstorming to all employees and to ride shotgun with them for the better part of a year, until they got the hang of it.

7. You also need to be prepared to bring in new talent that can support the newer products you'll end up making. These will be very different from your traditional products so it will take a different skill set than you currently have. And unless you have unlimited money (who does?), you'll probably need to swap out older products

employees for newer products employees. But at the same time, you need to make a commitment to the employees you keep that as older products phase out in favor of the newer products, they will be trained in the new products that are coming.

8. Now comes the really fun part. Recognize, reward, and reinforce. Every time my team comes up with a really creative idea, I bring a professional photographer in to take a group picture. And then I put the picture in a full-page 4-color advertisement in the city newspaper congratulating and commending them for their achievement. You wouldn't believe the motivational power of this. People love to see themselves in the paper. And they love to brag to their neighbors about being in the paper. And here is a bonus – it becomes a great recruiting tool when potential hires see how we recognize our employees.

But like my old Uncle Jim used to say, "If money isn't number 1, I don't know what number 2 is." You can talk intrinsic rewards until you're blue in the face, but without the money side, you're only giving people half the equation. I always give each member of the team a crisp $100 bill. And I give it to them in front of the entire company.

One Final Word

I've spent over 40 years in leadership positions discovering what works and what doesn't in creating high-performing organizations. And I can tell you with complete certainty that the principles and practices I outlined here won't work unless your entire workforce is engaged, enlightened, and enthusiastic. You need Cirque du Soleil™ performers. People who are jazzed up when they come to work, totally committed to doing better today than yesterday. That perfectly describes the employees at my company, Miller Ingenuity.

If you want super-charged employees, give them something to get super-charged about. Create a culture with foundational values that people can feel good about and get behind. Values that serve employees, shareholders, customers, and the communities within which you operate. Values that people are proud of. So proud they brag to their neighbors. If you do this first, you will be amazed at how your Innovational Potential™ effort will soar!

About Steven

Steven L. Blue is the President & CEO of Miller Ingenuity, an innovative company revolutionizing traditional safety solutions for railway workers. Its products protect assets, preserve the environment, and save lives.

Steve Blue is an internationally-recognized expert on leading change and business transformation, showing companies how to double and even quadruple growth. Steve regularly contributes to leading media and industry outlets, including FOX, *BusinessWeek, Forbes, The Huffington Post, Entrepreneur Magazine, AMA, Europe Business Review, The Adam Carolla Show* and *The Wall Street Journal.* His insights have led many media outlets to refer to him as one of America's Leading Mid-Market CEOs.

Steve holds a Bachelor's Degree from the State University of New York and an MBA from Regis University. Steve's *7 Values of Ingenuity™* is the preeminent system to exponentially growing a business. His Innovational Potential™ offers a roadmap on how any company can ignite its creativity and innovation capability.

Steve is the author of three highly-acclaimed books that target executives, leaders, entrepreneurs, and anyone seeking to learn the secrets of success in the corporate world. His latest book, *American Manufacturing 2.0: What Went Wrong and How to Make It Right,* was published in 2016 and offers an in-depth take on American manufacturing, inspirational success stories, and a guide on how to regain the key position America once held in the manufacturing industry. Steve's additional books include: *The Ten Million Dollar Employee: When Your Most Toxic Liability Meets Your Most Important Customer,* and *Burnarounds: Unlocking the Double-Digit Profit Code.* He is delighted to be co-authoring with Jack Canfield (*Chicken Soup for the Soul* Series) in *Mastering the Art of Success.*

Steve serves on a variety of boards in safety, banking, healthcare, and university business schools.

You can connect with Steve at:

- Website: www.StevenLBlue.com
- Facebook: fb.me/StevenLBlue
- Twitter: @StevenLBlue
- LinkedIn: LinkedIn.com/in/stevenblue

CHAPTER 10

CREATING CHANGE IN UNLIKELY PLACES: THE DNA OF SUCCESS

BY DR. KAREN HARDY

It's called Human Genome Mapping. My master's dissertation focused on the business and ethical implications of genetic testing. I embarked on this subject matter because I was fascinated by the fingerprint of our personal DNA. I spent twenty years at a renowned national medical research agency dedicated to making important discoveries that improve health and save lives.

One of the organization's biggest affiliated activities, "The Human Genome Project," was an international scientific research project with the goal of determining the make-up of the human DNA, and of identifying and mapping all of the genes of the human genome[1]. The project took 13 years to complete, ending in 2003. While the "Human Genome" represents a collection of DNA imprints, the "genome" of any given individual is **unique** – one of a kind.

I worked for the brightest minds in two biomedical research labs. When you are in the presence of such magnificent science, it's hard not to become fascinated with the science of possibilities and the risk-taking embedded in discovery. This is what dreams are made of. Having an understanding that possibilities are random opportunities disguised as impossible feats and that risk-taking is a key strategy for achieving success, is what separates opportunity thinkers from wishful thinkers.

Just like the human genome, I am convinced that our success patterns have a unique DNA sequence that doesn't lay dormant, but is mapped in real-time and created only as we actively engage in our life space. And if we catch it and take note of it early on, there is a story that comes through, providing us with a glimpse of the hidden messages to help us take inventory of who we are and who we are destined to be.

It's been said that Success is an art, rather than a science.

Perhaps, if it were a science, there would be a set formula for achieving it—like the human genome map. Believing that success is an art, it therefore should not be pre-defined, and is shaped and imagined by the artist at hand. Using life as the canvas, there can be many variations of success, just like there are many variations of paintings.

My variation of success has been a combination of chaos, insurmountable odds, and instinct.

You see, I was one of eight kids. My mom and dad were from North Carolina. My mom worked on a farm and dropped out of school in the 8th grade before moving to Washington, DC. My dad was a packer and truck driver. We were raised in a 900 sq. foot home that was built in 1911. Because the home was so small, the family story is that I was placed in a chest drawer instead of a crib to save space. So early on, there were success mapping signals in the works on my behalf. From time to time, we all find ourselves in situations that do not seem promising, but for every stumbling block there are strategies for succeeding. As I collectively amass these signals, I unveiled a trend of events that map a story about how I function in the world and how I succeed.

As a result, there were a few core principles that I embraced as a code of success as I pursued my life goals.

Principle #1: Have the courage to replace things that have good intentions.

I learned early to make the best of hand-me-downs. Hand me downs are in the eye of the beholder. I remember one occasion when my mom bought me a pair of multi-colored shoes for the new school year. I loved those shoes. But because we were so poor, she could only afford to buy me a new pair of shoes once a year. One day, the tip of the toe of the shoe wore out and my big toe stuck out. My mom lovingly sewed the top of the shoe back together, so you could easily see the threaded stitches. This was great for saving my favorite shoes, but not without consequence for a young schoolgirl like me. As suspected, I was the brunt of school yard jokes like every kid. But, I survived. That experience taught me that I should never be comfortable with trying to make something that's broken whole again. It is ok to move on.

Sometimes, it is just best to enter a new experience, rather than be reminded of what doesn't work. You don't have to wear worn out shoes… forever. Worn out shoes do not have to become a long-term lifestyle. Even your favorite things with good intentions have expiration dates. No need to keep worn out jobs, worn out careers, worn out associates, or worn out ideas. Appreciate the temporary fix, but make provisions for getting something better—whether that's education, a new job, a new home, or new associates.

Principle #2: Make your presence known. Find your space and occupy it.

As part of a big family, I had to fend for myself. There were no leftovers from meals. The only way to be the only child was to be the only one in the room. When you are a part of a big family, make no mistake about it: You are part of a crowd. Crowds aren't known for their uniqueness. In a crowd, you are one of many and nothing really sets you apart. Early on in my career, I realized that I knew a lot of successful people. The only problem was that no one knew me! It finally dawned on me that sitting behind a desk waiting for my boss to thrust me into the limelight was not going to happen. So, I purposely set out to ask myself some introspective questions, like, Who am I? What do I stand for? What makes me tick? What is my voice and message? I let my presence be known by making an appearance.

Principle #3: Make your voice heard.

Now how does this happen? I have 7 siblings. They all have distinctive voices. But on any given day, those voices can all sound the same. There were plenty of times when my mom would call me by my siblings' name because my voice sounded like one of theirs from a distance. I faced the same experience in the work force. A light bulb went off in my head one day about the number of people who can have the same voice in the professional arena, but how it is up to you to make your voice distinctive from the rest of the noise. Think about it, there are thousands of lawyers in the U.S. and yet law school applications are still submitted by many for a chance to join this profession.

Being a part of the crowd has its benefits because it helps to establish a level of identification for yourself and personal growth. But your voice, or message you want to send to the world, is up to you. How you say the message; the tone in which you deliver the message; the level of energy you send out with the message, are all ingredients for establishing your voice. Your voice means that what you have to say does and will make a difference, and it is important to release that voice where it is needed.

Principle #4: Seek to position your inner and outward power.

You don't need a title to be a game changer. Coveting titles can get you in a lot of trouble. What type of trouble? The trouble of "limitations." If you think about it, your soul is too big for a title. A title cannot possibly describe the magnitude of our potential or ability to create change. Early in my career, one title I always coveted was an executive title. There are certain expectations that come with executive status and it is usually reserved for those who can create change across a broad spectrum with far-reaching impact. In my three decades of public service, I finally learned that I didn't have to carry an executive title to create change, though I finally reached my goal.

Despite many setbacks and disappointments, I was able to influence public policy and work for the White House Office of Management and Budget right beside my colleagues from Yale, simply because of my talents, drive, and gift for strategic visioning—not because of a title. I was a risk taker. That made all the difference in the world. Even then, many people thought I held an even higher position when I didn't. This fascinated me. I was obviously giving off the Executive scent of success. That scent is the combination of identifying opportunity, calculating risk, and confidence and sends a message to the universe. The combination of these elements creates a confidence that is perceived by others.

Every business and organization can also give off a scent of success by clearly understanding the relationship between risk taking and opportunity thinking. We all exude a power that far exceeds any title you can hold. *Rather than seeking a title for a position, seek to POSITION your inner and outward power.*

Principle #5: Learn to embrace disruption.

To increase your odds of success, you should seek opportunities that don't attract a lot of attention. Some of the best opportunities are those that don't sparkle or seem that rewarding. Finding such opportunities will require a sense of strategic visioning – being able to see opportunity where others see lack. To be an effective strategic visionary, you should engage in the extensive reading of trends, ask many questions, and inquire of greatness. Strategic visionaries need time to take-in their surroundings, assess the landscape, and observe activities. One gift of a strategic visionary is the ability to see what others do not or to anticipate what others cannot perceive, while tapping into their reservoir of instinct. It also includes the ability to embrace disruption.

To achieve a level of change that sticks, the status quo will have to be abandoned to some extent. Old ways of doing things will have to be tested, reinforced, or thrown out altogether. Disruption is not something to be feared, but an energy to be embraced. Used properly, it can lead to phenomenal discoveries and effective change management. One of the most memorable experiences I had as a strategic visionary was working with the Controller of the United States to make policy changes that impacted the entire federal government agencies. There were several conceptual tools and approaches I applied to create change in the policy arena.

Six approaches for creating change that sticks:

- Maximize informal networks
- Operate through unstructured groups
- Start organically – grow individual relationships
- Fill a void – find that missing piece, then build it
- Utilize group energy for temporary gain – the highest point of production is the outcome, not the formation of a permanent group
- Don't hesitate to be disruptive - don't aim to build coalitions. Disrupt coalitions instead for maximum impact.

And finally, know that You are enough.

- Own your throne.
- Don't accept limitations.
- Find your voice.
- Speak your truth.
- Create change in unlikely places and you too will Master the Art of Success.

---

1. Robert Krulwich (2001-04-17). Cracking the Code of Life (television show). PBS.

About Dr. Karen

Dr. Karen Hardy is an Award-Winning author with a career that has spanned 30 years of public service. Prior to public service, she worked for a Fortune 500 financial services corporation. Dr. Hardy is known for her innovative approaches to creating change management opportunities. Her work has been recognized by a former Controller of the United States who noted that her ability to plan a strategy is outstanding.

Dr. Hardy's mission is to use her gift of strategic visioning and innovation to help individuals and organizations seek and think through opportunities for competitive advantage. Dr. Hardy has organized grassroots and internal business networks to advance policy change on a large scale, and offers her expertise as part of Boards, Executive education, and other platforms. She is a founder of a Risk Management association for the public sector and served as a Board Vice President.

Her work has included a workshop presentation on Managing Risk and Performance to the United Nations departments and offices, which was attended by members of its 24 component organizations including the Department of Peacekeeping Operations, the Economic Commission for Europe, and the Office of the UN High Commissioner for Human Rights.

Dr. Hardy's Award-Winning book, *Enterprise Risk Management: A Guide for Government Professionals*, is a recipient of the 2017 Most Promising New Textbook Award and also reached #6 on the Amazon Top 100 Best Selling List for Risk Management. She is the recipient of two bronze medals for Superior Performance in public service, and received the Outstanding Alumni Award from Strayer University.

She is a sought-after speaker on the subjects of leadership, entrepreneurship, and performance management. She earned a Doctor of Education in Organizational Leadership and Human Resource Development from Nova Southeastern University, a Master's in Business Administration and a Bachelor's in Media Arts and Journalism from Hampton University. In her spare time she enjoys playing the saxophone with her band.

CHAPTER 11

THE ART OF SUCCESS
—CREATING YOUR LIFE'S MASTERPIECE

BY EDYE ST. HILL, MBA

Gaining clarity about the vision of your ideal life is an important "propellant" for creating and mastering personal, organizational and ultimately, global success.

The quality of your life intricately depends on the clarity that you have around your top passions, strengths and values. When working in synchronicity, these things guide you to mastering a fulfilling life. This insight can be as exciting as it is worthwhile! You are an integrated, complex, and amazing creation. How much impact could your life have if you were able to show up authentically, inspired and excited about your life and feeling in alignment with your work – even at the end of a long day? Today, there is a global shift created by like-minded people connecting through meaningful initiatives to improve lives.

The greatest danger for most of us is not that our aim is too high and we miss it, but that it is too low and we reach it.
~ Michelangelo

Organizations that support their members in connecting with their passions, talents, and strengths, and help align them with a compelling vision, gain an important edge. These initiatives are a "propellant" that taps into the discretionary efforts of people – even when no one is watching. They simply do, because it feels right. They have clarity of a vision that speaks to them intrinsically, affecting how they act and approach decisions. The satisfaction that is derived from this offers a natural flow for someone that works in conjunction with their personal integrity, and authentically follows their own best practices. People win, including clients, employees, governments and families. It is a first step to creating an interdependent, symbiotic planet aligned globally by leveraging our individual and collective strengths.

Clarity is the biggest challenge in this pursuit, and for many it can take time to achieve. Much research has been done on the value of engagement at work. The most recent study I reviewed by my alumni association, Queen's University in Kingston, Ontario found exceptional results in businesses that focused on engagement, noting 65% greater share price, 26% less turnover, and up to 30% greater customer satisfaction levels. These benefits and others accrue when an engaged work force is dedicated to ensuring the organization's vision of success. Imagine the benefits we could derive by applying the same energy we do at work to living our best lives, or fulfilling a global vision?

THE IDENTIFYING FACTORS OF SUCCESS

We can secure a successful future best by committing to our personal contribution that comes from leveraging our passions and strengths, stoking them with life-long learning that leads to mastery, and moving out of our comfort zone when necessary.

Being engaged in our own personal development and paying attention to our passions is necessary to gain an understanding of which way our internal compass will point us. Through all the research that has been done, most agree that there are four elements which have a significant impact on engagement at work, and from my experience, are the same factors that are connected with personal passions. They include meaning, autonomy, mastery and connection. These four elements played an important role as I grew more intentional around my life and work goals. They very much aligned with what I came to recognize as some of my top passions. Clarity came with time and attention. While I eventually became very clear on the specifics of my passions, in the beginning they were more general.

It is our unique preferences and experiences that form these passions and values. My journey began as one of five children to parents who lost everything during the war, arrived in Cincinnati as sponsored refugees, and went on to build a successful family business near Toronto, Canada. They worked hard and taught me to do the same. I worked from the young age of 14, eventually taking on three jobs when I was in high school and just sixteen years old. I began to learn early on that I had a sense of certain values I deemed important to me. I knew that I valued the freedom to accomplish things my way. Also, it was important to understand how I contributed and to feel connected – to treat people well and be treated well. I needed to have fun while learning and growing. Later in life, my passion for freedom meant balance. Balance proved to be the grounding element that made the rest possible – time to step back, reflect, and move forward rejuvenated.

When I turned eighteen, I considered going to University for psychology, but was dissuaded by my mother because I had an opportunity to go from a part-time teller job at the bank to a full-time banking career, which Mom deemed to be, "pretty good for a girl." I took the advice and entered into a full-time career, learning quickly something that has become one of my "propellants." By acting like it was my own company, I was naturally adding value for my customers and the bank. Hearing about the challenges of my family's business in the early years taught me to take nothing for granted. Driven by goals that resonated from within, I saw a pathway to help me contribute and create opportunities which led to more freedom and choice. Being driven, not by competitiveness or finite goals, but by what's possible, I often had "ignited moments" that came from challenging myself to move beyond my comfort zone. One of these came from pushing myself to gain confidence speaking in front of people. This eventually became a strength that often led to exhilaration and some of my greatest successes. With this empowering mindset, I was able to keep moving forward in my career while experiencing joy and fulfillment for twenty-six-and-a-half of my twenty-seven-year career.

During this time, I was often approached to apply for promotions and eventually became a senior executive of one of the most highly-recognized corporations globally. Originally, my goal was to be a senior clerk, but through knowing and staying true to my passions, values and what served me best, my career blossomed. The tangible evidence came when I accepted a national Project Manager's position that took me away from customer service. At first, it was an enjoyable challenge because

I was given total autonomy. While the project was successful, I lost my zest for it when it became operational and I missed more direct contact with customers. Career growth needed to stem from leadership around an exemplary customer experience and creating a great place to work. Very quickly, I was offered the next "right step" and several promotions that were aligned.

WHEN CHANGE FINDS US FIRST

Clarity allows us to identify better decisions about when it's time to accept new challenges, or time to move on to continue to grow. We no longer strive – we are guided.

"Coincidental events" often shape life's opportunities. With clarity, you see these events happening more succinctly. Imagine being in a plane that is ascending, going through the thick cloud cover that doesn't even allow you to see the tip of the wing of the plane, and then bursting through it to reveal a clear blue sky and endless sunshine. This is clarity, and I had a defining moment with it.

I faced an extreme challenge with a set of circumstances I was in, which included continuing on in my career, completing my MBA, and supporting my father through cancer treatments. All of this was important, but something had to give. I innately knew what my priorities were, as well as what worked and what didn't. The level of autonomy I wanted was dwindling and furthermore, at age forty-four I couldn't see a path that offered growth while remaining staff and customer centric.

My top priority was to be there for my father, which meant that my opportunity to continue my career at the bank came to an end. It was time. I was so grateful for that extra time with Dad and the renewed connection it offered us both, and sadly he passed away rather quickly. His illness and passing was difficult, but it was a catalyst to an opportunity that I hadn't had before. These stressful circumstances had an amazing silver lining. I could take time out and do something new. I could live like I was dying! I thought about all the friends and family I had that ran out of time before they were able to live more unabashedly. That could not be me. It was time to learn and experience the adventure of life in a manner that fulfilled my desires including my passion for life-long learning.

This shake-up shocked some but made me feel vigorously alive and free. To describe it best you can look at the serious condition of Post-Traumatic Stress Disorder. PTSD can either debilitate someone addressing intense life experiences or it can actually have the opposite effect – offer intense feelings of positive energy. This is what I had and I knew I was being given a real opportunity. In psychology, it is known as "ecstatic growth" and through this I gained a greater perspective of what my life could entail after the age of forty-four. This was my moment, and connections I'd made over the years and people I'd sat beside showed themselves to be more than "coincidental events." At the time, I had not been exposed to information around the power of intention, that our thoughts are important in shaping our lives. I was skeptical at first, but once exposed to the power of the subconscious mind and the latest discoveries in quantum physics, I became curious and open minded. This prompted me to get clear and live even more deliberately.

Early in the process of gaining clarity it is important to pay attention to your emotions. What thrills you? What do you dread and what is the opposite of that? I had an unexpected revelation about these things at what seems like a most unlikely time. An MBA class on global trade agreements culminated in the professor ending the lecture with the possibility of ending poverty, something I had never considered or even acknowledged any passion for. I was overwhelmed with emotion at the thought, to the point of holding back heaving sobs. It was a transformational moment that led me to complete my global business project with a team that assisted a village in Tanzania with their challenges for meeting the most basic of needs.

The synchronicities that occurred to support this effort are too numerous to delve into with great detail, but one stands out distinctly. I wanted to continue work with the village after our MBA project was complete; however, my resources of time and energy were limited. What had been a joy was beginning to weigh heavily on me. Then I met the connection I needed, quite coincidentally. I happened to sit beside the founder of Developing World Connections at a conference and they began participating in the project, which led to the village becoming one of their most successful volunteer destinations for the next eighteen months. Numerous teams completed several worthwhile projects there - a water catchment system, plus homes for a medical doctor and teacher. I then had the joy of leading the team that completed the final project – eight years after my first visit. It was a most fulfilling dream come true. The connections were so amazing!

At this point in my life, the more deliberately I lived, the more prevalent the synchronicities became. I was invited by a former colleague to go through a process to get crystal clear on a career goal. Again, within eighteen months, I was living the dream! Just before my intended date to end my two-year sabbatical, I had lunch with my former boss – the first time we had spoken since leaving the bank. I was recommended for an opportunity that led to an amazing contract that exceeded the vision of my ideal work. I was now part of a "dream team" that allowed me to travel for work and add on play days, while delivering amazing programs and connecting with fabulous people. All this and I still had a very flexible schedule and earned my executive income! The bonus was an opportunity to travel to Europe and return to Africa on a lucrative contract with a bank where one of the greatest takeaways for the executive team aligned with my passion. They had declared their culture as "punitive" and through the program self-identified the power of collaboration and autonomy to engage their team. My heart sang!

Today, my life involves helping people and organizations around the world connect with passion and purpose in a way that aligns them with their highest vision of success. My passion for growth continues to be fueled by learning and the thrill of working with several like-minded authors delivering programs that focus on passion and mastery of consultative sales and leadership skills as a foundation for engagement. People leave these events excited about the possibility of achieving the highest vision for their life and livelihood. Because of this I also continue to grow and learn. I recently moved from a large home to a condo near the water and my sailboat, giving me simplicity and freedom to travel extensively and to follow the opportunities I love.

FULLY ENGAGED

Our ideals resemble the stars, which illuminate the night. No one will ever be able to touch them. But the men who, like the sailors on the ocean, take them for guides, will undoubtedly reach their goal.
~ Carl Schurz

To help with this, I created a game that is devoted to finding clarity and can be played as solitaire or with others. It can be found on my website www.passionclarity.com. There is also a list of entertaining and informational books that support all of this and my commitment to helping others be inspired by lifelong learning. They include more recent radical scientific discoveries behind mind-over-matter and enthralling accounts of near-death experiences by a well-respected neurosurgeon and an anesthesiologist that point to a benevolent universe, a loving source of life. Once a skeptic, I am now a passionate advocate of the power of intention. I also believe we can all learn from the evidence that consciousness survives our physical bodies. Truly, we are eternal souls having a physical experience.

Our passions and beliefs may vary individually, yet when we leverage and engage them together with our collective strengths, through this, we create our personal life's masterpiece. I continue on my path toward my highest vision – a global declaration of interdependence that elevates lives ignited with love, passion and abundance.

About Edye

Edye St. Hill, MBA, is the founder and Chief Ignite Officer of Ignite Consulting Group, dedicated to connecting individuals and organizations with passion and purpose. Combined with mastery of sales and leadership skills, Edye's approach propels organizational performance, tapping into the talents, passions and discretionary efforts of all team members. As an executive within one of the world's highest-rated banks, Edye achieved top awards for sales excellence, leadership and project management. In 2005, Edye completed her MBA from Queen's University in Kingston, Ontario and began helping her clients create a competitive edge.

Edye is a member of the National Association of Experts, Writers and Speakers. She ignites and delights audiences around the globe with humor and inspiration to live their ideal lives and livelihoods.

Over the past several years, Edye has also worked as an independent consultant delivering advanced sales, negotiation, coaching and leadership programs with global leaders in sales training. She has taught workplace communications for international master's students and has worked with two management development centres to create and deliver programs in leadership and advanced facilitation skills.

As part of her commitment to life-long learning, she has certifications to coach and deliver several programs by bestselling authors. She is a certified Canfield trainer in *The Success Principles*. She has also certified to deliver Mike Dooley's *Infinite Possibilities*, Steve Farber's *Extreme Leadership*, and Janet and Chris Attwood's *Passion Test* as well as offering her own customized programs.

Her personal development includes learning that supports a broad spectrum of skills that she brings to her individual and group programs. She is certified in Deep Democracy, training in skills to facilitate through deep-rooted conflict based on Jungian psychology. She has certified in hypnosis and been a member of the Association of Integrated Psychology as well as being an NLP Master Practitioner and Train the Trainer of NLP, based on the gestalt theory of psychology. She has gained exposure to various modalities through certifications in Reiki and other intuitive development programs. Edye is a certified Yoga Siromani and meditation teacher.

She is a committed philanthropist who serves on a Business Advisory Board, for www.enactus.ca., an organization that engages young action leaders, business leaders and academics in an entrepreneurial World Cup Challenge to create meaningful progress toward the United Nations Global Goals for Sustainable Development. Edye leads volunteer teams with Developing World Connections (www.

DevelopingWorldConnections.org) and is active in her local community. She is a co-founder of Team Canzania, an MBA team that climbed Kilimanjaro to raise the capital for a global business project to assist a village in Tanzania.

Her favorite pastimes are hiking, sailing and travelling around the world for work, play, life-long learning and to lead volunteer teams. Edye's highest vision is a planet that taps into the passions, talents and strengths of individuals that collectively, through meaningful initiatives, create a global connection and interdependence that elevates lives.

Play Your Way to Passion:
In order to assist people and organizations to connect with their highest vision, Edye has developed a game that can be played as solitaire, with families and friends, or at conferences – a game of connection and meaningful pursuit. It will get you started and lead to crystal clarity on your top passions. This ultimately has the potential to elevate the trajectory of your life and put you on the most direct path to your ignited life!

To connect with Edye and get more information on this game or engagement programs, visit:
- www.passionclarity.com

CHAPTER 12

WOMEN TOO BUSY TO LIVE: STOP... RECLAIM YOUR LIFE

BY JACQUELINE BURNS

It was 3:00 a.m. on a Wednesday morning. I was in the kitchen preparing vegetables for the Cajun cabbage recipe I'd have for dinner that evening. The rhythm of the chopping and shredding was almost hypnotic. The house was otherwise blissfully quiet. As I brought the knife down through the cabbage for the last time, the thought came to me that I was up early doing something that I needed to do for *myself*—for me—not my family.

How many of us have unconsciously ignored our own needs because we were too busy devoting ourselves to our families that we lost ourselves in the process? Being available to help our family is the loving thing to do. However, it is possible to become so distracted by our involvement in their lives that without realizing it, we neglect our own life. It's not until something happens that jolts us out of our trance that we awaken to find that while we were busy helping and supporting everyone else, we've put our own life on hold.

This chapter is for every woman who has been so devoted to helping her family that she has lost her sense of self and her own dreams in the process.

For more than 30 years, I was that woman. My life consisted of working, raising my daughter, caring for my mother and developmentally disabled brother, and supporting the dreams and goals of my grandchildren. Somewhere along the line, I'd forgotten about my dreams of learning to ballroom dance, of traveling to a foreign country, and of completing the children's book series I'd started long ago. I also hadn't taken the time to develop meaningful relationships that could have led to a loving, healthy marriage.

I have no regrets about devoting myself to my family. Every moment spent serving them was motivated by my love for them, but there was a point at which I realized that I was so focused on my family that I was completely unaware of what was missing in my own life. My joy in seeing them happy and fulfilled blinded me to the truth that I needed to make room for the creation of a life of my own. I was loving them, but neglecting me. It was time for me to acknowledge the cold, hard truth: thirty years had passed without me pursuing the dreams in my heart. It was time for me to examine how I'd allowed my dreams to slip away from me.

HOW I GOT THERE

I was 23, divorced, and raising my daughter alone. I had dreams of creating a better life for us. If I wasn't working two jobs, I was working and going to school. I knew what I wanted and I was focused on making it happen. Then, as it does for so many women, the responsibilities outside of my own home began to grow. One piled on top of the next until they became mountainous.

The Social Security Administration assigned financial responsibility for my mother and brother's benefits to me. My oldest brother, who was 34 at the time, was developmentally disabled. According to psychological assessments, he had the mind of a ten-year-old. He loved to laugh, and he called me Jack. Whether on the phone or in person, he always affectionately greeted me with an upbeat, "Hey Jack." Along with taking care of his finances, I took him shopping, to the barbershop, to movies, and did whatever else he needed.

My other brother was nine years older than me, but he, too, needed my help. After returning from the Army, he began abusing alcohol. When Children's Services threatened to take his six-year-old son from him, he prevailed upon me to raise him. I was happy to do it because, after all, he was family.

A few months before I took custody of my nephew, I'd entered college and sometimes had to take my daughter to school with me for an 8:00 o'clock Saturday class. I'd make a palette at the top of the lecture hall so she could sleep while I took notes. Juggling my classes and my responsibilities at home became infinitely more challenging when my nephew came to live with us. Around the same time, it became apparent that my mother needed more help budgeting her money, so I began doing her weekly grocery shopping and making sure that she had a reasonable amount of spending money. As the responsibilities of my family mounted higher and higher, I began to lose control of my own health. I was in my thirties by then. I had entered college at a lean, firm, and shapely 136 pounds. However, with the added responsibility I blew up to over 200 pounds. I wasn't taking the time to eat properly, to exercise, or get enough sleep. Anyone who knew me could have seen the toll all of this was taking on me physically, but I still hadn't woken up to what was happening.

By the time my daughter became an adult, I was full throttle and out of control with feelings of responsibility for helping my family. Here's what I mean. My daughter was working, but decided to take an evening class to add to her skill set. Even though she hadn't asked me for my help, I offered to support her by staying with my seven-year-old grandson while she went to class. In order to do this for her, I would leave work and travel nearly twenty miles—in the opposite direction of home—through rush hour traffic to get to her. Instead of staying at her apartment where I could rest, I'd entertain my grandson by taking him to the local Barnes and Noble. Afterwards, I'd make the long drive home and arrive around 9 p.m. – completely exhausted from a sixteen-hour day.

Let me ask you a question: Do you recognize this woman? Does any of this sound familiar? Is this you? Like so many of us, I wanted to support my adult child's dreams. I wanted to be an involved grandmother who provided my grandson with rich experiences and an abundance of love. I had the right ideas and motives, and I would never suggest to anyone that they should not be there for their family. What I had to learn was that helping my family didn't have to translate into overloading myself to the point that I neglected my own needs.

My wake-up call came in the form of an old photo and a journal entry. I had been arranging some old photos when I came upon the one that I often used to show friends what I looked like with my hair braided. I smiled, remembering a very different time in my life. I remembered wearing the jeans, the t-shirt, and even the Avon Cherry Jubilee lipstick that was my favorite. In the picture, I saw the sparkle in my eyes and my joyous smile. All of it gave me a warm glow inside until I turned the photo over to see if I'd dated it. To my surprise, it had been twenty-four years since that picture was taken. I was so shocked about all the time that had passed since I looked so young and hopeful that I wrote about the picture in my journal. Here's the entry from that day:

April 6, 2007

Until today the picture had evoked pleasant memories. I kept it where it could be easily accessed in order to show friends how I looked with my hair styled in French braids.

I'd looked at it many times over the years without checking the back for a date. Today, I decided to turn it over to see if it had a date on it. There it was—November 1982! The energy within me shifted. I froze. I couldn't believe what my eyes were seeing. November 1982. "My God, this was twenty-four years ago!" As my body became nearly catatonic, my mind reeled turbulently, and the only clear thoughts I could muster were the usual clichés: "Where did the years go? How did I let this happen?"

As quickly as the smiles had come, they left. The photo of a younger, firmer, more vibrant me became a bold indictment of years of living half a life…one more day, week, month, year of the constant beat that had become my life—a life of being tired all the time due to taking care of everyone but myself. My family's needs always came first. The sudden torrent of emotions was so overpowering that I collapsed in the over-stuffed chair behind me.

It was as though I had been awakened from a long, deep sleep. There it was in bold print: November 1982. The date loomed as a cruel reminder of years of not pursuing my deepest desires. It was an unforgiving attestation of youth taken for granted—the assumption that there would always be another opportunity. The only animated part of my body was my right arm, which was holding the photo. It extended the photo away from my body just long enough for me to feel relief from the painful truth I was facing, then just as efficiently as the arm had extended, it returned in lever-like fashion for another close examination of the date. I repeated this ritual until I heard myself utter the words spoken by Tim Robbins' character in The Shawshank Redemption, "It's time to get busy living or get busy dying."

I had no idea how much I needed that wake-up call, but it jolted me out of three decades of doing too much for everyone but not enough for myself.

I've been living ever since!

If you have been lured away from a life of your own by the seductive call of taking on too much responsibility for your family, this chapter is your wake-up call, and it's time to help you reclaim your life.

HOW TO RECLAIM YOUR LIFE

To get my life back, I made three major changes that I refer to as *shifts*. I believe that if you make these same three major shifts, you will get your life back as well. To reclaim your life, you must: *shift your place in line, shift your level of commitment to your dreams, and shift the way you see time.*

A. Shift your place in line so that you become the most important person in your life.

At first that may sound selfish, but really it isn't. With you as the most important person in your life, you will do everything in your power to make sure that you have what you need to always be at your best. When you are at your best, you can serve others from a place of fullness. One way to stay full is to ask yourself two essential questions when faced with a decision on whether or not to help someone.

1. In order to assist the person who needs my help, what will I have to give up in my own life?
2. If I give that thing up, what are the consequences?

Let's say that your Aunt June is moving to a new apartment, and she's asked for your help on Saturday afternoon. What would you have to give up to do that? Are you giving up time that you have to spare, or is that time you've set aside for some needed reflection and renewal? If the answer is that you need that time for yourself, it would be best to let Aunt June know that although you won't be able to help her move, perhaps you could spend a couple of hours with her helping her get organized after the move. If you really *want* to help, find a way that works for you. Save your energy for the right opportunity, for when you can be at your best. Everyone around you benefits when you've taken care of number one—*you!*

What action can you take today that will *shift* your needs to the front of the line?

B. Shift your level of commitment to *your* dreams.

You keep your commitments to your family. Why won't you keep your commitments to yourself? If you say you're going to start saving a certain amount of money—do it! If you say you're going to walk 30 minutes a day five days a week—do it! Those tasks can seem overwhelming, but break each goal into tiny pieces, set milestone goals, and don't forget to reward yourself at the milestones you set! Maybe you'd like to cross skydiving off of your bucket list. Take the first step, contact a skydiving instructor. Have you been wanting to take that dream vacation, but find it hard to save for it? Download a savings app on your phone that allows you to round up all of the purchases you make with your debit or credit card. Before you know it, you'll have painlessly saved enough money to do something you've always wanted to do. Imagine the possibilities if you did just one small thing each day to get you closer to achieving your goals and dreams!

What commitment to yourself do you need to make good on—today?

C. Shift the way you see time.

Instead of seeing each day as having 24 hours, *shift* your perception to seeing each day as having 1440 minutes. I call this the 1440 Rule. I created it as a way to make myself do what I didn't want to do, but needed to do—like exercise. To get myself to walk when I don't want to, I'll say "There's 1440 minutes in a day, you mean to tell me you aren't willing to use 15 of them to go for a walk?" Fifteen was the number of minutes I would commit to when I'd stopped walking and wasn't motivated. I'd start small and increase over time. When you look at that large number of 1440 minutes and compare it to 15, 20, 30, how can you not do what you need to do? I mean seriously!

To what important task can you apply the 1440 Rule? Do it now!

As you apply these changes to your life, remember that for years you've ignored your life. There is no quick fix for that. You must be patient with yourself, but more importantly—be patient with the process. You've embarked on a journey—the destination being a wonderful life of your own. I'm confident that if you see the reclaiming of your life as an exciting journey, you will find the same or even greater satisfaction in creating joyful experiences for yourself as you did for your family.

About Jacqueline

Jacqueline Burns is a certified business and life coach in the area of leadership development. She specializes in equipping and empowering women to reclaim their lives and reconnect with the dreams they've laid aside. A key component of her work with her clients is teaching them that in order to enhance the quality of their lives, they must learn how to treat themselves as if they matter. Her mantra is, "Women must learn to keep themselves full—to stop running on empty."

As an experienced coach, Jacqueline works alongside her clients to help them develop strategies that move their life forward to the achievement of their specific goals. With over a decade of experience, she has observed patterns that hold people back and has created programs of personal growth, self-leadership, and spiritual transformation to help them eliminate self-defeating patterns and experience lasting change.

Jacqueline's focus is on helping women break out of what's holding them back from living the life of their dreams. In her mastermind courses and seminars, she teaches women how to take action right where they are—regardless of circumstances. Using timeless wisdom, proven leadership principles, and insights from the field of human potential, Jacqueline engages, enlightens, and empowers women to take ownership of their life.

Jacqueline holds a Bachelor of Science degree in Psychology and a Master of Arts in Educational Administration. She is the CEO of JBurns and Associates, a coaching company specializing in personal growth and leadership development, and is a co-author with Jack Canfield in his new book, *Mastering the Art of Success,* to be released in Spring 2017.

Jacqueline is unmarried and lives in Dallas, Texas.

You can connect with Jacqueline at:

- jb@jacquelineburns.com
- http://jacquelineburns.com

CHAPTER 13

BEGIN BUILDING YOUR DREAM TODAY... NO EXCUSES!

BY NAUMAN KHAN AZEEMI

You don't have to belong to the rat race. Join the race where you can build a passion-filled business and life!

How many of you have had dreams that got abandoned? Maybe it was work, family life, or just life in general consuming all of your time. This is most people's stories, but sadly, it leaves a gap in their potential. Because so many people are designed for so much more. Ask yourself if you really have to surrender that job that pays the bills in order to start the new business that builds your dreams? I'm here to tell you that you do not! How do I know? Because I've proven it to be true. I've managed to build up five businesses independent from holding my full-time job. Each one got the attention it deserved, the resources to flourish, and is thriving today.

You can also start a new business without sacrificing everybody and everything. It doesn't have to be uncertainty battling stability. Do you have what it takes? You will need:

- A positive attitude
- Consistency in your efforts
- A fearless attitude toward hard, meaningful work

These things may seem hard to come by, but they are not. Why wouldn't you have all these qualities in your heart and mind if you're pursuing something you're passionate about and want? There is no valid reason, only excuses. Toss excuses out the window! We all have them at times, and what they really are is an alert to what is definitely important to us, and what, perhaps, is not.

You will have a thousand reasons not to start a business. But…you only need one solid reason to make your dream come true!

It isn't always easy to make it and sometimes the odds may seem to be working against us. However, if we dig in and identify with our passions, things do happen.

I came to the U.S. from Pakistan when I was nineteen as an immigrant. In order to make ends meet, I began to work in retail and I worked hard. Yet, I knew that I wanted more in my life than just that job, so I began investing in real estate. Things took off for me and by the time I turned twenty-one, I made my first fortune. Much to my surprise, by the time I was twenty-six, I was dead broke again. I'd lost it all.

A big decision had to be made: surrender or start again? I chose to start again. I was young and it was the time to take risk from a wiser perspective. Why not do it?

My bounce back opportunity came from the IT industry, an industry that didn't quell my desires and passions. It made me desire so much and this energy flowed through me that I could not ignore. This is when things grew exciting—and everything began to happen. It's these lessons that I want to share with you, regardless of where you are now. If anything, never fail to recognize that you do not have to choose risk and reward over family and security. You can do things the right way, so long as you have a positive attitude and focus on what's necessary to succeed, and not on reasons why others (including yourself) may suggest you cannot.

LESSONS IN SUCCESS

Never let anything stop you from pursuing your passions. Use the lessons and growth opportunities these situations offer and invest in your vision of where you want to be.

What a difference time, perspective, and initiative take. I've heard that your first million is the toughest to earn, and after that you have a strong understanding about the formula for success. I guess I cannot deny it, because after feeling and losing abundance all by my mid-twenties, my present-day life is one whose results prove this. With the five companies I've established while working full time, I have found that the quality of my time and the way I spend my days is good.

One of the keys to doing more than we may initially imagine is to recognize the value of a team of people who can help us create our vision.

As an entrepreneur and a president of an organization that is starting out, there is one thing you must remember: there can only be one leader. With one leader it becomes possible to build an entire team that can and will work together for the greater good of the organization, not necessarily you, the owner, in specific. But the rewards are the same; when your business prospers, you prosper. How do you become a good leader? There are three things to be aware of:

- Be optimistic
- Lead by example
- Share the vision with your team

As Alexander the Great noted:

I am not afraid of an army of lions led by a sheep;
I am afraid of an army of sheep led by a lion.

By using this approach, I found the answers to what I needed to do to take on my ambitious goals simultaneously. With start-up businesses, excuses as to "why" or "why not" something can be done always surface – excuses like not having enough cash, investors, etc. To start a business from scratch, these things don't have to be lined up. The problem only exists when you believe they never will be. You have to focus your energy on solutions because vesting your valuable time and mental resources on the problem cannot move you forward. You become the hamster on the wheel.

It's also important to remember that sometimes things won't just happen because you want them to. It's what you do in those moments that really defines the destiny you are cultivating for yourself.

Never give up! Learn from everything that happens and move on.

This is easy to say and hard to do. I admit it, but having patience and a positive attitude is the quality that will get you through those challenging moments where "things aren't happening fast enough." Through patience, I've found the best leadership skills to help me manage everything that comes my way. Of course, I wasn't a fan of this developed quality once upon a time. But I learned a lesson the hard way. I'd just gotten offered a "dream job" at Macy's in Chicago as a General Manager. It came with a great six figure income and I thought, yes, I've made it! Well, the door slammed in my face before I walked through due to a hiring freeze. I was devastated. Everything changed just like that, reminding me of how little control I had over other peoples' actions and decisions. That's when a friend suggested something life-changing to me: "Nauman, why not become an IT consultant while you look for another job." It was a simple suggestion that changed everything and a valuable lesson learned— one opportunity didn't happen because I was meant to have this one. If something goes wrong, be patient because there's a reason. As long as you're trying, what you need will come.

When you're trying to keep going despite obstacles and those "surprise moments" that come your way, it's important to find a way to remain motivated. It isn't always the easiest thing to do and it takes discipline to remember exactly why you should be motivated! After all, you're working toward something that will give you great freedom and rewards, plus a sense of accomplishment that cannot be had without the exciting experience of entrepreneurship.

Consistently follow your passion. Remember, there is no gain without the pain. But what numbs the pain? The <u>passion!</u>

When we want something at the deepest level, it is best achieved by consistently following your passion, as this cultivates motivation! I remember some wisdom I heard from a CEO of mine. He came in and told me this: "Everything you desire is going to bring stress." It seemed like a dismal message, but within its wisdom was sound knowledge for motivation.

There's no guarantee of "easy". What comes easy is a blessing, but the rest of it takes some serious effort, and it can stress you out. But what reduces stress? Acknowledging it exists and turning it on its ear, using it to help you. Understand that God does not bring anything to you that you cannot handle. If a problem comes to earth, a solution comes with it. Focus on the solution more than the problem. If your problem is a lack of money, your solution doesn't lie in dwelling on that. It lies in finding a way to get more money. How do you do that? Work, invest, and be motivated and inspired. Create a bold vision and become one with it. Know where you want to be and the rewards of the journey you are taking. This keeps you motivated because you are personally connected with it. If you cannot do this, it's usually because of the ugliest of emotions—fear.

Fear is a feeling which is self-created.

Most people will not start any business with the fear of losing. This is natural, and actually not bad, if... you also understand your chances of winning and losing! It all comes down to which feelings will overcome you. The one way to assure you lose is to not work hard or put any "leg work" into developing your business. Winning is great and the strategies to do it are available to anyone who wishes to seek them out. It's fortunate for you that you're right where you need to be, because I am going to share this great insight with you.

CREATING YOUR WINNING STRATEGY

When you build a culture from the start that has the right people to help you Succeed, you will be creating a situation where all people are operating on the same frequency.

Entrepreneurs love to think outside the box, and it's with good reason, as it's necessary! Some strategies are time tested and effective, while others need to be explored in a way that resonates with you, all while moving you forward. Here are four things that you should consider as you ignite your path to success.

1. **Know how to hire the right way.**
   A common thought is to grow the business and then hire. I challenge you to think differently. Hire first and then grow. Why? Because

you might be surprised about the potential that the people you hire bring. It could ultimately be more than what you're targeting. For example, I may want an IT company in the Chicagoland area, but maybe someone I hire can make it expand further. Why limit growth? It doesn't make sense, as it will limit your success.

2. Your network is your net worth.

Who you know is who you're going to become. If you want to be an entrepreneur, you had better develop relationships and mentorships with entrepreneurs. Take their wisdom and experience. You don't have to do this part on your own! I own an IT training institute, and I'm excited about how successful it is. I've trained over twelve-hundred students in the greater Chicago area, and half of them make pretty substantial incomes. But to learn this, I took advantage of networking in a most unusual way. I volunteered as a teacher at another school to learn what I needed to know, better honed in on my teaching skills, and took advantage of what I could gain at someone else's expense. Honestly, it's one of the smartest decisions I ever made. And those who have followed the suggestion have experienced the same thing.

3. Understand what your best efforts are. Learn balance.

I think of a plant to demonstrate this point. If you water it too much, it dies, despite water being necessary for it. If you don't pay attention to the little things like tiny insects, it dies. Through being a part of the process you are creating, you learn the things to look for. This, in conjunction with your network and volunteering, make for a powerful ability to gain invaluable insight.

4. Use your time wisely.

On average, people spend four hours a day browsing social media and watching TV. It's almost unbelievable! Imagine cutting that down to even two hours a day. Suddenly the "time" to pursue your passions becomes available. And it adds up! Do this for a year and you'll gain a total of 91 working days. How? Take 2 hours per day x 365 days and you end up with 730 hours! This equals that coveted 91 days. This is a powerful way to realize just how you spend your time and the greater potential you have with it!

IT'S TIME TO IGNITE YOUR PASSION

Move forward in faith and believe that with your commitment and effort, you will build great things.

There's nothing easier in life to give than extra effort when you're breathing and playing witness to the rewards of this. No one can do this in a more profound manner than an entrepreneur. So go ahead and give some extra effort; take some calculated risks. When you have patience, it does pay off.

Through all that I've been through, I've never been more excited to help coach people who want to invest in their own outcomes. It doesn't have to be all or nothing. Start that business on the side while you're doing your full-time job.

If you can dream it, you can achieve it!

About Nauman

Nauman Khan Azeemi is an Entrepreneur and Technologist. Through his desire to succeed, he has seen many ups and downs on his journey. However, he has always walked away with a valuable lesson and a renewed desire to keep trying. And it has worked. Today he is the President and owner of five businesses, four which are in IT and one is a retail establishment and things couldn't be better.

In Nauman's inspirational story and message, he has experienced and laid out a pathway for those who have entrepreneurial dreams to achieve success in them, without having to quit their full-time job or main means of income. Nauman, himself, did this same thing, rising to an elite level in all the businesses within just three years. A natural leader and teacher, Nauman is passionate about helping others realize their fullest potentials.

Nauman's success philosophy is a powerful concept, involving developing the right mindset, a consistent and positive attitude, and the commitment to achieve your dreams. This is a philosophy he has inherited from his spiritual mentor Khawaja Shams-Uddin-Azeemi. He uses this guide in all he does, including mentoring youth and working with an organization called *Tech in Pakistan* that focuses on a concept called, "Empower the Technologist." He's excited about being a co-author with Jack Canfield in his book *Mastering the Art of Success*. Nauman sees this as an incredible opportunity to reach more people than ever, sharing the ideas they must know and helping them organize their lives to make room for their dreams!

Today, Nauman lives in Chicago with his wife and two kids. He likes reading books and the opportunities to present his motivating speech and story to others. His upcoming projects include a course and book on "How to establish your business while doing a full-time job."

Nauman love to help people achieve their passion and can be contacted through his website:
- www.naumankhan.com.

CHAPTER 14

SEVEN SECRETS TO CREATING THE RESULTS YOU'VE ALWAYS DREAMED

BY MICHAEL J. KESSLER, CPA
Business Profitability Visionary

THE BUSINESS PROFITS

1. "Always do the right thing, Michael!"

My maternal grandmother taught me this one. And when you were growing up you may have heard the same from your loved ones, friends and mentors. Some of us may have let it go in one ear and out the other, so challenge yourself today by picking your favorite person who may have said that to you during your life and use them as your point of reference. For example, every action I take in business and in life I ask myself (consciously or subconsciously): "Would Gramma approve of this?" It's an amazing filter that helps me make the right decisions quickly.

If you're a small business owner, you've built the culture of your business. Webster defines that 'Culture' as: The set of shared attitudes, values, goals, practices and beliefs that characterizes an institution or organization. And it's your culture that breeds the environment in which your organization operates.

2. "It's the environment, stupid!"

I learned this one in the first moments leading my first small business. Behavior of many employees was in direct conflict with what we really wanted our culture to be. It was the result of the negative environment that evolved over decades under previous ownership, so we immediately set out to change that.

When bestselling author and leadership visionary Simon Sinek was a guest on my weekly radio show, he was so eloquent in articulating how an organization's environment can profoundly affect the behavior of its people and the organization's ultimate success.

Simon said: *"Leaders set the tone and the tone sets the behavior. We're social animals and we respond to the environments that we're in. You can take a good person and put them in a bad environment and they are capable of doing bad things. You can take a group of people who society may have given up on, maybe they've even done some bad things, but if you put them in a good environment, they're capable of turning their lives around and becoming remarkable members of society."*

Simon cautioned: *"The way we run our companies today, so often, it is the complete antithesis of how the human being is actually designed to operate. The reason we have stress problems, the reason that things like 'work-life-balance' are an issue today, has nothing to do with how much yoga we do. It's because we feel safe at home but we don't feel safe at work...THAT'S THE IMBALANCE!*

When you create an environment that is poorly led, stress is one of the results...work dissatisfaction is one of the results...being tired when you come home at the end of the day is one of the results... being afraid of your boss is one of the results...being paranoid, gossip, politics, these are all the results of bad leadership! In well-led companies there IS NO politics...there IS NO gossip... people come home energized, they're passionate, they're inspired, they're joyful...they LOVE their job! You feel taken care of by the other employees, you feel taken care of by leadership. You don't feel that they would sacrifice you to save their bonuses...rather they would sacrifice their bonuses to save you!"

Simon sums it up: *"When we FEEL that our leaders are trustworthy...when we FEEL that our leaders would take care of us...when we FEEL that our leaders would sooner sacrifice the numbers to save us, but would never sacrifice us to save the numbers, we will reward them with our love and our loyalty, we will offer our blood, sweat and tears to keep each other safe, to keep them safe and to advance their vision."*

So surround yourself with the right people to create an environment that takes care of your people who will in turn take care of your business and your customers without you even asking! It could bring your business to the very top of your industry!

3. "Your family, your religion, and the Green Bay Packers!"

NFL Hall of Fame Coach Vince Lombardi's famous pre-game speeches set strict priorities for his players. It was that set of priorities that created the winning formula to carry The Green Bay Packers of the 1960's to an amazing five World Football Championships in seven years.

As the working parents of three millennials, my wife Karen and I chose to share equally in our childrens' upbringing. I am truly blessed to have a true 50-50 partner in love, parenting and in life. That enabled us both to maintain the "family first" priority in our careers and businesses and we never failed to take care of our family, get the work done, take care of our employees and take care of our clients. In the end, I never heard any parent, man or woman, say: 'Damn, I wish I had spent more time at the office!' You have but one life to live and one family to love, but you have many chances to live life and love your family.

Today, Karen and I are most proud of our kids, not only because of their careers serving our nation, but because of the lives they lead. Oh yes, and proud that they are all financially independent of Mommy and Daddy!

And no matter your religious or spiritual beliefs, make those a part of your family fabric – it will be the icing on the cake!

4. "You miss 100% of the shots you never take!"

Wayne Gretzky said it; we entrepreneurs live by it. As the ones who take the initiative to found, organize and manage a business or enterprise at considerable financial risk, entrepreneurs usually don't take just one shot. With the rate of business failure at a well-known 90%, entrepreneurs relish the challenge. To discover whether you are up to the challenge, ask yourself:

- Do I need to be the smartest person in the room?
- Do I have trouble asking for help?
- Do I talk when I should listen?
- Do I have trouble holding myself accountable?
- Do I constantly obsess over my competition?
- Am I too busy to read for at least one hour per day?

If you answered yes to any of these questions, you and your business could be at risk. Food for thought on the above points:

- You just need to have access to the smartest person in the room
- Asking for help is a sign of strength not weakness
- Speaking last will help you avoid talking when you should be listening
- Never ask anyone to do anything you wouldn't do yourself
- Doing the opposite of everyone else is often the best approach
- Constantly educate yourself – READ, READ and READ some more

Take the time to talk about any or all of these with someone you trust – it could help you create the results you've always dreamed!

5. "Consistency, Authenticity, Empathy – it's YOUR brand!"

I got this from my mother who is the hallmark of these three. None of us is perfect, but when you are lucky enough to be able to put these all together and make them your brand, you become unstoppable.

When you're consistent in everything you say and do, and it's really you, authenticity becomes part of your brand. And if you have the true ability to understand and share the feelings of another, that's empathy. It should be empathy for your customers, your employees and your prospects alike. When empathy becomes part of your brand, you connect very powerfully with your clients and prospects on a deeply emotional level that will trump your resume every time.

People really don't care what your bio says. What people care about is whether you understand and connect with what they are going through. For example our hopes, our dreams and frustrations are all extremely personal to us. And when we FEEL that you understand and connect with those, chances are we have put you at the top of the list of people we want to do business with – absolutely HAVE to do business with – it's that powerful!

Every situation you've personally experienced has deepened your ability to empathize with certain clients and prospects. If you think about those experiences, both good and bad, it could help you focus on certain groups of clients and prospects you can help the most. Write those experiences down and develop a written plan to close those deals – it could help you generate more business than you've ever dreamed!

6. "Market, Message, Media – Yes, in that order!"

Target a specific Market (prospects or customers), with a compelling Message directing them to take a specific action, and deliver that message through measurable Media of advertising? That's Direct-Response Marketing and as you become better and better at it, your business could grow exponentially once you master it. Another great quote from Simon Sinek:

> *"People don't buy what you do, they buy why you do it. The goal is not to do business with everybody who needs what you have; the goal is to do business with people who believe what you believe."*

So what do you believe? And does everything you say and do serve as proof of what you believe? If yes, chances are you're building a loyal stable of customers. And your level of consistency, authenticity and empathy should help define your target Market. The more clearly you can define who you're really targeting, the better your results. A good way to do this is to describe (in writing) your ideal customer or prospect in terms of an individual person, not a vaguely defined market. For instance, saying "I want to market to people looking for a new franchise opportunity," is too general.

Instead, be specific! Is your ideal client female and/or male? How old are they? Are they married or single? Do they have children? What is their annual income? Do they live in a specific country, state, city or neighborhood? What do they do for a living? Are they interested in a specific hobby or activity? Do they have a specific problem they are looking to solve? And we're just scratching the surface here! Get laser-focused on your target so you don't waste your marketing spend. Getting the highest possible return on those investment dollars puts you way ahead of your competition.

Now, what's the *Message* you want to convey? Once you have your target market well defined, you'll want to tailor your message to attract that market.

What is it specifically that you want to say to them? Does your message contain an attention-grabbing, compelling headline that strikes the right emotional chord? Grabbing their attention emotionally is vital, as you want them to read your message and keep reading to learn more. Do they FEEL like you identify with their needs or wants in your opening statements? They should feel like you "get them", and you understand specifically what their actual need or want is.

Your *Message* could provide a solution for their need or want on the "WHAT Level" by listing the features and benefits of your product or service. Better though is to convey your message on the "WHY Level" that strikes an emotional chord. The emotional reasons for "Gut Decisions" are hard to put into words but your emotional gut is really what drives decision-making.

Finally, your *Message* should end with a "call to action." What action do you want them to take, specifically? "Call this number for more information," "Enter your email to watch this amazing video," "Click the add-to-cart button to buy now!" If you've done well to target the right market with the right message, you should generate a nice pipeline of prospects trying to reach you to learn more.

What *Media* to use? Once you have your target market well defined and your message is emotionally compelling, how are you going to deliver that message? What advertising *Media* will most effectively get your message in front of your specific market? Maybe it's sending them a letter through direct mail, or placing an advertisement in an industry publication. Maybe it's through email or text messaging or social media. The key is find the most cost effective way to deliver your compelling message to your target market...and actually have it read, so they will take the action you desire. This is a skill that takes time and practice to develop, so don't expect to get it right the first time.

But, keep practicing and persevering. Continue seeking to be more specific on whom your ideal prospect really is. Re-write your message as many times as it takes to get it right. And keep experimenting with different advertising media until you find the ones that deliver the highest return on your advertising investment. I've had winners and losers in my marketing campaigns...and you will too!

7. "Give back. . . No strings attached!"

Serve on a not-for-profit board, give to charity, introduce two colleagues to each other, put out free educational content, mentor a young person or help a friend in need. And do it when the cameras are off.

Detaching yourself from the outcome is never easy. But that is exactly what you must do if you are to truly give back. When you expect nothing in return, that's when it will come back to you . . . TENFOLD!

About Michael

In everything he does, Michael J. Kessler believes in challenging the status quo. He believes in thinking differently from traditional accounting. The way Mike challenges the status quo is by bringing his clients and their families into a world where their stress is reduced and their quality of life improves with an increased net after-tax cash flow far exceeding the investment they make in their relationship with him.

Prior to founding his Profitability Consulting and CPA business in 2011, Mike spent over 25 years as a small business CEO in private industry. Mike's businesses grew more than 400% in a transformation he likens to "hitting the business trifecta." Starting as a family-owned group of businesses, the group became employee-owned and then was acquired four times in ten years by multi-billion dollar public companies.

Mike's business achievements include the Rockwell Collins President's Award, election to the Rockwell Collins Supplier Alliance Advisory Council, The Best of Long Island Business Award, SmartCEO CPA/ESQ Award Winner and Long Island Business News Business & Finance Award Winner. Mike is honored to be your host for his weekly radio show, *Business Profits In The Real World*, on 103.9FM LI News Radio. He has been interviewed on America's PremierExperts® TV show seen on NBC, CBS, ABC and FOX Affiliates around the country and is a frequent guest commentator of 103.9FM LI News Radio morning host Jay Oliver on *LI in the AM*. Mike educates his audiences with his weekly *Real World Strategy Blog* and by speaking before various business forums including The Hauppauge Industrial Association, The Accountants Resource Group, The Long Island Advancement of Small Business and The Long Island Profitability and Economic Conference.

Mike's education includes a unique blend of four financially-based accreditations: BS in Accounting, BS in Mathematics, Certified Public Accountant and Chartered Global Management Accountant. Mike is very active in his community supporting the Down Syndrome Association, The Independence Fund, the Leukemia & Lymphoma Society and has been honored as one of Long Island's Champions for a Cure for his work in support of the Arthritis Foundation.

Mike and his wife Karen reside on Long Island where they raised their three sons, who all served in our armed services, and are blessed with four beautiful grandchildren.

You can connect with Mike at:
- Michael.Kessler@CPA.com
- www.MichaelKesslerCPA.com

- www.Twitter.com/MikeKesslerCPA
- www.Facebook.com/MichaelKesslerCPA
- www.LinkedIn.com/in/MichaelKesslerCPA

CHAPTER 15

CREATING TRANSFORMATIONAL CHANGE AND LEADERSHIP

BY JEFF TURNBOW
(aka 'Turnaround' Turnbow)

INTRODUCTION

I can't ever remember a time when I felt limited. I certainly was, if you measure our family in financial wealth, connections, and social status, but I never knew it. My family and support system did an amazing job of constantly reminding me of my blessings rather than my challenges. I certainly wasn't blind to my challenges, but I didn't fear them. Instead, I always saw light inside the tunnels. In fact, I often feel as though I possessed some super power to see the path to change.

A few years ago, I was struggling with direction in my life. My career was fast and the number and weight of my responsibilities was growing. I completed the Joel Osteen Study Guide – *Your Best Life Now*, and it helped me enlarge my vision, live with favor, and refocus my goals. It was certainly a turning point for me.

This personal breakthrough catapulted my career. It almost seems to be an overnight success where my career immediately launched to a higher level. Literally the next day, the perfect client (according to my workbook goals) called, referred another, and another! I have found no special secrets to success. My success happened due to hard work, initiative, and blessings from God.

Sometimes a business or organization reaches a point where they feel limited or stuck. Regardless of financials, human resources, or brand status, any organization or team can experience a turnaround. They can breakthrough any perceived limits. This has been my focus over the past seven years. Here are some of the keys I have discovered for creating significant organizational turnarounds.

THE CHANGE PROCESS

When a team needs to move in a new direction, change the status quo, and transform in very significant ways, designing and executing a strategic change is often placed on the shoulders of great leaders with no previous experience leading this level of big change. Leadership experience and talent alone cannot create this kind of change. Most leadership and management training cannot teach the necessary art and science to create transformational change. This type of big turnaround requires the boldest leadership.

Turnarounds must have specific and attainable goals, yet unlike other change, the goals may seem attainable without sufficient documented or historical evidence. Gut instinct and big change experience helps here. I remember the day I was labeled "Turnaround Turnbow" during a conference call, and somehow the branding spread to other clients until it really got me thinking: What is it that creates successful "turnaround" within an organization?

During my time in consulting and training large and small organizations, I began to identify a similar strain of struggles, regardless of the type of organization, such as:
  - complacency
  - inability to reach goals
  - ineffective management styles
  - employee churn

Often, I hear about employee resistance to change. Employee resistance is often measured in proportion to the degree to which people are kept in the dark and left out of the change process. This is very common.

Unfortunately, we have all contributed to the rise of standardized environments and teams, therefore we all must contribute to the deconstruction process necessary to become extraordinary.

> *Problems cannot be solved by the same level*
> *of thinking that has created them.*
> ~ Albert Einstein

Turnarounds happen through radical breakthroughs in thoughts, beliefs, and actions.

#1.   Change The Environment.

We have standardized work environments. Sure, some companies hung a few motivational posters, but as I walk through most offices I notice how they almost always look similar. I often recall my amazing sitter telling me "Your environment is stronger than genetics." I never realized the power within that statement until I studied human behavior and what motivates people. I believe she was correct. While I certainly can't settle the lifelong battle of nature vs. nurture today, I can tell you that when I make changes inside an environment, attitudes, behaviors, and results always change. I have learned that big change requires the team to buy-in to a large specific strategy or roadmap. The map must lead to an attainable, collaborative goal, including an attitude adjustment for all involved. Finally, there must be a very obvious adjustment within the physical office design and purpose. When I have performed or helped create these shifts, I have witnessed extraordinary – actually astounding – results! Oftentimes without a change in staff! Today, I simply will not attempt a Turnaround without this first element of change.

#2.   Train / Educate / Empower

Employees perform better when they are educated, empowered, competent and confident. Companies often rush their teams to market or task far too fast. Training and educating creates the confidence and will improve all efforts. Through training and education, you can increase overall confidence, desire, and competence. However, the trainers must be excellent. Great trainers understand the training, and education process must be frequent and with hyper-focus. Broad classes yield very little progress over concise chunky power sessions. The learning must become immediately applicable and frequent "check-ins" are necessary to measure retention. I use the 20/80 rule in almost everything. For example, before I implement a training session, I write down: What is the 20% of content within this class that everyone must retain today? Do not move forward until everyone is ready to move forward.

Once the team members have become an integral part of the organization, they should be empowered within their scope of work. Limited employees cannot adequately serve the company, plus they slow down the momentum and pace of change being implemented. I often tell managers, "If you cannot trust this agent with your company's best interests, they shouldn't be here." Trust, cooperation, and empowerment are critical components to a healthy team. Sure, boundaries are necessary, but employees must be fully aware of the boundaries and empowered to maximize their opportunities to reach goals.

#3.   Create Momentum

Goals during transformation and turnarounds are unique. There must be a groundbreaking shift in the roll out and appreciation of new goals. These goals must look and feel different than ever before. First, make certain the new goals have a clear roadmap to attainability. Define what you are going to accomplish, why you will do it, what the benefits of change are, and what the dangers of not changing are. The Bible says, "Without vision, the people will perish." Vision is the energy which creates momentum. The vision must be clear and constantly in front of the team. Next, create a sense of urgency and maintain this urgency throughout the process. This maintenance is very similar to that of a point guard maintaining or adjusting the tempo of a basketball game. Remember that bodies in motion will stay in motion – at the tempo created and maintained by the leadership. This leadership position is the change agent and the team will respond to their cadence and calls.

#4.   Create Trust

I have learned in twenty years that teams become cooperative and successful faster when they want to be, rather than when someone attempts to force them to be. To create a Turnaround Team, you must balance control with letting go. If you are using the words "required" and "mandatory" to lead your team, there is a significant breakdown in the relationship. This breakdown almost always rests on a lack of trust. This foundation is not ready to build upon. The trust and cooperation must be mended. Begin by never asking the team to do something you are not willing to lead and participate in. Successful teams see their leader out front and fully engaged in the process. They are inspired by their leadership and expect leaders to correct the course during the event rather than post event.

The injection of constant force is usually happening because the team doesn't want to do the work. Force and stress will only destroy teams. Sure, pressure and stress are motivators, but they almost always motivate good people to leave. You must look inward and the first question should be: Why? You may learn the team holds a better process or idea to obtain the desired result. You may learn the team is frustrated and stuck because they simply don't know how (usually due to lack of proper training and education), or you may learn that you have a few wrong players on the team – but more trust, not force will create success.

Big change agents focus on creating visceral levels of trust, creating smoother opportunities for their team, and removing roadblocks swiftly along the course. These deeply-committed teams are totally engaged with leadership and eager to reach the highest levels of success.

#5.   Reward Success
The taste of big victories should be so sweet that it is never forgotten and constantly craved. The pushback I get here is almost always related to costs and expenses. My answer is always this: "If you run your company based on standard formulas, you will continue to get standard results." To be extraordinary, you have to toss out the standards and the "industry standards." *Think shock and awe!* If you have invested in the other steps, then set the bar high, attainable, then shock your team with the sweetest reward possible! Suddenly, more of your team's engines fire and excitement is running everywhere!

Remember, when more people enjoy the environment, you become the place where all the top team players want to work, and everyone in the community is talking about the excitement and energy on YOUR TEAM! This creates exponential returns on your investment.

#6.   Create Healthy, Inspiring and Passionate Teams

Organizations must become less self-centered and more interdependent. Today, our lives are filled with information about tragedy, political discourse, and conflict. More family members are working and juggling the busiest schedules. Many companies are fueling this reckless behavior! We can never obtain long-term employee/team success until we become a part of fostering better holistic lives. We spend so much time at work, why can't we become a resource far beyond paychecks and company goals?

Holistic team leadership includes motivation, hope, and inspiration. Yes, I am talking about having a real relationship with your team. Without this focus on the whole health, we will drive ourselves into peril by pushing our teams until we are recruiting for the churn we actually created. Unfortunately, many companies calling me are already stuck in this vicious cycle. Ultimately, people will perform their best when they enjoy their work and when they feel like they are a part of a focused team – rather than operating as a tasked robot. Their best performance is something we need, it is not optional.

In order to create significant turnarounds, we must be able to cultivate and activate the health, spirit and energy of our people. This is passion, and passion comes from the heart. To ignite passion, you must move beyond critical thinking, analytics, and facts. Igniting passion comes from learning about your people on an emotional level and connecting with their deepest aspirations. You cannot find or measure this on a spreadsheet.

IN SUMMARY

Creating Turnarounds in a team, department or whole organization is not for the inexperienced. It involves taking bold steps into what most would call an uncertain future. Most seek out Turnarounds when they see limitations or opportunities. They just need assistance in executing the big change.

While this listing above will help serve as mile markers on the road to transformational change, remember that you will need someone with big change experience to lead true turnarounds. The success is found in the methodical and powerful execution rather than simply completing the steps. This is where the art of change becomes significant. While the tactics and steps can be carefully organized and executed, the style, cadence, energy, intuition, tenacity, and resolve are all part of the secret sauce for successful and significant turnarounds.

About Jeff

In addition to leading ReachTurnbow.com, a digital marketing and media company, Jeff Turnbow has extensive experience working on a broad range of organizational change-related topics in a variety of industries, including: auto, media, nonprofit, legal, and industrial companies. Jeff possesses considerable expertise in talent and leadership development, performance management, marketing, and capability building. In addition to serving clients on these topics, he works as a marketing strategist for a few large clients. He serves as a public speaker and adjunct professor on similar topics.

His recent client work includes:
- designing and implementing the integration of digital sales into two top broadcast organizations. A key element of this project was training, goal setting, and momentum.
- helping a leading RV and Boating company expand its marketing and sales to a more regional brand.
- launching startup companies, including attracting diverse talent and pursuing opportunities in unfamiliar markets.
- leading a retailer with organizational structure and strategy in order to expand brick and mortar sales with ecommerce.

Jeff Turnbow spent the first twenty years of his career in sales and marketing leadership. He is actively involved in staying at the forefront of transformational leadership and marketing through continuing education and thoughtleadership. Jeff was recently interviewed to appear in a ThoughtLeader show on FOX, CNN, and MSNBC.

Jeff is certified in Digital Strategy at Harvard University and serves as a paid Expert Consultant for national research firms. He is an adjunct professor at Universities, is Certified by Google, and is Certified by E-Cornell and by LinkedIn University. Jeff was recently inducted into The National Association of Experts, Writers, and Speakers.

CHAPTER 16

WHAT DOES THE WORLD NEED NOW?

BY OLIVER BENNETT SCHLAFFER

Serve the needs of others, and all your own needs will be fulfilled.
~ Lao Tzu

THE NEED SHARED BY 7+ BILLION PEOPLE

During her 2013 Harvard University commencement address, Oprah Winfrey shared what she called the single most important lesson she has learned, after 25 seasons on television:

> *The common denominator that I've found in every single interview is that we want to be validated. We want to be understood. I've done over 35,000 interviews in my career. And, as soon as that camera shuts off, everyone always turns to me and, inevitably, in their own way, asks this question: "Was that okay?" I heard it from President Bush. I heard it from President Obama. I've heard it from heroes and from housewives.*

In this speech, Oprah identifies the need that we all share for validation as the driving force behind our decisions, our conflicts, our actions and our happiness. In reflecting on this, I have often contemplated how this need is connected to the quest that all humans have (myself included) to find their *raison d'être. . .* or life's purpose.

155

Perhaps this story will shed a little light on how I found mine.

THE SOURCE OF INNER STRENGTH

"So...where are you from?"

This was always a very difficult question for me to answer, as I had an unpredictable childhood moving between twelve cities across six states throughout the United States. I attended seventeen schools from Kindergarten through college, never staying at any school longer than three years, and sometimes multiple schools in the same grade.

No, my parents were not in the military – they were professional musicians, and their work would end up taking my family all over the country. After spending middle school in six different locations, I remember feeling like a "professional" new kid by the time I was in eighth grade, adopting a carefree attitude when approaching new people that I hadn't met before.

You would think that disrupting a child's environment and relationships so many times might cause one to become introverted and reclusive, but I was just the opposite. I remember how liberating it felt, not needing or hoping for the approval of others

"Hello, nice to see you!" I would say at the top of my voice while extending my hand to a stranger...they would stare back at me as if I had two heads! Although I could have easily felt awkward in those situations, I never expected to stay in any one place long enough for their opinions to matter.

Ironically, that led to me becoming one of the more popular kids by the end of middle school... as in the movie "Groundhog Day", when the main character (played by Bill Murray) became so skilled at dealing with all the people he encountered for the hundredth time, after living the exact same day over and over again.

Back then I believed that it was all the constant moving around which gave me the confidence to overcome those challenging times. However, thinking back over the years to where my inner strength originally came from…I realize now that, in fact, it came from something else entirely.

The cello.

LOVE AND THE PASSION FOR MUSIC

My mother played the piano and the violin, and my father played the violin and the viola. I guess I was destined to become a musician too, since my parents had both decided before I was born that their first son would be a cellist… I was actually never part of that discussion.

My loving mother would tell me that when she was pregnant with me, she would always listen to cello music, and pray that her baby would have the soul of a cellist. While it may be difficult for me to unequivocally know the absolute intention of my soul, I know I always loved the sound of the cello, so I was always happy that it was chosen for me.

My early years were constantly immersed in music from the beginning, and I began attending concerts when I was only a few months old. My parents performed often and also taught music lessons at home. Music was always being played in the house, in the car, at dinner time, and at all other times of the day and night.

When it came time for me to start my cello lessons, I was only four years old. I think something interesting happens when a child is constantly immersed in something like music at such an early age. For me, music was much more than a form of entertainment, it was part of my everyday thoughts and feelings, and it became my identity.

Not only did I feel love *through* music, but I also experienced every other human condition that the greatest composers throughout history could convey via their art. Up until the age of eleven, I can remember spending hours on the floor of my room, staring up at the ceiling while listening to the great classical cello concertos (solos with orchestra), and imagining that it was me on that stage, connecting with the audience.

I have always believed in the power of intention, and have been applying it (albeit unknowingly) since I was a kid. My assumption that I could achieve the highest level of mastery on the cello was something I never doubted I could accomplish. Even though I would experience various setbacks and challenges along the way, in my young mind it was inevitable that I would succeed, it was just a matter of maintaining a steady course to get there. As it turned out, it would be another ten years or so before I would actually step onto the stage to perform at Carnegie Hall in New York City.

Achieving a certain level of competence on the cello early on was key to developing my confidence and a positive self-image. Not a lot of my classmates in school were musicians or even understood what studying music was all about. When I was in elementary school, I remember often dealing with the typical amount of ridicule that is common at that age. There were always other students who found it enjoyable to poke fun at me for playing my instrument, which wasn't anywhere as cool as playing sports... but it was through those experiences that I learned very early on not to put much value into negativity from others, a strength to which I still attribute most of my early success.

People who hear my story often remark that it must have been difficult for me to study music in any kind of productive way, when I was constantly relocating from one city to another, which is certainly true. Most of my colleagues in music had the luxury of geographic stability, so that they could learn the art of music from one or two main teachers.

In my case, I would need to change teachers every time I moved to a new location, so stability was hard to come by. However, the hidden benefit that I later discovered, was that having so many different mentors in music also gave me a broader perspective on all things technical, musical and philosophical. When it comes to studying music, there are many different layers of proficiency that have to be mastered, and what I came to later realize was how many of those layers are also synonymous with key skills needed for living a fulfilling and successful life.

SEVEN CELLO LESSONS FOR LIFE

Now I am a mentor myself, and I have come full circle in the learning experience. It is not uncommon that my students initially think of me as just a music teacher, but this is only partly accurate. The truth is, like my mentors before me, my aim will always be to pass on the tradition of defining excellence to the next generation, music is simply a vehicle I use for accomplishing this goal.

Over the past 30 years, there are certain life lessons that I have taken away from my life's dedication to studying, teaching and performing music at the highest level, which I feel would be beneficial to any person, regardless of background and experience.

LESSON #1 – THE IMPORTANCE OF MENTORSHIP

Whenever you want to learn how to be the best at something, whether it is for your business, your relationships or your life, you need mentors. We all do, and how lucky we all are that we have access to generations of people that came before us, who could figure out the answers to many of the greatest challenges you will face in any experience, because you are not the first person to have that experience.

I am often surprised at how today's younger generations don't seem to value the older generations for their knowledge and experience as much as my parents and grandparents' generations. I think that this trend could be reversed as long as we make a concerted effort to teach this fact to our children, and show them that the true strength of our future generations lie in what we can build on the wealth of knowledge from the past.

I have worked with mentors my whole life, since I was four years old, and they have taught me what was important to focus on, what kind of standards to live up to and how to achieve the results that I desire, far better than I could have ever achieved them on my own. Obviously, the easiest and fastest way to gain the help of a mentor is by simply picking up a book and reading it. But beyond that, the value of having an interactive relationship with a mentor, one on one, is priceless.

LESSON #2 – IMAGINATION IS POWER

Anyone who has read *Psycho Cybernetics* by Maxwell Maltz or *The Vortex* by Esther Hicks already knows this fact. Anything that you can visualize you can realize. The mind is a sort of future projector, that can manifest into reality anything that you desire, all you have to do is focus on the thing you want. Often, where people go wrong is they tend to focus on the negative, or what they do not want, which only draws the negative closer.

Our society and news media are partially to blame for this, because negativity tends to draw greater attention than positivity. We don't always realize that we are not using the full potential of our minds for the good that it could create, both in our own lives and in the lives of others.

Training your mind to focus on what "should" be in the future is infinitely more important than what is "realistic", or how things are now. When people say they are being "realistic", they are not focusing on the future good, they are focusing on the present. But by looking past the present to what the future should be, you automatically begin to change the present.

Motivation, discipline and work ethic are all natural byproducts of intense focus and visualization on an intended result. I would say that anyone who is either not goal oriented, or has trouble reaching their goals or staying motivated, would benefit the most from understanding the power of this concept.

LESSON #3 – YOUR STANDARD IS EVERYTHING

The opposite of success is not failure, we all know this because we see the most successful people in any industry overcome massive amounts of failure to achieve success, or failing their way to success in other words.

So what is the opposite of success? In a word, mediocrity.

I have come to believe that a person's standard is unavoidably linked to their level of self-respect and personal self-image (see lesson #2). My grandfather always told me that in order to be successful, you must willingly do all the things an average unsuccessful person would be unwilling to do. So, logically, all you have to do is just make a list of all the things an average person wouldn't want to do, and make that your 'to do' list!

The standard in music has always been perfection, and although it takes some time for one to learn how to reach such a standard, there is no room for mediocrity in music.

When it comes to your standard, honesty is key. You need to be honest with what you know in your heart to be true. Sometimes it hurts to admit that we are only achieving average results, because we don't want to be average. The truth will set you free.

LESSON #4 – LEARN TO BE EFFICIENT

This lesson was learned the hard way, after much stubbornness and difficulty. Often, we mistakenly think that just working more hours than everyone else will give us an edge, and sometimes we think we can take shortcuts to success.

These two things are not dissimilar, because they are both examples of what happens when you aren't working to solve a problem efficiently. I have made both mistakes in the past because I hadn't yet adopted the best practices to achieve the highest and best result in the shortest period of time. Short cuts are often the long way around in the end.

This is one of the most important reasons for working with mentors, so you aren't wasting valuable time going down the wrong path. . . efficiency is key to preventing burnout and frustration, and achieving desired results quickly.

LESSON #5 – PATIENCE IS THE ADVANTAGE

If someone told you that it would take you at least three years to develop an even basic proficiency on the cello, would you ever start lessons? I have found that the determining factors in the equation for patience is this:

Self-Belief + Determination + Accurate Expectation = Patience

Usually when someone starts to lose one of these three factors, they begin to lose the patience necessary to achieve the intended goal or result. Frustration always sets in when expectations are not in line with what is reasonable or achievable. This can also be avoided with the proper guidance from a mentor who has already been down the path you are taking, and can guide you to know where you should be and when.

LESSON #6 – LEADERSHIP REQUIRES HUMILITY

One of the greatest gifts of studying music is the ability to collaborate with others in a large or small ensemble. While playing in an orchestra is definitely a team sport, it is a very different experience from playing on a team. The world's best orchestral musicians are selfless, and understand all too well that the whole is greater than the sum of the parts.

There are no individual statistics like in sports, as an orchestra can only be as good as its weakest player, which is why every single member has an overwhelming sense of self-responsibility to be personally prepared. . . but that is only the beginning. The goal of each and every musician is to have the best unified performance possible, the highest form of excellence, and everyone's sense of success is 100% tied to this result.

Sometimes a player has to take an important solo, and other times fade out of the way to listen attentively as another player whose part has become more important takes the lead. There is absolutely no room for ego, only humility and precision can help to bring out the best from others around them.

LESSON #7 - EMPATHY IS THE KEY TO HUMAN CONNECTION

From the study of the great music written throughout history, I have come to understand that music is a bridge that transcends words, time and space; it is a direct connection from the heart of the composer to the heart of the listener.

Over the past 500 years, every person who was ever moved to put their divine inspiration to pen and paper did so because they felt something emotionally, or had a message they wanted to get across to other humans around the world, both present and future.

Every time I take the stage to perform in front of an audience, I am aware that it is not me that is speaking to the audience, it is the inspiration from the heart of the composer that I am honoring. It doesn't matter if I had a good day or a bad day, if I got a good night's rest or no sleep at all, my commitment to express the heart of the composer must be 100%, or there cannot be a connection to the listener. In my case, it was that human connection which became the fuel behind my passion for music.

CONCLUSION – MY LIFE PURPOSE

I have always sought to inspire people, of all ages, to find greater meaning and fulfillment in life by experiencing a deeper and more empathic connection to the world around them through the art of music; for when we can experience the joys and sorrows of the past with the power that only music brings, we can truly have a better understanding of who we are, what we share, and what we can be grateful for.

While reflecting on Oprah's important lesson, it became clear to me based on my own experience as a mentor and concert performer, that validation is simply what we crave when we are ego focused, which is a natural condition that all humanity is born with. . . perhaps it is nature's gift for self-preservation.

The biggest lesson that I have learned over the years is that when we turn our focus outside of ourselves, and strive to serve others with love and admiration, our hunger for validation tends to evaporate.

In other words, we must learn to move ourselves away from our natural ego-centered tendencies, by simply training our focus on understanding and helping others. It is empathy, or the ability to feel for and relate to another, that is the secret to fulfilling the greatest human need. You could even say that empathy is just another form of love.

In a world driven by the internet and social media (which seems to me to be anything but social), we tend to see a great deal of negativity, ego-centeredness and divisiveness on a grand scale never experienced before in history. Never before has there been a greater need for human connection and empathy on a global scale. When we live to serve, we truly make this world a better place for all, no matter what our race, religion, political views or social and economic status.

Not too long ago, my dear friend, Dan Greer, sent me a note after a performance I gave for some of his clients. I am choosing to share what he wrote here, because it is so relevant to how I regard the true purpose of what it should mean to be a musician:

"A very dear client shared what I found to be a beautiful observation with me last night ... in short, he commented on how we all typically live our lives feeling and acting as individuals. He pointed to areas of philosophy, religion, politics, social issues and so on and so forth as mechanisms we can use to actively/passively separate ourselves from one another.

He then went on to talk about how certain events/moments (like your performance) have the ability to literally connect/transform a group of individuals into a collective sharing an experience – when the organization and the organism are one, if you will. . . or maybe better put, when the organism is not at odds with itself."

He stated it more eloquently than what I've written here, but his point left me thinking about the complexity/intricacy of life, and the ability of art to transcend even our own conceptions/perceptions of ourselves.

Just as your playing helps me communicate things to clients that I cannot achieve with words, I believe the above observation helps me express my gratitude to you more than a simple "thank you" ever could.

. . . That said, as always, thank you."

In closing, my reply to Dan:

Thank you for sharing that wonderful observation...I think that also sums up why I wanted to become a musician in the first place.

For me, music has always been a bridge to a higher level of consciousness and connection to each other. Call it love, or spirit or what have you. . . but while it can be argued that oftentimes words serve as the catalyst to create a gap between that connection, music tends to do the opposite.

Being at the center of that experience brings with it a sense of purpose, and a degree of value that cannot be quantified monetarily, and so I just want to thank you again for the opportunity for me to give what I have to give to your colleagues.

Your friend,
Oliver

Only those who have learned the power of sincere and selfless contribution experience life's deepest joy: true fulfillment.
~ Tony Robbins

About Oliver

Passionate about inspiring a more unified world through the art of music, Oliver Bennett Schlaffer is a classically-trained concert cellist, author, public speaker, coach, mentor and devoted husband and father.

He has performed on stages around the United States, Europe and Asia, including seven appearances at Carnegie Hall in New York City. While still a student, Oliver was highly praised by international cello soloist Yo-Yo Ma, for his performance in a masterclass recorded by the international broadcasting network CNN.

Oliver has performed in over a dozen orchestras across the United States, including the Chicago Symphony Orchestra and the Dallas Symphony Orchestra; he is currently principal cellist of the Dallas Chamber Symphony, which is well known for its innovative joint projects with film composers and directors of silent films.

Inspired by today's YouTube generation, Oliver has begun a series of collaborations with directors from around the world to create new video content that combines the music of the past with the possibilities of the future. A versatile performer, he has collaborated with a variety of genres and mainstream artists from outside the classical realm, including live concerts with Josh Groban, Gloria Estefan, Richard Marx and Andrea Bocelli, in addition to nationally-televised appearances with rappers P. Diddy and Snoop Dogg on MTV's Video Music Awards.

Oliver is also actively sought after as a teacher, public speaker and presenter; providing a unique and interactive "informance" experience to a broad spectrum of audiences that is both engaging and entertaining for all ages.

A champion for excellence through music education, Oliver has captured the imagination of over fifty-thousand students through his live presentations. He also maintains an exclusive teaching studio in Dallas, Texas, where his private students have consistently ranked in the top 1% of music students across the state.

In 2013, Oliver founded an annual music festival that takes place each Spring in Plano, Texas, for the express purpose of bringing free concerts to families in the community. He currently resides in Plano, Texas with his wife, a concert harpist; his four-year-old son (who does, in fact, have his own mini cello); and their little dog, a Japanese Chin.

Oliver holds degrees in Cello Performance from Southern Methodist University and Northwestern University, and has studied under the principal cellists of seven major symphony orchestras, including the Chicago Symphony Orchestra, New York

Philharmonic Orchestra and the Vienna Philharmonic Orchestra.

Two of Oliver's primary teachers include Orlando Cole, of the Curtis Institute of Music in Philadelphia, and Danish cellist Hans Jørgen Jensen, who was highlighted in the book, *The Talent Code*, by Daniel Coyle in 2009.

More information about Oliver, his music and his upcoming projects can be found on his website:

- www.OliverCello.com

CHAPTER 17

SUCCESS BEGINS WITH "C"
LEVERAGING CLARITY TO MASTER
THE ART OF SUCCESS

BY IRIS POLIT

Paul[1] was feeling restless and dissatisfied with his career progression. Like many "successful" mid-career professionals, he excelled at his job and was paid handsomely. However, contrary to these traditional satisfaction indicators, he was simply miserable. Each Sunday afternoon, a feeling of dread came over him as the start of the work week loomed. Moreover, occasions that would usually be cause for celebration – such as receiving accolades and awards for his contributions to the company – were no longer a source of comfort.

He decided the only solution would be to dust off his resume and look for an exciting new opportunity. Paul reached out to a personal branding expert that came highly recommended by a friend. Much to his surprise, the first question he was asked was "What's your definition of success?" Not "What sort of role are you looking for?" Or "What new skills have you acquired that need to be added to your resume?" Or a basic inquiry regarding his LinkedIn account. This was not at all what he was expecting. It made him feel uncomfortable because he knew that his current situation WAS many people's definition of success.

This would not be the first or last time he felt uncomfortable during the time we worked together. Nevertheless, after fully committing to the process, he learned to appreciate the probing questions and felt empowered

169

by my "no excuses allowed" approach that held him accountable. Finally, he reluctantly admitted that even a "realist" (a label most pessimists hide behind) such as himself couldn't help but be swayed by my contagious positivity and optimism.

Our work together enabled Paul to discover a path to a new role with which he felt intuitively aligned. He was thrilled to learn that leveraging his newly found self-awareness, coupled with his years of experience, allowed him to transition into another role that will serve as a gateway to a new career path. Paul is now a believer. With a fresh tool kit of skills acquired during our coaching sessions, his transition took only a few months and brought with it a substantial salary increase.

****

With Gallup data[2] indicating that actively disengaged employees represent nearly double the percentage of engaged employees (only 13% of employees worldwide are engaged), it is no surprise that more and more professionals struggle with success and happiness in the workplace. Like Paul, many of them feel that the only option is to chronically switch jobs. This trend is supported by data from the Bureau of Labor Statistics[3] with employees' median tenure decreasing to 4.2 years as of January 2016. It is as if today's professionals are simply sleep walking through their careers – on a never-ending set of conveyor belts through the assembly line of life – awaiting the ability to retire. This leads to a vicious cycle of added stress – from job searches, starting and acclimating to new companies, ending up in the same dissatisfied state again – and a grave impact on their personal lives including health, family life, and overall happiness.

So, what is the solution?

We need to STOP! and realize that everyone deserves, and is capable of, having a career and life full of happiness and prosperity. Furthermore, all of us have the power to create success in our lives by employing our unique strengths to set ourselves free from the "conveyor belt" mentality and accomplish anything we desire. To help my clients identify and achieve success in their lives, I have developed and regularly utilize the *Ace Success Formula*. The formula is simple; however, this does not mean it is easy. It demands honesty, commitment, and discipline as well as a high level of self-awareness and an open mind.

Here's the formula:

$$3C - C = C$$

(Clarity + Certainty + Commencement) – Control = Creation

It all begins with clarity. It is nearly impossible to be successful or even develop goals without first getting really frank with yourself. By focusing on what it is you actually want for your career and in your life, you are able to block out distractions, expectations, and perceived societal judgments to more easily identify what success truly means to you.

Too often, when we begin the journey to success, we cast the net too wide. The average person believes that there is a universal definition of success that applies to all and only achievable by a few. The truth is that there are many definitions of success and paths to it. Unless we first define what success means for us individually, we'll continue to chase someone else's dream, follow someone else's rules, and remain wanting. To get out of your own way and find success (regardless of what it means to you), you must first get some clarity.

Here are five key steps that Paul followed to gain more clarity and so can you. Are you ready to begin creating success in your career and life leveraging clarity?

#1: GET HONEST

This is the most difficult task, not because people are inherently dishonest, but because it is so easy to lie to ourselves. Getting honest about what is working and what you really need and want is not easy. For some, it is tough because they cannot fathom that the traditional definition of success is not a generic one-size-fits-all. For others, it is challenging due to a sneaking suspicion that their true definition of success does not align with their current life and commitments.

Do not focus on what is not working. You already know what is wrong and, if you continue to concentrate on it, you will only manifest more of it in your life. I have worked with several sales executives that couldn't understand why – even though they very clearly knew what they disliked about their current work environments – they kept choosing companies that were exactly the same. Same toxic environment. Same unmotivated teams. Same stress inducing leadership.

In order to get clarity to work for you, a shift is necessary. Just as the acknowledgement of an illness does not represent health, being aware of what you don't want does not represent what you do want. Focusing on what is working and what you really need and want is necessary to be able to recognize it when it comes your way.

Aspirational Action: Make a list of what is working and what you would like to see more of in your life and career. It helps to consider what energizes you and brings you joy. Both of these are indications that you are on the right path.

#2: EMBRACE IPP

When we endeavor to seek clarity while still wearing the blinders of our current reality, it is impossible to see the opportunities that present themselves. Just like an NYC carriage horse only sees the road in front of it and misses the glorious beauty of Central Park around it, so are people blind to the coincidences and "miracles" that are around us. It is only when we shed those blinders and truly embrace IPP – Infinite Possibilities Perspective – that we are able to discover new (and in some cases, easier) paths to success.

Lift yourself out of your current state. Do not get dragged down and limit yourself by existing circumstances. Move past what you perceive as "realistic". This thinking keeps us on one path, a path that may or may not get us to where we are trying to go. I have worked with my share of entrepreneurs who kept restricting their options because they were holding on to what they thought they could "realistically" accomplish. It wasn't until they embraced IPP, that they discovered a multitude of alternatives and were able to see synchronistic moments that kept popping up in their lives to propel them forward. Just as today's weather doesn't predict tomorrow's forecast, your current state does not predict your future.

Aspirational Action: Ask yourself positive "what if...?" questions. What if I couldn't fail? What if there IS a greater power conspiring to help me? What if I already know the people that can help drive my career or business forward? What if the realization of the goal I'm trying to accomplish is closer than I think?

#3: BE STILL

We all possess the answers within ourselves. However, sometimes life is too noisy for us to hear them. We are constantly "on" and do not realize that modern technology – while providing many advantages and conveniences – makes it impossible for us to be still. There is always a text to respond to, a post to like or a phone call to answer.

Give yourself permission to be still. This is probably the step that my clients fight me most over. You don't understand, they often say. I have to get up early to go to the gym. I have to get the kids to school before my morning team meeting. I have to <insert your favorite excuse here>. The ironic thing is that once they do make a slight effort to complete this "homework assignment," they discover that the rest of their day flows more smoothly. Solutions and opportunities – which would usually go unnoticed due to distractions, stress, and lack of IPP – are easily identified.

Aspirational Action: Spend at least 5-10 minutes each day (preferably in the morning) in tranquil silence through prayer or meditation. Allow yourself to hear the answers that may emerge out of that silence. You will find many responses to your "what if...?" questions in this space that will enable you to take prolific steps toward achieving success.

#4: FACE FEAR

On the road to self-discovery, many uncomfortable feelings will surface. The harder you try to push them aside the longer it will take to get clarity. Instead allow yourself to feel them. Wallow in the discomfort. Face the fear head on. It is within these negative forces that you will find your breakthrough. It is only when you take the time to examine the fears – and shine a proverbial flashlight inside dark corners of the closet looking for the monsters – that you discover that they are baseless.

Make sure you move on and focus on your newly found courage quickly. I have found that, when clients focus on the fear for too long, they are held back by false justifications of the fear. When they shift to focus on the truth, they are empowered to burst through these fake barriers.

Aspirational Action: Write down your fear. Think of a time when you overcame a similar situation and write down the steps you took. If this is a new fear, examine it from a fact-based perspective and visualize yourself successfully overcoming it.

#5: PRACTICE VISUALIZATION

Once you get to a place of clarity make sure you take every opportunity you can to visualize your perfect life. Closing your eyes and "seeing" your ideal future state, as if you were already in it, is a valuable tool. It allows us to better embrace IPP and maintain integrity with regard to what we really need and want.

Get very specific. Many clients find it easy to identify where they'd like to work or what kind of life they'd like to have and imagine what it would be like. It is not until they pay attention to how it would feel – down to every little detail – that they tap into the true power of visualization. When you take the time to focus on the feelings and detach from the physical things, you will find yourself getting closer and closer to achieving your goals.

Aspirational Action: Create a vision board. It will serve as a frequent reminder of your ideal future state and will help keep your IPP top of mind throughout the day.

****

Robert F. Kennedy made an astute observation of human kind during a speech[4] in 1968 and it still rings true today. We all share "the same short movement of life" and people seek "nothing but the chance to live out their lives in purpose and happiness, winning what satisfaction and fulfillment they can." That is the basic definition of success and the formula for that success begins with clarity. Once you know your purpose and what happiness looks like for you, you have a solid foundation to achieve any goal and master the art of success.

Reference Notes:
1. Customer's name has been changed to protect his privacy.
2. http://www.gallup.com/businessjournal/200108/damage-inflicted-poor-managers.aspx?g_source=EMPLOYEE_ENGAGEMENT&g_medium=topic&g_campaign=tiles
3. https://www.bls.gov/news.release/tenure.nr0.htm
4. https://www.jfklibrary.org/Research/Research-Aids/Ready-Reference/RFK-Speeches/Remarks-of-Senator-Robert-F-Kennedy-to-the-Cleveland-City-Club-Cleveland-Ohio-April-5-1968.aspx

About Iris

Iris Polit is a personal branding and success coach, inspirational speaker, and corporate trainer. Her mission is to help professionals and entrepreneurs confidentially pursue their life's purpose. She leverages positive psychology methodologies and proven success principles to help her clients get clarity and achieve a career and life full of happiness and prosperity. Having lived most of her life in New York, she employs a direct (no nonsense) yet friendly approach to guide her clients to their best potential.

Iris is also an award-winning marketing professional. With a career spanning over two decades in both non-profit organizations and corporate environments, she is intimately aware of the many challenges facing today's professionals. This familiarity with various workplaces enables her to truly understand the hurdles her clients are facing. In one-on-one coaching or in group trainings, she utilizes the *Ace Success Formula* to facilitate the discovery and application of signature strengths to help clients get unstuck and thrive.

Iris currently resides in Florida with her husband, Paul, and furry baby, Layla, the German Shepherd. In her spare time, she enjoys traveling, listening to music, reading, eclectic dining, and, most importantly, spending time and laughing with family and friends.

If you would like to learn how to better leverage clarity (or other tools) to master the art of success, contact Iris at: www.yoursuccessace.com

CHAPTER 18

CUSTOMIZED SUCCESS:
—CREATING A THRIVING PERSONAL AND BUSINESS CULTURE

BY CHRISTINE MARCELLO

Finding a successful business structure requires more than a one-size-fits-all formula. You must customize to maximize.

My childhood was filled with fun adventures and opportunities, mostly having one thing in common—I approached them like a business. I don't know why this was always my focus, but it was. Perhaps it stemmed from my passion for the independent, smart, and fearless characters in *Charlie's Angels.* I naturally wanted to be to my world what they were to my TV land.

Being independent was natural for me; however, I never wanted to be "the face" of anything. I loved being behind the scenes, helping everything run smoothly, and be organized. Ah yes, organization. If you remember Suzie and Suzie's Lemonade from the Verizon commercials, you'll get the idea. She was a master of organization. So was I. Even something as simple as creating and designing a play as a child, or making sure everyone else knew their part so they could excel at it was of interest to me.

It was no surprise I went with a business degree for college. I didn't know what I wanted to do and that was an all-encompassing degree. After college, I started working in Boston's financial district, finding a good fit for me with my company. I grew up professionally being part of a good corporate structure. Strangely, the corporate structure was also my biggest challenge.

When structure is too much about processes and follow-ups, but not good for employees, it doesn't work. What is meant to keep order becomes overbearing, and certainly not motivating.

Despite loving my career, my creative side was suffering. Thinking outside the box or in different terms was discouraged. The corporate world didn't embrace it the way I did. To me, it was something I gravitated toward and longed to explore.

The other cultural norm I conflicted with was how anything you said could and would be used against you in the court of corporate public opinion. Fear-based operating such as that was (and is) counterproductive to moving forward and flourishing. And what business doesn't want to more forward to a stronger, more viable position? The resistance bothered me, as I knew it was based in fear and excessive constraints, likely put in place out of ego more than necessity.

I'd had enough and after seven years, I left the financial industry. I had an opportunity to move to Vegas, so I quit my job despite not having anything else lined up. My connections took note of my knack for organizing and thought I might be a great fit for an unexpected, non-corporate industry—construction.

I became a project manager and it was definitely "anti-corporate" in culture. Although completely different from my past experience, I was open about the opportunity and learning more. What I discovered was quite incredible, actually. My prior work experience transferred to this arena in regards to structure. And this business had no structure. I was able to help put a set of strategies into motion that really helped this business, especially with a major project they were having problems with. However, as much of a free spirit as I was at heart, I didn't resonate with a complete lack of structure.

Okay, so what else was out there?

The need to find a place where both creativity and structure existed was important to me. I sensed it was also pivotal in creating a winning business formula.

My next experience was working for a prominent entertainment company in Las Vegas. The organization had decent structure, but chaos in it, mostly due to the diverse range of creative personalities. I noticed the "human factor" to organizational success in an entirely new manner. This challenge excited me and I learned three important things:

1. Organizational dynamics are everything. This includes individual skills and characteristics, as well as policies and procedures that are in place (or the lack of them).
2. The blend of structure and creativity together is powerful, offering opportunities to expand in ways that we may not consider without an outside perspective.
3. In order to have an effective system, you need the right people in the right positions and you need to let them thrive.

I was at this job a half a decade before restlessness set in again. I'd accomplished a great deal, but had grown stagnant. Another change was in order. I moved to the hotel/casino industry, revamping a VIP department. The corporate chaos came back in a whirlwind and I learned that implementing change is often met with resistance. Others fear it and will resist—even if it doesn't directly impact them. It was threatening, which was more shocking than it should have been. Consequently, I learned something valuable: keep your ego in check and make sure you incorporate the people you're going to rely on for changes. Save stress and hassles by doing this, while elevating your success.

Again, it wasn't "for me", leaving me wondering: what am I supposed to be doing? I wasn't finding it in Vegas and moved to LA, where I began working with an interesting venture that had wellness, hospitality, and entertainment all inclusive. It was an amazing and challenging opportunity. One I couldn't wait to start and be part of.

This change of pace was exciting, but I kept noticing what wasn't working. People weren't in the right positions, the Executive Vice

President struggled, and for as innovative as the idea was, it was a toxic environment for everyone. Ultimately, the project was ahead of its time and failed, but I did gain insight from it.

Over the next few years, I worked in the real estate industry and when that lacked what I was looking for, I ventured out as an entrepreneur in my own business. I tapped into my dormant creativity and began designing jewelry. Had I finally found it? No, but I found that designing jewelry and the lack of security was not a good fit. The question was there again— what was I meant to do? While trying to determine this, I went back to work with the entertainment company as it launched a new show in LA. There was a lack of vision and strategy, sprinkled with assumptions. The show closed after two years and I went on a year hiatus, working with entrepreneurs, helping them to organize their business plans and structures.

It was great. Connecting with people and assisting them with their dreams was exciting. Still, it wasn't "it"!

I began seriously thinking there was something wrong with me. I recalled words from an old college professor telling me I'd likely switch jobs about ten times in my life. I'd thought it was an exaggeration and that he was crazy.

THE PIVOT POINT

When things are bogging you down, you must do what is necessary to clear your mind and give a serious evaluation to the questions that are plaguing you.

My skills were good enough to find another job, the job changing easy to explain. But, I didn't want a repeat of days past.

One of my favorite exercises is walking. I find that it clears my head and helps me gain perspective on most everything I contemplate. I went for a walk and some self-talk one morning, moving along and thinking about my career path thus far. I'd worked successfully in a great number of industries and added value, but none of them were for me. Why? A thought came to me. I'd yet to work in the medical field. It was followed by a warm flashback of my childhood and playing medical office, not doctor. I never wanted to be the actual doctor, but always wanted to run the operations.

I decided to pursue that avenue next. I came across a plastic surgery practice management position in Beverly Hills. I was able to show my value and got the opportunity. The position required a lot of communication and coordination with various corporate, onsite, accreditation and regulatory agencies. Although I was enjoying learning the business, I took note of the constant barrage of exhaustive requirements being asked of everyone. So many things were being done with no real purpose or understanding as to "why". People were in the wrong positions creating additional issues. I thought, *the same problematic scenarios, again.* What wasn't working and how to fix it was so obvious to me. It was a defining moment – one that revealed to me that my purpose was to be a business consultant.

With my diverse experience in various businesses and natural alignment with processes, structure, and creative influence, I could do something special. The key? Never dive into structuring a business with a cookie cutter approach. Look at the individual identity of the business and you'll truly understand what its needs are, and how to best elevate their effectiveness.

THE 7 PIECES THAT MAKE UP THE WHOLE

It takes a lot of courage to release the familiar and seemingly secure, to embrace the new. But there is no real security in what is no longer meaningful. There is more security in the adventurous and exciting, for in movement there is life, and in change there is power.
~ Alan Cohen

Through consulting, I can use a combination of logic, life experiences, creativity, corporate, and entrepreneurial practices and structures to bring out the best in organizations and their employees. By coming in as an outside source, I am able to help businesses organize meaningful change. At times the ones who bring me in resist and challenge the very change they requested, but this is good, as it helps me grow and reminds me of the importance of communication and clarification throughout the process.

These seven pieces are the parts that make for a whole transformation to a more successful enterprise.

1. **Understand the goals and intentions from owners, direct reports, and higher-ups, developing good relationships and rapport with everyone who impacts the business.**
Knowing this helps you to understand what you can suggest and develop, how you can implement it, and the manner in which suggestions may be received. In addition to personnel, vendors and outside sources are an important determinant in how a business operates. Strong, authentic, and respectful relationships help you get things done more efficiently, creating win/win scenarios for everyone. In addition, this can halt any intentional or unintentional sabotage of your efforts.

2. **Prepare to deal with the good, the bad, and the ugly.**
Not every company needs a complete overhaul. You have to learn to look at the employees, their roles, likes, dislikes, any special arrangements and the best solutions for "problem people". One employee in the wrong place can have a negative trickledown effect that can greatly impact the team. Take time to get to know employees, understanding their interests, passions, and motivations towards work, so you can try to incorporate those into the overall plan and each person's role. This helps create a powerful team and allies aligned with strength and purpose to accomplish action steps. Additionally, it curbs negative criticism (which is inevitable to face at times). You want thick skin and the information to back it up!

3. **Understanding negatives and ulterior motives, as well as the company culture.**
Not everyone is candid in their disclosures. You must be able to look at the source of the problem to see where any ulterior motives, road blocks, or kinks in the working relationships may lie. This includes paying attention to gossip. While it may not seem kind or productive to do this, knowing what employees say about each other helps you identify problematic individuals and connect with staff.

4. **Access, review, and live out the current structure.**
Know the operational flow from all aspects including the space, technology, policies and procedures, employees' roles, personalities,

complimentary and uncomplimentary traits. Additionally, learn about vendor roles and processes along with customer and outsider experiences. Do these policies and processes add value or appear to be "needless work" exhausting employees? What are the problems and what are the strengths? Physically get in, roll up your sleeves, and do the work. Understand the reality of what people are living day to day.

5. **Use creative processes.**
Through visualizing what you are dealing with and what needs to happen you can create plans to revamp or modify accordingly. You'll also want to incorporate feedback and analysis of these ideas, as what may appear unnecessary or unstructured often does have a good reason behind it. Employees should know what that reason is and feel empowered to be part of the creative process that defines the new structure.

6. **An organized plan that you can adhere to is essential to implementation.**
To be organized you need to have a to-do list, a plan of action with a calendar showing timelines for task completion, plus a commitment to continuous reorganization as changes are made and feedback is given. Once you've strategized out a plan, you want to make sure it goes smoothly, as this will alleviate stress and anxiety. This means adhering to established timelines. Have a plan that factors in tasks, resources, overall structure, completion dates, and communication of efforts.

7. **Be attentive to what change results in ensuring continued success.**
Change without evaluation and constant follow-up seldom lasts. It's important to be mindful of the evaluation process of what works, what does not, and what can be tweaked. Be sure to ask for feedback and collaboration from the team. Typically, the more engaged employees or key players are in giving input, the higher the success rate will be to keep the new set-up functioning. Don't forget to thank and reward those that participated in the journey to making the process successful.

FULL CIRCLE SATISFACTION

Happiness does not come from doing easy work but from the afterglow of satisfaction that comes after the achievement of a difficult task that demanded our best.
~ Theodore Isaac Rubin

Change is seldom easy for us, especially when we resist it, which is often the case with human nature. However, through using our talents and natural gifts, we can find ourselves thriving and doing work we are meant to be doing.

For me, as a consultant I help evoke excitement for positive and meaningful change in a manner that helps create a powerful state-of-being in an organization and its employees. Anyone can extract on these principles and the 7 pieces that make up the whole for improvement and change.

From my personal experiences with professional results I can tell you this – when you are finally doing something that deeply resonates with you and is of service to others, you naturally become a more complete individual. Customized success means treating businesses and their people as unique beings. It's through these life experiences that we can open our minds, fearing change less and create more positive results that truly make a difference in our lives, and in the overall structure of organizations. And that is something any person or business can bank on!

About Christine

Organizations seeking turnaround and stronger profits seek out Christine Marcello. Her 20+ years of experience in helping businesses identify their challenges and hindrances have given her a unique, sought-out perspective. Her extensive experience allows her to look at a business as a whole and also break down all the details, from the people in the organization to the policies and processes that are in place.

Christine is currently a Director of Operations working in the plastic and reconstructive surgery industry. She brings numerous years of experience with her as a consultant and proven business leader. She works closely with management and all levels of employees to help businesses begin to flow and function better, utilizing her breadth of experience in operations management, marketing, and business development. As a specialist in strategic planning, processes and performance, customer service and satisfaction, plus resource management and profitability optimization, she has a unique perspective that makes her a turn-around artist for the businesses she works with. Over the years, she's worked with renowned companies such as Cirque du Soleil, MGM Resorts International, as well as in the medical, entertainment, hospitality, financial, real estate, retail and construction industries.

Attending Johnson & Wales University in Providence, Rhode Island, Christine graduated Summa Cum Laude and holds a BS in Business Administration and an MS in Management. According to Christine, "Continuing to pursue opportunities to learn and grow is fundamental to my success as a business consultant. I have to keep up with changing times and new business concepts to successfully implement effective change." She is also a certified life coach and a co-author with bestselling author Jack Canfield in his book *Mastering the Art of Success*.

The hours Christine spends helping her clients create stronger, more vibrant businesses are exciting. She is also passionate about supporting educational, cultural, philanthropic, wellness and social endeavors that enrich the community. Christine loves spending time with her seventeen-year-old Pomeranian Santino, friends and family. Walking outdoors for fitness and emotional health are always a pleasure, as well as a good book and opportunities to help people in some way, whether large or small.

For Christine's complete credentials, see her LinkedIn profile:
- Christine Marcello, Beverly Hills, CA.

Or
- Email Christine at: christinemarcello@christinemarcello.com

CHAPTER 19

WHATEVER YOU'RE THINKING… THINK B.I.G. "R"
—BETTER INVESTMENTS… GREATER RETURNS

BY DEATRA STEVENSON

As a man thinketh, so is he.

Many of us have heard that quote countless times. But have you ever stopped and thought… What am I thinking about all day long? I spent several years working in Human Resources for two Fortune 50 international companies. A huge part of their success was their ability to master inventory control. So, when I realized that my thoughts were the root cause of my returns, or lack thereof, I began to think of my mind as this huge distribution center of thoughts. Some of those thoughts were old and outdated, rotten even and simply needed to be tossed out. Another set of thoughts were good, but had been there so long and unused that they were way in the back, up high on a top shelf and forgotten about. They just needed to be rotated down and recirculated. And lastly, there were some thoughts and beliefs that were missing all together: positive thoughts, thoughts of being successful, independently wealthy, having time to spend with friends and family doing the things I really enjoy.

This is how I began my self-inventory process. I remember walking into one of the Wal-Mart Distribution Centers with over one million square feet, and thinking: "Oh my goodness… how on earth do they keep track

187

of all this stuff?" It was overwhelming at first, until I learned the system. Effective inventory control is a science. This scientific, constant self-inventory process is crucial to changing how we think.

This chapter is designed to show you how a change in our habitual thinking can lead to better investments for greater returns in both our business and personal lives. Are you experiencing only a fraction of the success, joy and satisfaction that life has to offer? Do you want more? There are investments that each of us can make that will position us for greater returns in every aspect of our lives.

THINKING

For years, I questioned how others seemed to achieve their goals and dreams, while I struggled to find my path. To my natural eyes, we appeared the same; educated, hard working, talented... yet my goals remained outside of my reach. Finally, I figured out that the biggest difference between those who are successful and myself wasn't talent or work ethic or even luck – it was our way of thinking.

I had a mentor and friend that constantly encouraged me to "take your dreams off the shelf and believe in yourself." He would say: "If you worked as hard for yourself as you do for that company, do you know how much more successful and happier you would be?"

I was at my wit's end and completely frustrated with where I was in life, when a light bulb went off in my mind. In all of my setbacks, failed businesses, failed relationships and other disappointments, *I was the common denominator*. I remember asking myself: "What on earth was I thinking?" Well the answer was clear. I simply applied this formula T^B $(w+A) = t$ in reverse. My **THOUGHTS** multiplied exponentially by the power of my **BELIEFS** multiplied by my **WORDS** plus my **ACTIONS** equals the manifestation of thoughts in the form of **THINGS**. I looked at my outcomes and they could all be traced back to some crazy thought, belief, spoken word and action that I had unconsciously given energy to.

Has something bad ever happened and you found yourself saying: "I knew that was going to happen." Well ask yourself, which came first? – the thing that happened or the thought of the thing that happened. Now imagine if you had simply thought something different, something better, something bigger. Now think on those things all day long! Thinking, believing, speaking and acting upon those things is the investment that ALWAYS yields a positive return.

INVESTING

The best investment you can make is in yourself – Do This First!

It's never a waste of time or money to invest in yourself, no matter the source. True wealth begins inwards and emits its light outward into everything else, including the people you surround yourself with.
~ will.i.am

One might think that investing in self would be the easiest investment of all. However, when we stop and really take self-inventory of where we spend the most time, money and energy, it is not usually on ourselves in the form of an investment. Great leaders of people are first great leaders of self. They understand that leading by example is an investment not only in oneself but ultimately in others. We can do less by becoming more.

Many times, the day-to-day rituals of working, taking care of our loved ones and basic "busy stuff" becomes so routine that over time we are functioning at a much lower level than what we are capable of. Thus, we are not giving our very best to anything or anyone.

As leaders, we are called upon to pour into others so often that it becomes second nature – so much so that we forget to replenish our own well. When we invest in ourselves first, we frequently have a better version of ourselves to offer to others. Consequently, we reap what we sow and receive the best in return. Do something today that your future self will thank you for.

No Man Is an Island - Invest in Others

True leaders don't invest in things. They invest in people. Why? Because success without a successor is failure. So, your legacy should not be in buildings, programs, or projects; your legacy must be in people.
~ Myles Munroe

Humanity is the Universe's greatest asset, always evolving, always impacting and never dying. Payroll, in many companies, is the largest ongoing line item expense. Industry leaders across the globe compete for the best talent through competitive salary packages, benefits, and promises for training, development and growth, etc., to separate themselves from their competitors. Why? Because they understand that when they invest in people their company reaps the return. Investing in others is as much of a science as any other business process.

Payroll alone is not a viable investment. This is where many managers fail but where leaders shine. People, unlike other investments, need to feel like they are valued. Figuring out how to meet that need and doing so is the real investment.

Effective leaders have a diverse leadership style that allows them to discern the unique individual needs and desires of others that stimulates a sense of self-worth. These leaders take advantage of that knowledge to create an environment and culture specific to people in their own unique ways. It's the only investment where insider information is not only allowed but encouraged. These unique investments increase the value of the relationship, and by default the return is increased. Staff for tomorrow's success – not today's needs. Then train, develop and consistently invest in your people. Mentoring, both professionally and personally, is a great way to invest in others. When the people around us grow, so does everything else.

INVEST IN CHANGE

The definition of insanity is doing the same thing over and over and expecting different results.
~ Albert Einstein

If you want a different result, you have to do a different thing. It's not about doing the same thing better or faster; *it's about doing and thinking something different.* There is an entire industry surrounded by the concept of managing change. This is because change for whatever reason is very difficult for most people. Many great ideas have failed miserably before they even got off the ground, because the mere thought of change shut down the people that were in the positions needed to execute the change.

Leaders understand this and invest in managing the process. Do not be discouraged if the followers do not get your vision at first. Henry Ford said it best: "If I had asked people what they wanted, they would have said faster horses." Press forward; the result you are looking for is at the end of a road called "Change."

THE INVESTMENT SELF-INVENTORY

For where your treasure is, there will your heart be also.
~ Matthew 6:21

When we subscribe to this philosophy, "where your treasure (resources – time, talent and treasure) is, there will your heart be also," it is easy to see where our priorities are. Wherever we are spending the majority of our time, talent and treasure is by definition our top priority. Sometimes this is a hard admission to make. However, the good news is that we have the ability to not just take the self-inventory, but also to make the necessary adjustments. We are the decision makers of how we invest our personal resources. So, with a few strategic shifts in our thinking and some better investments of our resources, we can align these three up to fit what we say we want.

Five Things to Factor in When Evaluating Your Resource (Time, Talent and Treasure) Investments:

1. You are your greatest asset. You cannot expect others to value your time, talent or treasure more than you do.

2. Think of time as a commodity to invest, not to spend. In life and particularly in business, there are all sorts of time robbers. Just like you guard yourself from someone running up and stealing your wallet, guard yourself against people that rob your time with conversations, requests or actions that are not a part of your vision and goals.

   Separate income-producing activity from non-income producing activity. In business, everything has an impact on the bottom line directly or indirectly. It is easy to get lost between the two.

3. View all the money you spend as an investment. Are you going

to see a movie? That money is an investment. Review all of your investments at the end of every month. Are they in alignment with your vision for your business and personal life? Now make the adjustment for the following month. With every expenditure, you are either adding/multiplying (good investments) or subtracting/dividing (just spending money).

4. We all have natural, God-given talents. Those talents become marketable skills when we perfect our craft. Read books, watch videos, attend trainings, volunteer, etc. to gain more experience and assist in growing your talents. Stay relevant and ahead-of-the-curve in your thinking.

5. Give Generously. In all our getting, remember to give. We have a solemn obligation to help people who are in genuine need. Investing in the principles of God always has a positive return.

Give, and it shall be given unto you. . .
~ Luke 6:38;

He who sows sparingly will also reap sparingly, and he who sows bountifully will also reap bountifully. Each one must do as he has made up his mind, not reluctantly or under compulsion, for God loves a cheerful giver.
~ 2 Corinthians 9:6-7

ROI (RETURN ON INVESTMENT)

The RETURN! This is why we do the things we do. Whether the investment yields a return in the form of some sense of personal fulfillment, the joy of making someone else happy or a financial gain... the bottom line is the bottom line. Use this knowledge to your advantage. Begin with the end in mind.

Get a vision for what your ideal return looks like for every investment you make. Once you have that vision set in your mind, start developing a plan of action. A vision without a plan is just a dream. Every business and life goal needs a plan, a strategy that defines your vision, and goals that set measurable benchmarks. Measure what matters. Knowing your numbers, both real-time and future projections is a phenomenal tool to use to make adjustments along the path to your end result. Whether you are a new business owner, or already have a small business, a simple business strategy can take your business to the next level.

TAKING THE NEXT STEP

Over the years, I have worked for a variety of companies and business owners. Large and small businesses, start-ups and established, growing and struggling. The thing that consistently seperates those that I could help transition to the next level and those that I could not is the mindset of the leadership.

I have client and great friend, Dr. Chambers. Dr. Z as we love to call her, has owned her own practice for over 25 years and is a notable leader in her profession and community.

One of the services I provided for her was a full financial review and assessment of her practice. My accountant and I spent hours and hours combing through her records and computer files. We were convinced that we were missing documents. Finally, we accepted that numbers do not lie and our conclusion was correct. Unfortunately, in spite of the respectable volume of revenue the practice was not profitable. I contacted Dr. Z to deliver the news. I shared my findings in accounting terms and she replied: "I don't understand." I said: "Sweetie, you're not making any money." She then shared: "I know, that's the problem." We both broke out in laughter! From that day moving forward there was a concerted effort to begin Thinking B.I.G. "R". We had several conversations about how the practice could run more efficiently. However, the vast majority of the strategy talks dealt with what could be done different... new... outside-the-box.

Later in the year, Dr. Z attended one of her annual medical conferences. There she met several equipment representatives advertising their products and services. Three of them were of particular interest to her, which would help her offer three new services to her clients. After returning home and doing her homework, she decided to make the investment in all three new pieces of equipment! In addition, she hired and trained staff to support this new division of her business. One month into the first quarter of the following year, she is already cash-flow positive and on track to increase her bottom line by more than six figures!

One of the many things that is so exciting about this story is that Dr. Z has always attended medical conferences, and they were always filled with representatives marketing their products and services. The right people and opportunity were there all along. However, as her mindset began to shift, her vision became clearer and her investments began to line up with her desired outcomes.

Many people believe that life and business are hard and filled with sacrifices. I choose to believe life is a lot less complicated than we think and that it is filled with choices. The sooner and more consistently we line our decisions up with what we say we want out of life – the less complicated life becomes.

Trust the process, consistently execute the formula TB $(w+A) = t$, expect great returns. And if your vision does not scare you just a little bit, you probably need to Think B.I.G. "R"!

And God is able to provide you with every blessing in abundance, so that you may always have enough of everything and may provide in abundance for every good work.
~ 2 Corinthians 9:8

About Deatra

Deatra Stevenson is Founder and CEO of DEARS, Inc. and specializes in leading companies through strategic growth with an emphasis on people, processes and profits. She and her team pride themselves on <u>NOT</u> being consultants, but rather **business partners** who provide the expertise and resources needed to grow businesses. Whether the focus is on starting a new business, transforming an existing business or sustaining performance and building on achievements, Deatra and the DEARS team can help improve any organization by examining everything from core management and business processes to future directions and opportunities for growth.

In addition to DEARS, Inc. Deatra also founded The DEARS foundation, which funds qualifying organizations in four categories: Benevolence, Educational Excellence, Health and Wellness, and Small Business and Entrepreneurship Development. Deatra believes in leading by example and inspiring other business owners to be generous in their corporate stewardship. The foundation matches individual donations dollar-for-dollar and has zero administrative cost. All funds raised go directly to the receiving organizations.

Deatra's professional career spans over 20 years serving in several leadership positions in the non-profit sector as well as working in Human Resource Leadership for two Fortune 50 companies. She has led senior leadership teams both locally and throughout the Midwest region in Talent Acquisition, Labor Relations, Profit and Loss, Team Building and Communication projects. She has provided HR Management for as many as 900+ employees at one time. Among her corporate achievements include being recognized for successfully leveraging $8.5 million annual payroll budget for two consecutive years, national most improved safety record, and creating and implementing new logistics university curriculum.

In addition to helping clients in the areas of Operations and Strategic Planning, Human Resources and IT Support, she is also a private investor for start-up businesses, including: Staffing, Child Care, Accounting and more. She is very passionate about sharing the expertise she has gained from working with corporate giants and entrepreneurs to accelerate the success of her clients.

Although she is serious about business, she loves to have a good time – which she defines as being with the people she loves no matter what the activity, and helping people overcome obstacles and achieve their dreams. Deatra also enjoys traveling, speaking and inspiring ordinary people to accomplish extraordinary things. She attributes much of her success to her parents and is often quoted as saying: "My mom is by far my biggest cheerleader. People say you can't choose your family. But I believe that even if God had hung me over the edge of humanity, offered me a sea of beautiful, kind, smart, loving women and said: Here, you can have any mom you like; I would have sifted through them all just to find her. She's not only my mom...she's my best friend. I am so grateful for her example and support. Everybody needs a W. Ruth Stevenson on their team!"

You can connect with Deatra at:
- Deatra@DEARSInc.com
- Deatra@DEARSFoundation.com
- www.facebook.com/DeatraStevenson

WHATEVER YOU'RE THINKING...THINK B.I.G. "R" is not just a chapter; it's her way of life.

CHAPTER 20

THE SUCCESSFUL AND CONSCIOUS CAREGIVER

BY DIANN MARTIN

INTRODUCTION

As I take my seat in the airplane, the stewardess gives the standard litany about trays, seatbelts and also reminds me, "In the event of a loss of cabin pressure, the oxygen mask will fall from above your seat. Pull the plastic straps to place the oxygen over your mouth and nose. TAKE CARE TO PUT ON YOUR OWN MASK FIRST, AND THEN ASSIST OTHERS." The same concept applies to caregivers – it all must start with taking care of YOU. Caregiving is a natural and common role in today's world. Being a caregiver represents a life experience that can range from running simple errands to 24/7 total physical care and being a virtual nurse. Likely, you are somewhere on this continuum, or, it's very likely that you will be.

I want to share some insights or keys, both concepts and practicalities, to love YOU as a Conscious Caregiver. What is a conscious caregiver? It's a helping person who is mindful and aware that they share accountability for both self-care and care of another. The role of caregiver in the absence of self-care is doomed. Caregiver stress becomes burdensome, annoying, fearful, draining or overwhelming. Burned-out caregivers of spouses, family members and neighbors turn into martyrs, have significant health problems, and are drained – this presents an inability to fulfill their own passions.

How do I know about caregiving? My years as primary caregiver to my quadriplegic boyfriend when I was a young adult, along with my years as a nurse (42) and executive leader and educator in nursing grant me credibility on the subject. Moreover, I spent 30 years as a home-care nurse showing families how to care for their loved ones as a major part of my job. I have seen caregivers who thrived, but have also seen too many good people with good intentions who crashed and burned. Before we get to the three keys to being a conscious caregiver, let me frame our discussion with some basic facts about caregiving roles.

CAREGIVING ROLES: THE INFORMATION

At the present time about 30% of us provide care to someone who is sick, disabled or aged. This figure is expected to grow as the population ages. In fact, the fastest growing part of the U.S. population is the group over age 85. These folks are referred to as the "old-old". Most often they have significant functional impairments requiring varying degrees of assistance with activities of daily living. They likely need help with daily care including medical procedures. About 60% of family caregivers are women, but men are a substantial source of caregiving for their aging wives. A national study of family caregivers conducted in 2015 noted the following:

- 34 million unpaid caregivers provide significant care and services to someone who is ill or disabled—usually a family member.
- 25% of caregivers are taking care of a person with dementia or Alzheimer's Disease.
- 21% of families in the U.S. contribute in some way to caregiving for a relative or friend.
- 59% of caregivers report not taking care of their own medical or social needs.
- 1/3rd of caregivers provide high level medical care and spend an average of 62 hours/week devoted to caregiving—most often to a spouse.
- Caregivers over age 75 are growing in numbers, they live with their recipient of care and provide over 36 hours of heavy care a week. They provide an average of 5.5 years of caregiving.
- Caregivers report high levels of stress, declining health and isolation.

It's clear from this report and from my own experience that caregiving is a heavy load that adds demands to individuals and families. The need for self-care, respite and support is crucial.

KEYS TO CONSCIOUS CAREGIVING

While this article is not a "how-to" for caregiving, it offers a set of keys to care for your soul and your spirit when facing the responsibilities of caregiving. The ideas come from my own journey – both professionally and personally. I hope you find them to be helpful as you face this important role.

My boyfriend Michael broke his neck in a car accident at age 16. His mother was emotionally unable to care for him and she put him in a nursing home. I met him when he turned 26 and I was a nurse at the Rehab Institute of Chicago. I worked on the pediatric unit with teenagers who had spinal injuries and they all talked about this very cool guy who was on the independent unit. Michael had been sent to Rehab by vocational services in Michigan when a social worker realized that unless his situation changed, he would never leave the nursing home where he was surrounded by frail elderly people and had no opportunities for the future. Despite this living situation, I fell for Michael the first time I met him. He glowed from the inside and had a serenity and loving kindness way beyond his age and situation. He loved living and was joyful to be a source of information and guidance to younger patients who were just learning what life in a wheelchair would bring. I ended up moving to Detroit where he lived and eventually we got an apartment and he started college.

Despite my love and good intentions, we both burned out. I worked full time as a visiting nurse, then came home to care for Michael. Michael suffered one healthcare crisis after another and his stamina to continue in school faded. Right before the holidays in 1977, he spilled an entire carafe of coffee onto his legs and they were severely burned. Following a one-month hospital stay and skin grafts he came home in an ambulance and when the drivers put him in the bed I gasped. Though I had been with him daily, I was shocked to see his skeleton frame in our bed. He was about 6 ft. 3 inches tall and he weighed 84 pounds.

Two weeks later, Michael took all of his medications including narcotics and tranquilizers and committed suicide. His note for me expressed his love and also expressed his belief that the quality of his life no longer allowed him to pursue his dreams. That experience, so long ago, gave me grace and insight into the emotional and physical commitment required of a caregiver. I realized that I had isolated myself, separated from my family and friends and put my life on hold. Looking through the rearview mirror years later, I want to share some strategies that will help you be a more conscious caregiver than I was as a young nurse in love.

Key One: Start with YOU in Mind and with EYES WIDE OPEN

Conscious Caregivers benefit from deep knowledge and attention to their inner life and connection to Source Energy. Taking regular daily time to set intentions, meditate, and reflect all reduce stress and promote living your passions, even in the midst of taking on a caregiving role. When the role of caregiving begins, or if you are already in this role, I recommend that you read, complete, and live by The Passion Test (Attwood and Attwood, 2010). The Passion Test is the premier internationally-recognized tool to identify and prioritize the elements of your ideal life. As a conscious caregiver, you are 100% responsible for creating your life and making the time and space for your own needs. In using the Passion Test, you will identify and prioritize your top five answers to complete the sentence, "When my life is ideal I am…." It sounds simple, but requires going inward and opening your heart to what will fulfill you. You can also visit the website: www.thepassiontest.com and take the test online.

The alignment of your passions with caregiving responsibilities may present conflicting feelings and thoughts. Many caregivers feel that they have no choice or alternative to being in the role. I urge you to enter the process with your eyes WIDE OPEN. Make sure you know the exact nature of tasks and caregiver responsibilities. Is the care recipient facing a short-term need, or are they likely to decline and have an increasing need for care? What are the duties and tasks that you will have to take over? These range from those called Instrumental Activities of Daily Living such as shopping, bill paying, cleaning and yard work to Functional Activities of Daily Living, which includes, bathing, grooming, toileting, assistance with feeding and monitoring the safety of the care recipient.

Another, even more intense level of caregiving, is providing nursing care such as tube feedings, bladder catheters, home IV therapy, giving injections, administering medications and caring for stomas or skin wounds. Be sure that you know what is expected and determine if you are both able and willing to step in as a caregiver. If you have doubts, research the potential and availability of a paid caregiver. It may be that a combination of family members and paid caregivers are needed to meet the needs.

I urge you not to take on more than you are able and willing to – along your other life responsibilities such as your job, your own family/spouse and your free time. You can get help from hospital or community social service agencies to locate care providers. You may need to investigate the availability of local long-term care residencies such as assisted living, group homes, and skilled nursing facilities.

Key Two: Develop and Stick with a Mindfulness Practice

I recommend a regular practice of Transcendental Meditation for 20 minutes twice each day. TM is scientifically proven as a major way to shed daily stress and the practice deepens over time. Most cities and larger communities offer TM training, or you can look online for training in your area. In addition to calming the mind, performing a daily ritual such as lighting a candle, repeating an affirmation, reading from a sacred text or chanting will prepare you for a mindful day. I wear a simple bracelet with a locket that vibrates every hour reminding me to NOTICE what is surrounding me and how I am responding to the present moment. (see website: www.meaningtopause.com for information). Living in the present moment reminds me that I am a just fine and have all that I need in the NOW. I made it through whatever I faced in the past – and I am curious and prepared to live in whatever the future brings, which is as yet to be lived. Both the future and the past are really just stories that I created in my mind and neither warrant fear or remorse. The only moment I can be in is the present (NOW).

Living in the present does not mean that you have no plan. It's important that you keep a schedule of the daily or weekly appointments, visits, errands and chores in your own life and those that you are performing as a caregiver. Make sure to schedule YOU time –uninterrupted time to think, play, stay connected to your friends and regularly experience JOY. You may need to arrange for a respite worker or sitter if your patient needs constant attention or safety in the home is a concern. When this person is present and oriented to the care needs and ways to reach you – LEAVE THE HOUSE AND ENJOY YOURSELF.

Consider: For your dependent care recipient, time away from you is also a break for them. Even isolated and debilitated people benefit from socialization with others. It would be a good idea to arrange vacations and weekends away on a regular basis. Remember, local assisted living or in-home workers can be scheduled in advance to cover for you.

Another suggestion I offer is a daily practice of gratitude. At the end of the day, make a list of three to five things you are grateful for. I call my list WWWT? – What Went Well Today? Do this along with reviewing and evaluating your intentions for the day. Begin to think about what you want to bring into your life on the next day and imbed the image of this actually happening into your head before you go to sleep. If your loved one is able to participate in any of your daily practices with you, it can help form a close bond and deepen the experience for you both.

Even highly-evolved mindful and/or enlightened beings experience the contraction caused by negative emotions and troubling experiences. As a caregiver, they are bound to happen. The issue is how you will handle these situations. Just as you noted your joys and gratitude, note your moods and stressors. Process your sadness and ground yourself by taking deep breaths, letting the feelings come and face them to let them go. An excellent way to let go is using The Sedona Method by Hale Dworkin. It's a simple yet profound way to look at a negative situation; look at it in a mindful way and then LET IT GO.

Take extra care of your health and wellbeing both physically and mentally. Caregiving is not a time to ignore regular medical care, dental care or treatments such as massages or chiropractor visits. If the role is causing you any anxiety, depression or other negative emotions, reach out to someone who can help and support you.

Key Three: Form and Use Your Tribe

Social support from friends and family may sound like another chore, but your wellbeing may depend on it. If you are in a book group, make sure you plan to keep up with attending it. Keep up with your regular contacts for going to movies, dining out and making appointments for yourself. It's likely that friends who learn of your role as a caregiver, may ask how they can help. TAKE THEM UP ON IT! Let a friend sit with your loved one while you go shopping, attend a movie or go for a long walk. You may want to put an ad in your local paper to find a companion/sitter so that you can have private time.

Some communities offer support groups for family caregivers, or you may want to do an online search for internet-based groups. Ask for help with chores, errands and other tasks. People who care about you will want to help and you are doing their soul a favor by allowing the gift. Joining a caregiver support group either locally or online can give you a chance to connect with other people who face similar challenges. Many of us have a tendency to see accepting or asking for help as a weakness. I view it as a strength and a form of self-care.

CONCLUSION

Caregiving is a bittersweet activity. It means giving back to a spouse, a parent, a relative or friend who likely gave to you and supported you along your journey in life. Sometimes the need may be greater than we can provide, and it's best to know this and work on resources to take over some aspect of caregiving. You need to start the process by taking care of yourself. If you are depleted it limits your ability to be present for your loved one.

My thanks to Michael and all of my patients over the years who taught me these lessons.

About Diann

Diann Martin, PhD, RN has been a nurse since 1974. She earned her BSN at Loyola University and her MS and PhD at Rush University in Chicago. She spent over 30 years in home healthcare as a visiting nurse and executive leader. She also worked as a national nursing consultant to assist hospitals with their patient management in the community.

Since 2004, Dr. Martin has been in higher education in nursing programs and has served as Dean at four colleges/universities nationwide. She currently owns her own business, RoadScholarsRN and The Conscious Nurse Academy, which seeks to transform the practice of nursing and inspire nurses to lead their ideal lives both personally and professionally. She is on the Advisory Board of the Center for Healthcare Innovation.

Diann lives in Wilmette, IL with her husband, John.

CHAPTER 21

SUCCESS BEYOND WEALTH
—FINDING TRUE SUCCESS BY INSPIRING OTHERS TO SUCCEED

BY SAM E. COHEN

Today, I am a successful business owner with over 30 employees doing $20 million in sales a year and helping hundreds of people find success in their own lives. It hasn't always been that way. Just a few years ago, in October of 2010, I hit rock bottom. I went from a high level executive earning six figures, to doing whatever it took to pay the bills. I was selling DVDs at local flea markets when I decided to get back into the e-commerce market by attempting to sell on e-Bay. I met a potential buyer who explained he was a third-party Amazon seller. I didn't even know this business existed, but instantly realized it was my opportunity to truly achieve and earn wealth and improve my lifestyle.

I jumped headfirst into becoming a third-party Amazon seller. The first six months were grueling, but the process of buying and selling came naturally to me. I gave it my all, learning the intricacies of my new business and working long, hard days. In six months, I went from selling DVDs for $1 each at flea markets to making a $100,000 in monthly sales on Amazon. Now, in my sixth year as an Amazon third-party seller, I am doing $20,000,000 in sales a year. My Amazon business is in the top one percent of third-party sellers, out of more than two million sellers.

By January 2015, I built a reputation as an expert on e-commerce and Amazon. I realized I was spending a substantial amount of time answering questions from struggling entrepreneurs on how to become a successful third-party seller. I truly loved doing it but realized it was consuming a lot of my time. Then I recognized helping others succeed as third-party Amazon sellers was another opportunity for me to give back while satisfying a passion of helping others. I could fulfill my love of helping others succeed, while simultaneously running my own thriving businesses. I launched Amazon Consulting Experts in July 2015 to provide personal, customized, and comprehensive services teaching the intricacies of being an Amazon third-party seller, along with business, life, and personal development skills. The results were amazing. My first group of consulting clients achieved a 98% success rate and 95% signed up for a second year.

Amazon Consulting Experts is a way for people to achieve the same success I did, success that brings true wealth and allows you to live the lifestyle of your dreams. Since mastering the art of success, I now jump out of bed at 5 a.m. every morning excited to start my day. There hasn't been a day in six years, since I started my own business, when I didn't want to go to work. I never miss any family events and I have free time to travel with my wife and children. I am truly my own boss and live by my own decisions. You too, are capable of finding the same freedom and success in your own life! Looking back on what I have done to master my success in the last few years, I realize the following six principled actions made a huge impact on my business and personal success:

1. Embrace Hard Work.
2. Leave Ego Behind.
3. Be Personable.
4. Share Success.
5. Delegate with a Giving Heart.
6. Ask "What Else?"

1. Embrace Hard Work

People often ask what I tell my clients and employees to encourage them to succeed. There are many philosophies and experiences that I share with them. Things like, "you can make excuses or money, not both" or "it won't work if you won't work" and "you don't have to be great to start but you have to start to be great." These phrases catch people's attention and almost always inspire them to action. The reason these messages work is because they encourage people to **embrace hard work**. Many new, struggling, entrepreneurs have an excuse on why they can't, won't, or haven't succeeded. It just comes down to hard work. To succeed in anything, it will take long hours and a lot of energy in the beginning. You can't expect to follow an easy plan and have success happen. A new business is like a new baby; at times you may have to stay up with it all night, change it, feed it properly, give it a lot of love and not expect much in return. If you do this, you will see huge results quickly. Don't focus on how much time or money you need to start. Just start with however much you have and get to work. There is no specific amount of time, money, or skills needed to master your own success, only the hunger to succeed.

2. Leave Ego Behind

Wealth, lifestyle, relationships, and health success must require the **absence of ego.** Being free of ego, even when society or other's standards give you plenty of reason for an ego, is one of the biggest assets an entrepreneur can possess. You must be one hundred percent responsible and accountable for everything that happens to you, rather than looking to complain and blame. When you focus on comparing your new self to your old self, rather than to others, you will make true progress. When you view others as people who can help you and people you can help, much can be accomplished. This may mean you need to admit your shortcomings and partner with others to make up the resources you don't have, whether it be financial resources, business, leadership, or technical skills. Having insight to understand areas that are not your strengths and seeking the right council from others enables you not only to succeed, but also to realize your strengths and the opportunity to help others.

A truly successful person will make time to listen to others because he or she knows everyone has something to contribute. You must always value others and realize no one is beneath you. If you have truly embraced hard work to reach success, you will recognize others doing the same. You will have no basis to view yourself as better than anyone else. This ego-free mindset will enable you to achieve true success that exceeds beyond wealth and positively overflows to your health and lifestyle.

3. Be Personable

Once you have freed yourself from ego, you open yourself up to **be**

personable. In my experience, this is the only way to develop great relationships. It can and should extend beyond personal relationships and to business associations. Being consistent with self, being your same self at work as at home or with friends, opens doors to creating a dynamic, enjoyable workplace filled with meaningful relationships with colleagues, staff, and clients. It builds mutual respect, friendship, camaraderie, and loyalty that retains good staff and clients, a necessity for a successful business. When good people stick around, good ideas are created and successful work inevitably takes place.

So, how do you become personable in your business world? Get to know your staff and clients personally. Find out what is important to them in life. If you know your employees personally, you can give them meaningful, personal rewards for a job well done, promotion, or work anniversary. For example, if you know an employee loves sports and values family time, give him a set of tickets to a live sporting event. If another employee has a tough commute, allow them to work from home when possible. Give time off at holidays and accommodate schedules. Joke around; allow your staff to be candid and feel valued. Share successes and failures. Simply being personable will go a long way in developing relationships which foster success.

4. Share success

On my journey to earning wealth and the lifestyle of my dreams, I feel most fulfilled when **sharing my success** with others. As I built my business, I learned many things from the experiences of others which helped me succeed. I now find the best thing I can do with the success I create is to help others create their own success. I did not get to where I am because I had special talents, great business skills, or luck, but rather because I had passion and perseverance. I created my consulting business to share my passion for success with others. After clients hear they can succeed, from someone who has succeeded, they have a stronger confidence in knowing there are simple actionable measures that will put them in the best position to achieve. They have confidence in themselves. I find great joy in leading people to understand their options while instilling confidence by explaining how to proceed. I encourage them along the way and offer an individualized approach. I found wealth through my e-commerce business, but wasn't truly satisfied until I started sharing my success with others in a way that can lead them to their own success. No matter how much wealth you earn, you will never feel truly successful in your life until you share your success with others.

5. Delegate with a Giving Heart

The ability to delegate is a well-known method to achieving success. The skill to **delegate with a giving heart** is a distinguishing factor and will yield even greater results. To achieve success, across all aspects of your life and improve your lifestyle, you must delegate not with an end goal of taking work off your plate (although that is a positive result) but rather to give others opportunity.

When you delegate, do so to help others succeed, not simply to make your life easier. Delegate big and meaningful tasks, ones that are worthy of your time, just as much as you would delegate less significant tasks. To truly provide others, such as your staff, with opportunities through delegation you must give them meaningful, challenging tasks. It may lead to some mistakes, or still require your involvement, but it enables you to use delegation as an opportunity to give to others development and growth.

Don't overlook your personal life when it comes to delegating. You can delegate home and personal tasks as well as work tasks. Of course, you may be able to clean your own house or maintain your own yard, but once you have the financial means to hire others to do so, you should consider it. You can provide meaningful work opportunities for those who need them while freeing up time to focus on your business, family, and personal interests. If your spouse or partner shoulders a large amount of the household duties, delegate some of that work for them and make their life easier, provide meaningful work for others, and help yourself by creating a happy home. It's a win for everyone.

6. Ask "What Else?"

If you think you are finished with something, ask "**what else?**" Mastering the art of success is not finite, but rather a never-ending goal. By simply asking "what else" of myself and others I always get more information. When you ask a broad, open-ended question, you find tremendous insight. You will find value in the thought process, which brings out unique perception and talents. It will set the bar for people to do more, in an encouraging way. When you ask "what else?" you guide others and can then lead them to develop and manage their own ideas. It is yet another way to work hard, leave ego behind, be personable, share your success, and delegate with a giving heart.

Over the last few years, I've helped many people find success with their own e-commerce businesses and watching them succeed was and is immensely fulfilling. People I work with who follow the principles and strategies outlined in my training courses have experienced amazing results. For example, Phillip went from losing his home to foreclosure to achieving amazing success with gross sales in excess of two million in his first year in his e-commerce business. Gus went from selling $30,000 a month to $200,000 a month in four months time. There are many more examples with very similar results.

You may ask yourself how the principles outlined in this chapter might be used when faced with difficult circumstances, similar to those mentioned above. How do I share success when I'm not in a position of success? The important things to remember are focus and perception. If you only look at what you don't have, you will have a difficult time understanding what advantages you do have that will help you succeed. If ego is your focus, your pride would be so hurt by failure that you would be less inclined to try something new or challenging. By focusing on being personable, you are able to concentrate on the importance of communication skills and reap the benefits of caring for people beyond yourself. Delegating with a giving heart provides others the opportunity for growth and opens valuable time for your family and self. Finally, by asking "what else?" you open yourself to endless new possibilities.

About Sam

Sam E. Cohen currently resides in New Jersey with his wife and four children and has been in e-commerce for 20 years. He started selling on Amazon in 2011, and founded Amazon Consulting Experts (ACE) in 2015. In that time, Sam's business has become one of the top 1% of all third-party sellers on Amazon. He employs 30 people, and owns and operates multiple Amazon accounts with express written permission from Amazon. Sam has been an invited guest at Amazon headquarters in Seattle to discuss current and future business goals and concerns, and was featured on National Public Radio's *Planet Money* and in *The Wall Street Journal.*

Sam is very passionate about mentoring, consulting, teaching, motivating and inspiring other business people. He has been helping other Amazon sellers for the past five years, both as a consultant for large businesses as well as entrepreneurial individuals just starting out and looking to get on board. From this experience, Amazon Consulting Experts (ACE) was born: an exclusive, custom-tailored consulting, mentoring and training program.

Sam believes in paying it forward by teaching people "how to fish" and the abundance mentality. Sam strives to find a balance in life and has a supportive family behind him. Sam also believes in employing as many people as possible given the sluggish economy, and routinely helps people who are financially struggling. For the past 25 years, Sam has worked closely with a charity for terminally-ill children all over the world, and a portion of what he earns goes to this amazing charity.

If you would like additional information on how the ACE program helps new entrepreneurs get started – or how it can help grow an existing business – by effectively utilizing e-commerce tools, retail arbitrage and Amazon third-party selling techniques, your inquiries are welcome via our web site.

Sam is available for speaking engagements and media interviews.

Contact us via our website or call us at:

- Web Site: www.amazonconsultingexperts.com
- Phone: (732) 695-6355

CHAPTER 22

MAGIC'S DETERMINATION

BY CORKIE MANN

Have you ever noticed those *Lucky People* in life, and wondered why some people get everything they ever wanted, and everything they touch seems to turn to gold? You know the ones. . . *Those People* who are always at the right place at the right time and whatever they want just seems to drop in their lap? Do you really think this is luck, or could there actually be a technique?

Years ago, I remember waking up to a pounding sound coming from outside. At the time, we were "living our dream" by living off the land on our small 16-acre farm, and our beautiful Bashkir Curly mare was due any day. I quickly ran outside to see what was causing all the commotion, and I found my expectant mare "Magic" running towards me and then heading back out to the far back fence line. Then she came running towards me again with her nostrils flared as she stopped right at the fence. She was trying to tell me something urgent.

As I went back inside to find my boots I could still hear the pounding of her frantic impatient galloping as she whinnied loudly. It was obvious she was panicked about something. I ran outside again and noticed that her large belly was quite a bit smaller than the day before, and as soon as she saw me she took off towards the back fence. I ran as fast as I could to keep up with her, and as I reached the far corner of our fence line I discovered that her newborn foal was outside of our barbed wire fence. The foal looked so helpless, and frightened but I couldn't concern myself with emotions or my curiosity as to how she was on the other side of the fence. I just needed to stay calm and cut the fence. "Magic" had tenacity, extreme passion, and desire to help her baby. She knew she couldn't get to her foal by herself, but she knew if she made enough noise and showed determination someone would come and help her. It seems that even animals have this God-given ability of determination within them.

This passion from deep within your soul is the rocket fuel that ignites your thoughts. You see, everything has to be a thought before it's created, it doesn't just appear, and it has to have fuel to create it! This passion comes from deep down in your heart, not from your head. It's a strong desire and a resilient faith in yourself. A faith so unshakable, that if someone told you, "It can't be done," you would just ignore them and know that it's "already happened" in your mind. Like Magic's passion, you must be willing to run back and forth with enthusiastic passion, and make a lot of noise until someone hears you, and you let all your passion explode, then you will receive your hearts desires.

I'm sure that the moments seemed like hours for Magic, for me to run to the barn in the freezing air to find wire cutters, and run back to open the fence. When I returned, I saw the small frightened foal still wet from birth stand on her wobbly legs as if she knew it would only be moments before she would be united with her mother. As soon as the fence was cut, she stepped out of the woods and was nuzzled up near her mother sucking and grateful to be safe. At that moment, I couldn't hold back the tears that filled my eyes as I watched this wonderful touching moment. Magic's passion, her love, her desire, made it possible for her to have her sweet baby by her side.

Have you ever sat down and really thought about your life? Have you thought about the way things are and what you really truly want? We all have this innate passion within us to receive our dreams! Maybe you have just gotten knocked down so many times, that you didn't realize that all you had to do was get back up, dust yourself off and try one more time. Having steadfast focus is what it takes to be one of the "lucky people." Most of the time we don't see the painstaking actions, the tenacity, and all the struggles that those people have, in order to be so Lucky.

Then there are those who try to steal your dreams by telling you, "You aren't capable of success, . . . you're too young, . . . you're too old." They say, "You're not pretty or handsome enough, not educated enough, not the right size, not the right gender." They knock you down so many times you feel . . . "What's the use in trying?" Are you the type of person who will just roll over and let them convince you you're not good enough? Or do you love yourself enough to succeed. Don't let your friends, your family, or your acquaintances tell you it can't be done. Dust yourself off and try one more time! You have the ability to be one of the "lucky ones!" You can be one of the "lucky ones" who succeeds on the 11th try, after having failed 10 times. You see, it's not really luck. It's tenacity, it's determination, it's a willingness to stick to it.

My favorite part in one of my most treasured books is, "And all things, whatsoever ye shall Ask in Prayer, Believing, ye shall Receive." Most of us get the Asking part down, and many of us can be gracious in receiving gifts. It's the middle part we might have a hard time with, "Believe." To believe is to trust completely, having immense Faith and passionate excitement and just, "know like you know like you know" that it's yours! To create what you want, you must believe that it will happen, know it's in the midst of creation. Like the scripture reads, Believe and ye shall receive it.

Bill Gates looked at the impossible, and he had a desire to create, and he had passion, desire, and he didn't give up. I'm certain that he had struggles, and some days he may have even wanted to give up. But he must have had a reason why, that was bigger than all the struggles. He had determination, stick-to-it-ive-ness, and he knew he wasn't going to give up until he created his dream. The same was true with Henry Ford. He wanted the V8 engine, so he hired people smarter than himself, and expected them to achieve it. He passionately believed it, and for two years his team continued to tell him that it was impossible to make a V8 engine. Henry Ford had tenacity, desire, and passion. It was impossible, but with passion and a belief so strong that nothing could waiver his knowing it was possible, and it was created!

I have found that the word 'Impossible' re-written is, "I'm Possible."

Doing what it takes to have the tenacity, and determination as my mare did, can be difficult, but if you never stop believing in your dreams and desires, and breathe life into them with passion, you will watch magic happen.

All doubting will block any desire you may have. All Complaining is Repulsive . . . It Repels all goodness. All Suffering and Blaming, Guilt, Fear, Hate, Sadness, Worry, Envy, etc., Repels Your Dreams and Desires. Holding onto Grudges will cause you to suffer. A negative mindset will not allow positive feelings in. Let the Negative Go! The keywords in your creation are Believe, Trust, and Enthusiasm.

I was born and raised in the San Francisco Bay area and was not accustomed to the freezing cold of West Virginia. Trying to live off the land was a huge desire, but there was a lot to learn. I found myself discovering creative ways to stay warm while doing my farming chores. Our first winter we had several kids born on the farm, not to mistake the word "kids" for my own babies, these were baby goats. Since we had little money I needed to be the Veterinarian for our little farm. A friend showed me how to take care of the newborn's horns, umbilical cord, shots, and castration (ouch). But it was snowing! And freezing! And I had no desire to get out in that kind of weather. So, when my children went off to school and I was home alone with my 2-year-old, I, in my infinite wisdom and with creativity, brought the baby goats and newborn foals into our nice warm home to take care of their veterinary needs. It worked perfectly, until my youngest who was home with me, started talking and told daddy "The horsy was in the house." It was linoleum though, and the animals were very cooperative not to make a mess on the floor.

Just as much as passion is important to having your dreams and desires magically appear. Gratitude is a necessary ingredient as well. When you are grateful for everything, even the upsets in life, you will then have the ability to receive. Your life is shaped the way it is, because of your good times and your bad times. We gain wisdom from our lessons in life and it's vital that we pay attention to them and learn from them. If you are reluctant in gaining wisdom from your failures, sad to say, you'll probably find yourself in the same situation again and again until you finally get it. You see, we are given troubles and trials throughout our lives to test us and to grow from them. So, pay attention, succeed in your tests, and get on with the happiness that's in store for you.

Years ago, when I first learned about Vision Boards, I had just discovered that I was expecting our 5th child. Up until that point, I just wanted a sweet little baby, and then it hit me. We're going to need a mini-van that my entire family could fit into. I started looking around and discovered that there were only two vehicles that offered seven seat belts. We had no money, no credit, and a car that was falling apart. Someone told me to put a photo of what I want on my wall. So, I went to the Toyota dealership and got a brochure of the van that had seven seatbelts. I cut the photo out of the brochure, and put it on the wall. Focused daily, and my heart was filled with gratitude of having this van. I called the dealership at least once a week, and they were working with me to somehow have this impossible dream. Then one day I received a call from the salesman, and he said they had my Previa van. It was over 150 miles away, but they could take my car as a trade-in. Somehow, we qualified for the loan, we drove the clunker over the 150-mile drive, and as we drove into the dealership it almost didn't make it. We chugged and chugged across the parking lot and it died right out front of the doors. They took our clunker as a trade-in, as if was a prize vehicle. We drove home with a beautiful used Previa Van with only 9,000 miles on it and it fit our family perfectly!

Since then, I've discovered five amazing techniques in creating dreams to come true. Not to brag, but to show you that it's like a muscle you develop over time. Later in life, we needed a home and were in a financial bind. We decided that we would find the best home ever, and it would be for FREE. Two days later we had found a half-million-dollar brand new home to live in for free. It had so many bedrooms that we were able to rent out two rooms with an extra income of $700 a month. We were also paid $1,000 when we moved out exactly one year later. These things actually can happen for you as well.

Bobby McFerrin says it all in one short sentence "Don't worry, Be Happy!" You have this great power to create your world anyway you want. What are you waiting for?

Having what you want is Hard.
Having what you don't want is Hard.
Choose Your HARD!

Now, with your chin up, shoulders back, and a great big smile, breathe passion into your hearts desires, and Live Your Dreams!

About Corkie

All her life, Corkie Mann has been in search of how to help people find joy. When she was ten years old she found the poem, "Don't Quit." From that moment on, she knew that to be genuinely happy in life, you must keep picking yourself up, dusting yourself off and going after your dreams again and again. Going after what she wants has always been a way of life for her. Corkie has discovered over the years how to quickly and effortlessly receive the Goals on her vision board. "It just takes determination and applying five easy techniques. It's like exercising your muscles, the more you exercise the easier it gets. The same is true for Goals. The more you stay focused on your Goals with some easy techniques, the faster they are accomplished." Corkie has tested and retested many methods to find the techniques that have skyrocketed her goals. She now does trainings that inspire and support you in having an amazing EPIC lifestyle, that's filled with Joy, Harmony, and Satisfaction.

In her spare time Corkie has written three books. These are quick read books that you can read daily in about ten minutes to "Set your mood right" in Living your Dreams:

1) *Today IS Tomorrow! 10 Minutes a Day to Live Your Dreams!*
2) *"And then HE Kissed me!" Daily Steps to a Passionate Marriage.*
3) *"And Then SHE Kissed me!" Daily Steps to a Passionate Marriage.*

She has five fantastic, positive, motivated children, and so far, nine wonderful grandchildren. She enjoys teaching them about the law of attraction and having their own Vision Boards, as well as giving them plenty of love, hugs, and kisses.

At 18, Corkie Mann went after her dream to become a Professional Photographer. She was so determined to succeed, she called up the best photographer San Francisco had to offer, and asked him if she could follow him around and learn from the best. Six months later, she opened the next best professional Photography Studio in the San Francisco Bay area, photographing weddings, families and babies.

Back in the mid 80's, she was a young wife and mother of three. Corkie and her husband had a dream to "live off the land." They bought 16 acres in West Virginia, and left the Bay area to live "back to basics." They had two more babies that were born in their beautiful, cozy underground home they built together. They used a wood cook stove to heat and cook, and they lived off a one-acre garden, along with their chickens, rabbits and an occasional deer. After ten years, they had had enough. As Corkie puts it, "I learned a lot, but It's hard work, and not as romantic as it sounds." So, in 2004, she opened 2-Curves for Women Franchises in the Carolinas. They were on her vision board, so of course they were a "hit" the moment they opened, and many women began to lovingly see themselves in a new self-confident way.

As you can see, Corkie Mann enjoys helping people find themselves, and when they find themselves, it's so exciting to say, "They love who they find."

You can connect with Corkie at:

- Corkie@CorkieMann.com
- CorkieMann.com
- Facebook.com/CorkieMann
- and all the other social media /CorkieMann

CHAPTER 23

STARTLING "SECOND OPINION" SECRETS FINALLY REVEALED
—SURVIVING DRUGS AND SURGERY

BY JOHN PARKS TROWBRIDGE M.D.

Maybe a laboratory technologist wasn't supposed to understand the elevator talk I witnessed – or maybe, as a hospital employee, I didn't have any business paying attention. But I was startled to hear three physicians joking when leaving a lunchtime continuing education lecture on molecular biology: "Do you have any idea what that professor was talking about?" "Not a clue! Glad it doesn't have anything to do with taking care of my patients." "Yeah, me too!"

As a future doctor, I was appalled at how these practitioners so casually dismissed advances pointing the way for improved patient care. They didn't *understand?* For my biology degree from Stanford just one year earlier, I had focused on molecular genetics and immunology. Some 47 years later, I *rely* on that and *all* my other knowledge – every day – when addressing complicated illness issues.

The Principal Part of Everything Is the Beginning

Most doctor visits presume that you need *"medical* care" (for disease or distress) which is far different from promoting longevity and preserving wellbeing, known as *"health* care." The advice in this chapter applies to

221

either … and hopefully your coming years will aim not at recovery from frustrating illness but rather at achieving optimal health. Now it's time to get started on your amazing journey.

Is there a way YOU could be empowered to get the very best results from any visit to a physician? You might not realize it – but *YES*, there is a "soft technology," a method to assure a brighter future and fewer problems.

Your doctor holds a special trust – with your comfort, your recovery, your very life in his or her hands. Seek a partnership that promises to go both ways. In the past, people seemed to have little choice but "blind faith" that prescriptions and advice were the very best. Today, just a few quick steps take off the blindfold so you can make informed decisions about *your* physicians and *your* care. Take note that you call the graduate at the bottom of his medical school class … "Doctor." You might be taken by his or her smile and gentle manner, sharp wardrobe, whatever … but do you *get what you need?* Should you expect more than just a "better Band-Aid®?"

Avoid Overwhelm – Start with the Basics

Doctor-time is precious, so efficiency is essential to meet the needs of all patients. Write down your key questions, even those of concerned family. Get the information you need, but realize this is not the place for casual conversation and direct answers aren't meant to seem rude. (You are the *only* judge of whether you feel comfortable – or prickly – or downright antsy during your visit. My job is set you at ease or send you to a physician who might be a better "fit" for you.)

"Specialists" are sometimes useful … but not always. Any puzzling, lingering, or worsening problem *might* deserve specialty evaluation sooner; if you're concerned, ask for referral. (My aim for every patient, through my efforts alone or along with other experts, is simply "Find it *now* – Fix it *right!"*)

Results should be your only guiding principle (after safety, of course). Sadly, modern medicine is "protocol"- or process-oriented rather than "product"- or results-oriented. Sounds strange, right? The medical culture decrees and imposes conformity. Doctors come under scrutiny when they divert from the outlined "standards of care" to evaluate or treat your problems. Even when **you** benefit from an unconventional treatment, **your doctor** could be called to answer to "the authorities" (and even disciplined) for departure from "the way they say." (I call this "One Size Fits None," because you are unique and have needs different than anyone else – don't you deserve *personalized* care?) Your wellbeing hangs in the balance ... *demand results.*

Finding the "right doc" might be an unpredictable journey. Be wary of frequent malpractice suits; state medical board websites have this information available. Allegations of "fraudulent practice" might simply reflect disputes for daring to step "out of the box" and offering "alternative" treatments. Patient results are the key standard to evaluate reports and commentary on the internet. Be mindful that you are seeking a savvy physician willing to offer his or her best remedy ... which might be reassuring counsel or timely advice rather than a pill. A winning selection is a skilled professional who helps you to achieve and accomplish more than you ever imagine, and your benefits can last for years of longer life. We spend more time reviewing restaurants or selecting a new car – odd, isn't it! Be sure to set aside money in a "Feel Better, Get Healthy" budget to invest in the care you desire and deserve. Let's get started!

Slip Into the Driver's Seat

❖   **Set Your Goals** – Your first step is to reflect on what is bothering you or seems "wrong" or different than you used to feel. This might appear obvious ... still, take just five quiet minutes to review how your life is affected. Next, put on your "imagination glasses" and **visualize** how you will look and feel and act when you feel better as this problem is resolved. (If you claim you don't have a good imagination, I say "just *imagine* that you do and give it a go.") Now ... *believe* that you could actually achieve your goal of finally feeling better.

When you "see" a detailed "mind picture," write down a *full description* of how you would look, where you would go, what you would do, how you would talk with your family and friends. *WAIT!* I said **write down** these details. This is *your* "ideal scene." Skip this beginning and you can stumble over yourself as we go further, sadly missing the results you truly deserve.

❖ **The Spider Web Theory of Medicine** – You want a doctor who "sees the big picture" for you, one who respects that "when you pull on *one* part of the web, the *whole* web jiggles." Remember: "the devil is in the *details*" ... *your* details, *your* situation. Expect your physician to seek to correct the "root cause" rather than just prescribe yet another "bandage" for bothersome symptoms. One more drug for your next new complaint? *No!* Insist on a blueprint with the prospect of the most benefit for the least risk or expense or effort.

Always act as if your doctor truly wants to share a caring relationship of warmth and insight. Then, after genuine eye contact and a welcoming handshake, your doctor's *first job is to <u>listen</u> to your details* – not just to what you're saying, but more importantly for what you're not telling him. On average, our attention span is about 8 seconds (down from 12 since 2000) – while a goldfish can last about 9 seconds! Oddly, your doctor waits 17 seconds before interrupting your story. How easy it is for you to feel misunderstood! Some 40 percent of patients feel rushed during their visit, which for about one-third lasts *less* than 10 minutes. Given these limitations and your doctor's need to hear *your* relevant details, stay focused on sharing step-by-step not randomly. Stay on-track with *your* concerns, not what happened last year to Aunt Matilda. If you're not sure you've explained yourself clearly, help your doctor to understand what you need to communicate.

Worried that you can't afford more time? The most expensive treatments you get are the ones that don't work. Chances are, you already understand *that* all too well! Remember your "mental image" of success? Focus on value not cost – your future, your comfort, even your life ... *you're worth it!* The tragedy is not that you "have issues" with your doctors, we all do – do what you need to do to get the very best care that your condition requires and you are willing to do.

❖ **"Close" Counts Only in Horseshoes, Hand Grenades, and Shotguns** – The *best test* to correctly understand and resolve your concerns is **not** in a lab or a hospital but between your doctor's ears! Perhaps 80 percent of diagnoses can be made from your history alone. All *you* do is outline your circumstances like a sharp reporter: "what, where, when, how" ... your *doctor* will seek the "why." Your physician needs to listen carefully as a specialist in how your body works and why things go awry: Correct *diagnosis* is key – Correct *treatment* is critical.

Where's the source? While "symptom" discomforts might center on a particular area, the actual cause might be quite remote, even hidden. Unless you and your doctor actually know the cause,[1] getting better is not a "hit or miss" proposition but "miss and miss and miss again"! *That's* why you're persistent in seeking a physician who is always learning newer and better evaluations and treatments – not just responding to a longer list of side effects with the latest "TV drugs." Ever wonder about advertisements for 1-800-BAD-DRUG – or *www.1800BadDrug.com* and *www.bad-drug.net?*

❖ **Gaze Into My Crystal Ball** – Could your doctor really *miss* your diagnosis? Consider this dicey picture for any physician: You don't *look for* what you don't know about – You don't *find* what you don't look for – You don't *treat* what you don't find – You don't *fix* what you don't treat. Understandably, doctors don't want to face things they *can't* fix becaue that betrays their inexperience, inattention, or simply fallible human limits. The avoidable result can be more and more drugs, more and more operations. More and more lingering discomforts and disappointments.

Staying up-to-date is difficult. *PubMed.gov*/MEDLINE is the computer search system for over 17 million published articles in over 5,600 biomedical journals ... but 20 percent of relevant papers in the database can be *"missed"* in each search. Articles before 1964 are not listed, even "old knowledge" that could be very pertinent. Critical research published in *most* of the 14,000 worldwide journals is overlooked because they're not accessible.

Doctors won't study tests or treatments they simply don't know about ... or don't understand ... or (falsely?) dismiss as quackery. Do *you* get "missed" in the muddle? Why settle for the blinders on a one-trick pony when you can locate doctors widely recognized for teaching and "thinking outside the box," pushing to the horizons of excellence. Even "TV hero" Marcus Welby, M.D., *could* earn accolades from peers across the country or around the world when offering effective innovative

---

1. Delightful concept: *Know The Cause* is a syndicated TV show for 18 years, hosted by my dear friend Doug Kaufmann, a medical tech whom I taught in 1984 to treat **The Yeast Syndrome** (my Bantam Books bestseller since 1986). He gained tremendous experience working with doctors who had not a clue that undiagnosed fungus/yeast could explain problems in 40 percent of patients and he has devoted his broadcast career to spreading the word: *www.knowthecause.com*.

solutions not widely promoted.

"Doctor Talk"

(Just so *you* know to investigate and inquire about state-of-the-art issues)

Details on emerging advances are available *except* in the major journals or at the "regular" continuing medical education conferences. Your doctor has to *prowl* for reliable evidence on evolving tests and treatments for *increasingly common* (and often poorly managed) illness issues related to The Yeast Syndrome[1] and mycotoxins (fungus), stealth parasites, chronic virus or bacterial infections more odd than MRSA, biofilm and gut microbiome alterations with disease, impaired digestive processes, induced autoimmune malfunctions, painful back or arthritis joints and sports injuries, mismatch of tongue-jaw size leading to an obstructing airway, central (brain) changes with worsening hypoxemia and resulting system malfunctions, pre-diabetes (cardio-metabolic syndrome), oxidative stress/inflammation patterns, hyper-reactive platelets and endothelial blood vessel alterations (causing strokes, heart attacks, gangrene), heart rhythm disturbances, hormone deficiencies and dysregulations, neurotransmitter imbalances, altered mitochondrial functions and energy efficiency, effects of toxic heavy metal exposures, GMO-food alterations, unhealthy cultivation and animal husbandry procedures, chronic "fertilizer"/herbicide/pesticide exposures, organic chemical poisoning, essential mineral and vitamin deficiencies, recognized adverse effects of routine drugs (statins for cholesterol, acid-blockers, anti-inflammatories, pain-relievers, others), emotional and psychological stress (mind-body medicine), and more ... also dramatic healing and rejuvenation possible with nutritional supplementation, reduction of body burden of toxic heavy metals and organic chemicals, frequency-specific microcurrent, revolutionary stem cells, and many other technologies being discovered or proposed ... or not yet imagined!

❖ **Smarter Than a 5th Grader?** – Some studies show that 40 percent of patients have already consulted "Dr. Google" about their problems. This *can* help you understand your doctor more quickly. A variety of revolutionary newsletters share breakthrough treatments that you might want to copy for, and discuss with, your doctor.[2] But if you trust these or the internet more than your current doctor – or if you feel

---

2. "Medical Establishment" newsletters review conventional care. Cutting-edge and ancient techniques are introduced in various monthlies, such as these published by my friends: Dr. Julian Whitaker's *Health & Healing*, Dr. Joseph Mercola's natural health website *www.mercola.com*, Dr. Jonathan Collins' *Townsend Letter for Doctors & Patients*, Dr. Russell L. Blaylock's *Blaylock Wellness Report*, Dr. Jonathan Wright's *Nutrition & Healing*, Dr. Frank Shallenberger's *Second Opinion*, Dr. Chauncey Crandall's *Heart Health Report*, Dr. Bruce West's *Health Alert*, Dr. David Williams' *Alternatives*, and *Life Extension* magazine; refreshingly for network TV, Dr. Mehmet Oz has broken the glass ceiling with The Dr. Oz Show and *Dr. Oz The Good Life* magazine, educating millions on alternative health ideas that lie outside the medical mainstream.

the need to "Ask your doctor if [the newest TV drug] is right for you" – rethink your approach or maybe find a new doctor … certainly consider requesting a "second opinion." If you remain unsettled, summon the courage to make the choice to tell your doctor "You're fired!" and find one who produces results for you.

Even "complicated" medical care is easy to understand in the framework of **"Blockers-Missing-Switches."** *Whatever* is **"blocking"** your body functions needs to be discovered and reduced or removed – think of tossing the shoe that's causing the blister. *Whatever* is **"missing"** but you need for healing and repair must be provided – think of adding compost, lime, sand, and other amendments to garden soil. *Whatever* **"switches"** need to be flipped on to start your systems will need to be set and balanced (thyroid, other hormones, even oxygen) – besides fruits and yogurt to make a smoothie, you must hit the "START" button. These are critical factors your doctor needs to address, regardless of your "problems."

ACTION ITEMS

When you start taking responsibility for finding *your* "best doctor," some simple steps will help create an effortless working relationship. Here's how *you* can set the stage:

- *Be on time (even early)* – "Just a few minutes late" squeezes all the staff into "rush-rush," trying to take care of patient needs, since you and everyone *following* you could be cut short. Emergencies happen … but your being late doesn't really count. And please – be patient, kind, and courteous when unexpected events delay your visit; ask to reschedule if needed. Always expect the doctor and staff to be respectful to you as well.

- *Know why you're there* – "Follow up" or "Doctor wanted to see me" doesn't give details to nurses who strive to have everything ready in the room for the physician.

- *Know what pills and potions you're taking* – That "little white pill" could be one of thousands available. Mixing ingredients can make a tasty dish for supper; mixing (or mixing up) medications can be *deadly*. Often overlooked is the list of nutritional supplements you take daily or often – while useful to "educate" some doctors not yet "in the know," it might be critical to help avoid interactions with some prescription drugs.

- *Know how you're feeling* – This might sound obvious but … you'd be surprised that your doctor needs a bit more to go on than "I just don't feel well." Describe in your own words what is *different* than earlier for you. Give numbers not conclusions: "My pressure at home has been 155 over 90" not "It's been pretty good lately." Keep a symptom diary between visits: what, where, when, how long, … and so on.

- *Be honest about what you've done … or haven't!* – If you've ignored or overlooked treatment plans exactly as intended but don't "fess up," then your doctor lacks critical information to conclude whether your treatments need to be changed. Bring copies of recent tests or notes from other doctors – also printed photos or close-ups on your smartphone. Reactions to any medications?

- *Time is ticking* – Place a high priority for your doctor to spend the time needed to discuss your condition and explain specific recommendations. Happily, almost 70 percent of patients bring a short list of questions to their appointment. That *one* proactive step can be critical, so long as you realize that only the most important items can be addressed in the usual 10 to 12 minutes. Act as if success is just within reach, so schedule and pay for extra time (even another visit) if needed – to get your concerns handled.

- *Schedule your follow-up visit right then*. Appointments are essential to monitor expected changes in your condition. Get seen when your doctor wants to reassess your program. Shortest wait times are "first thing" in the morning or afternoon.

Arrange quickly to see any specialist advised, so your doctor gathers all the perspectives he needs. Confusion arises with similar titles for doctors who treat an organ or system with *medications* and those who perform *operations* in the very same area. (Example: neurologist or neurosurgeon.) Expect consultants to join the team for your best results.

- *Immediately question if you are reluctant about a test or a treatment.* Speak up: an explanation right then might reassure you with any misunderstanding or confusion. If you still need more details, ask for the best information source and call back to the office to arrange for testing or treatments when you are satisfied.

- *Request your diagnoses and treatments in writing.* Medical words are weird, confusing, difficult to say, and often impossible to spell. *MedlinePlus.gov*, *mediLexicon.com*, and *MedicineNet.com* might become go-to resources to steer you in the correct direction. Written instructions from your doctor's office are helpful. Try this: on your smartphone or tablet, record your office visit and directions from the nurse, to review later. Search the internet for excellent dictation "apps" to download free.

- *Ask your doctor for copies of all lab reports and consultant notes* – Assemble these papers in date order, in a binder or folder. Get access details for any computer portal where your test results might be available anytime for download.

WHERE DO YOU GO FROM HERE?

❖ **Grab Your Shovel and Gloves.** If you are facing down serious medical worries – and especially if you are older – you might conclude that my advice sounds good but it's "too late" to help you. Take heed of this Chinese proverb: "The best time to plant a tree was 20 years ago. The second best time is now." Enough with regrets – get out there now and start digging!

❖ **Grandma Knows Best ... But You Need *Better*.** Georges Clemenceau, French physician who served as Prime Minister during World War I, proclaimed that "War is too important to be left to the generals." In the same vein, "Your health is too important to be left to the physicians" – meaning: just conventional doctors. Reducing risks is the hallmark of Grandma's advice: don't swim right after eating, get eight hours of sleep, eat your vegetables ... her prudent cautions and health habits form the basis of "*preventive* medicine." Once illness or injury has occurred, the setting has changed: consulting your doctor for a recent or urgent problem is "*reactive* medicine." *These* treatments, reacting to your concerns, are "regular medical care" at your doctor's office or the hospital and when successful, they *completely* solve your issues.

If your earlier health is not restored completely – without continuing drugs or repeated surgery – it's time for a physician or other professional with expertise in healing and repair. Ideally you continue to practice preventive habits and you achieve and enjoy a baseline "good health" condition. *Then* you should trust *"predictive* medicine" for "longevity" (prolonged, robust, vital survival), so-called "anti-aging" or "health optimizing" care. You simply make regular visits for usual *and* advanced tests that detect unsuspected patterns relating to crucial risk factors, so your doctor can give advice to reduce or delay the later surprise of nasty diseases. Advice on foods and supplements is critical in this modern (polluted!) era. *That's* the essence of *"health* care" in contrast to *"medical* care."

Elementary, my dear Watson. (Never actually "said" by Sherlock Holmes – but you get the idea.) Rarely do typical physicians (M.D., D.O.) without an advanced degree or extensive on-the-job training have any expertise in nutrition and suitable "integrative therapies" (conventional medical approaches enhanced by combining with ancestral knowledge and emerging discoveries). Seeking *other* doctors – a capable naturopath (N.D.) or chiropractor (D.C.) – might be your salvation. Internet reviews and websites *could* help but they present treacherous potholes … and finding "the best doctor" the same way you find a restaurant or plumber might be challenging. Has he or she written books or a well-researched website? Often given lectures? Developed innovative treatments? Been recognized by colleagues for notable accomplishments?

C + C Is Your Goal

In "the old days," we used to fear dying. Now, we fear getting sick. One major illness or injury – or lingering problems that never go away – these can cripple your activities, paralyze your optimism, and literally steal your assets and bankrupt your family.

While many claim they "want to live forever" – or maybe 100 or whatever … what you really mean is that you want to live as long as you remain both …

<u>C</u>omfortable
and
<u>C</u>apable.

For too many years, we've witnessed our seniors debilitated with aches and pains, where drugs provide little relief, longing for rest of any kind. Successful medical ***and*** health care, at the very least, keeps ***you*** living independently and free of misery or discomfort … for a long time to come.

"The best doctor in the world is the veterinarian. He can't ask his patients what is the matter – he's got to just know." American actor, writer, and humorist "Will" Rogers might be onto something there … but I haven't found a vet who will take care of *me!* So I have had to place my faith in …

THE SECRET FORMULA:

2 C + 2 C = A+

Honestly, there are no secrets. Mastering success with your doctoring is quite simple when you follow the guidelines presented. *Your* responsibilities are summed up as " **2 C** ":

<u>C</u>urious patient, <u>C</u>ompliant patient.

<u>*Plus*</u> the doctors you seek have obligations that also add up to " **2 C** ":

<u>C</u>ompetent doctor, <u>C</u>ommunicating doctor.

Not knowing what ailments or injuries will befall you, faith in the process I have outlined is your key to invaluable ***preventive* and *reactive* <u>medical</u> care.** When your attention turns to the future, this very same process will lead you to find the best in ***predictive* <u>health</u> care.**

Your goal is simple and achievable. Use the tools presented to enhance a purpose-driven life, one where you are empowered, passionate, enthusiastic, vibrant, vital, and robust. These rewards will enable you to engage in meaningful and joyous relationships, fulfilling work, and cheerful play. Keep your eye on the prize!

Remember, the insurance company is not your doctor. Your spouse is not your doctor. Your family is not your doctor. Dr. Google is not your doctor. "The secret" is simple: take full responsibility and choose *your* doctor wisely – there *is* a Marcus Welby, M.D., for you to find.

Subtle Implications For Business Owners and Managers

Should you be concerned about which physicians your employees can choose to see, often limited by your insurance plan? Workers who are absent or feel poorly are hidden *losses* to "the bottom line." More than a third of patients are *misdiagnosed* and over two-thirds are given an *incorrect treatment* plan. "Hoping to feel better" is a poor substitute for effective doctoring. Inadequate results can lead to years of unrecognized expenses: work inefficiencies, unnecessary operations and drugs, futile but costly doctor visits, tests, treatments and hospital stays, needless suffering, discouragement, even early disability or retirement. Employees getting the care they need reduces risks and saves company money. *Should I say more? I certainly can!*

About Dr. T

John Parks Trowbridge M.D., FACAM – "Dr. T" – as he's affectionately been known for 39 years – claims he's "just getting started," now asking better questions and finding superior answers for healing your body.

An Eagle Scout, National Merit and California State Scholar, he concentrated on immunology and molecular biology at Stanford University. "Medical school was so much fun I'd have been a permanent student if they just paid me," he recalls about Case Western Reserve University.

"I told the clerkship chief, a prominent heart surgeon, that eight weeks of surgery was about eight weeks too many, since I planned to be a 'medicine man.'" From day one, he fell in love with operating and later trained in general then urological surgery (at the celebrated Texas Medical Center). Plans changed: Dr. T realized that his superb medical training, coupled with a singular commitment to patient outcomes, meant he often "revised" the care plans of other doctors. Oops! That would mean bankruptcy because colleagues would not refer patients for surgery!

Entering general practice in 1978, he became a busy "industrial physician" serving 53 area companies, also chief medical officer of Texas International Airlines. Again, plans changed: disheartened with risks, reactions, and limited results from drugs and surgery, Dr. T explored other approaches. An advanced degree in nutritional medicine launched him on a journey with extraordinary state-of-the-art tools to repair illness and promote health.

Lingering questions: *why* and *how* do people get sick? Dr. T prowled around and stumbled on *obscure* toxic heavy metals (pollution!), becoming a preeminent educator in chelation therapy, the exclusive FDA-approved treatment. Further: *unrecognized* devastation by internal yeast, creating discomforts and diseases in 40% of Americans. Innovative treatments in his 1986 bestseller **The Yeast Syndrome** are acclaimed around the world.

Enthusiastic for patients to get exceptional care, Dr. T often lectures across the country, in Canada, Mexico, Taiwan and Brazil. His predictable success with complicated illness patients is endorsed in over five dozen volumes of **Who's Who** – and by a Distinguished Lifetime Achievement Award from the International College of Integrative Medicine.

Trowbridge hesitates to reel off professional organizations he has served as president. "Honors don't matter," he explains, "only the vitality and joy I produce for each unique patient." Dr. T talks about . . . BUSTING OUT OF THE BOX: "My clinical research focuses on identifying and treating diseases from unsuspected parasites (including *plant* fungus, of all things!), dramatic rejuvenation with exceptional stem cells, reversing heart disease, healing neck/back/joint pains without surgery. Literally, the list is long."

Dr. T's CDs, DVDs, books, articles, and lectures have opened eyes to healing beyond drugs and surgery. "I'm also proud of medical politics contributions: as a med student, I got leaders in AMA and Podiatry talking. Three years later, foot specialists were permitted to operate in hospitals."

The catchphrase for Life Celebrating Health in Houston has long been, "When life is your choice, failure is not an option." Dr. Trowbridge proclaims that every patient deserves leading-edge breakthroughs in diagnosis and treatment:

"Find it *now* – Fix it *right!*"

- DIAL: 1-800-FIX-PAIN
- www.healthCHOICESnow.com

CHAPTER 24

CREATE YOUR GENIUS ENTERPRISE

BY VICTORIA JENNINGS

I was first introduced to Jack Canfield and the book, *The Success Principles* in 2005. Around the same time; I had been introduced to the movie, *The Secret* and this is where I first saw Jack Canfield and he really inspired me. I resonated with his point of view that you had to do more than set the vision and feel it. He talked about breaking the vision into goals and then chunking them down into the action steps that needed to be achieved whilst at the same time, acting as if it had already happened.

This excited me and I went about creating my first vision board, set the goals and broke them down into chunks, as he had suggested. It was around this time that I had started my first Trade College in Brisbane, Australia, called "IPS Institute". We were quite a small team at this point, and I out-sourced a lot of work to contractors in the beginning phases. As I progressed through the action steps, my business started gaining momentum and started to grow through planned growth. My vision board began to move piece by piece into reality and it surprised me how quickly this occurred, and how easy this was.

As we began to grow, I realised that I knew very little about business. I had great knowledge in my expertise area which is adult education, but running a business was very new to me. Previously I had held senior positions in government and industry, however, my degree was in adult and vocational teaching. We were not taught how to run a business in this degree.

My Institute taught courses in business management, but that was focussed on the management team, not the business owner. In fact, I couldn't find anything that focussed on the business owner in main stream education. So, I quickly became a "seminar junkie" determined to find the secret key to unlock my business' full potential. At the same time, I was attending seminars, I was working through *The Success Principles* and implementing the strategies.

In part 3 of this book, it explains how to build your success team. Chapter 39 – "Stay Focused on your Core Genius" explained how to do what you are great at doing, what you love to do, and delegate everything else. This was key for me—a game changer. As a result, I developed my own position description that would only include the things I was great at doing and what I loved to do. This worked extremely well for me. There was only one issue, I know myself very well so it was easy to identify my core genius, but if I was going to delegate everything else, how would I know what my team's and contractor's core genius were? I found a profiling tool that identified my team's core genius, and I loved it so much I implemented it and doubled my revenue within six months. I wanted to share it in our classes, so I bought a global license from the developer, Roger Hamilton, and built another business around it, "Dynamic Academy". Dynamic Academy creates genius enterprises and entrepreneurs through a Dynamic Framework and workshops.

THE FUNDAMENTALS - THE FIVE FREQUENCIES

The Dynamic Framework that drives a Genius Enterprise is based on the 5,000-year old Chinese Philosophical Text called the *I-Ching* (literally translated as – The Book of Changes). This Chinese philosophy of life was recorded by many scholars and Emperors in China, and made its way to the west when Richard Wilhelm first translated it into German in 1923. In Zurich, in one of his Psychology Clubs, Richard spoke about his findings and shared it with one of the attendees, Carl Jung. Carl Jung too had a fascination about the book, which was a strong influence for his own book on Psychological Types and his theory on Synchronicity and the Collective Unconscious. And as many business owners and professionals involved in organizational training know, it is Carl Jung's work that forms the basics of psychometric testing today.

The Dynamic Framework I'm about to share with you is powered by unique profiling tools, which links the missing elements from the original *I-Ching*, that Carl Jung chose not to include in psychological profiling.

What makes it so different to other profiling tools for individuals? This one impacts business as it is not simply about the personality traits you embrace, although it covers that too, but more about the way you undertake tasks at work, and its simplicity so that all team members understand immediately exactly what each profile can do, and therefore can leverage their genius against others' genius that make up the team and the organisation.

Unlike any other profiling system, the Dynamic Framework has a close relationship with the cycles of time, which is one of the most important things to address in business today and talked about extensively by Jack Canfield. In today's market, things are changing so fast that business activities, projects and how people work, must nimbly evolve and adapt to the volatile markets. As such, this Dynamic Framework and its profiling tools not only draws upon characteristics of different personality types, but also scales the philosophy to the different stages of business that relate to these profile traits, and how all businesses go through cycles like the seasons of Earth. As businesses move through each season, how they operate in terms of leadership, strategy, and delivery, must change too. This is a core difference to the Dynamic Framework, which also happens to be core to the philosophy of the *I-Ching*. After all, it is 'The Book of Changes'.

To understand how the Dynamic Framework translates to business, it is first important to start with the *basic building blocks* of the philosophy, from which the entire genius approach to building a business is created. It is like a core fractal, once you identify and appreciate the form and function – it permeates and exists on an endless number of levels.

The *I-Ching* describes five natural *frequencies* or *energies*, each of which is linked to a different season and element, for making sense of the world, and the hidden order of life on Earth. The frequencies also help explain human relationship with time, and the nature of different people (archetypes) based on their propensity towards the different frequency traits. When all of this cycles together, trusted teams are formed, trust is enhanced in the marketplace and flow is created to ensure sustainability and profitability.

The frequencies are:

    1. Dynamo
    2. Blaze
    3. Tempo
    4. Steel
    5. Spirit

These are represented in the Dynamic Square below (by Roger Hamilton), which is a visual I will frequently refer to giving you a better understanding of how the frequencies interrelate.

Figure 1 – The Dynamic Square

Each of us has a mix of the above 4 frequencies which is unique to who we are. These 4 frequencies are measured in percentages for ease of understanding, and are representative in a unique footprint or 'fingerprint' for every individual represented in a unique graph. *(Note: the 5th frequency, **Spirit**, is infinite, accessible by all and is therefore not measured).*

A sample 'footprint' is illustrated in the chart provided below (see Figure 1). In this chart, there is a breakdown of: 52% Dynamo, 32% Blaze, 16% Tempo and 0% Steel (though this does not mean the individual has no steel at all, because we all carry a portion of every frequency, but in this representation, it just means the amount of Steel frequency is negligible in comparison to the others). These proportions give us a unique sense of someone's natural talent and strengths. That is, these are not learnt talents, but intrinsic and unconsciously competent, like driving a motor vehicle. Other tools I have used tend to label people, these tools do not. We could have 10 Creators in one team for example, and their individual graphs would look very different, because the percentages of each frequency are unique.

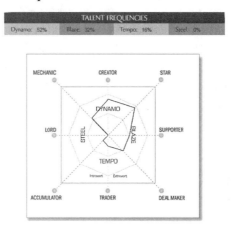

Figure 2 - Sample Dynamic Graph - Creator

The understanding of these frequencies gives us a sense of our natural genius, and reveals distinctions that explain exactly why we stress and struggle to complete certain activities in the workplace, whilst other tasks and activities come to us more naturally, and explain why we procrastinate when confronted with certain tasks. When you fully understand this, you can identify where your genius best contributes to yourself, a team, a division and the entire organisation. When you profile others, you will understand how they can best serve the team, the division, the organisation whether they are employees, suppliers or contractors. And here is the major difference of this profiling tool to others, everyone else will understand how to work with each other too! I will never recruit or work with anyone I haven't profiled.

1 – Dynamo

Is about innovation and growing the business, new beginnings, and is associated with the season of spring and the element of wood. When you think about spring time, it's where everything starts, animals are born in the spring and flowers bloom. These people are highly intuitive and often described as having their heads in the clouds – that's great because there they have the eagle eye view. They gain perspective. They can see five years into the future easily, future time is easy, they struggle with being in present time and this can make them impatient.

The same characteristics you observe in nature and spring itself, can be seen in our personal traits and business. Dynamo is all about innovation, vision, strategy, new ideas, new products, and the start of new projects. People with strong Dynamo frequency are great at strategic and visionary thinking (seeing the bigger picture). Dynamo is the fastest vibration of the frequencies. These people will often talk fast and think fast and they love to inspire others to the vision. They need to see the significance of the work they are undertaking to be engaged in it. The natural question for Dynamo is, "What?"

2 – Blaze
Blaze frequency is all around people and glowing. It is associated with the season of summer and the element of fire. When you think of the summer season, everyone is taking advantage of the warmer temperatures by spending time outdoors: at the beach, playing sport, having picnics, going to festivals and outdoor dance parties. People are out, interacting with each other. They need variety and give colour to everything around them. You can literally feel the heat!

Blaze is all about magnification of the business through communication and people. People with strong Blaze frequency are: extroverted ('out there'), passionate, outgoing, great at networking, and absolutely *love* variety - the "spice of life". In business, this is great for building and leading teams as well as marketing and sales!

People with strong Blaze can't help but connect and be around people, and are most energized when they are working through and with people. They work through conversation. The natural question for Blaze is, "Who?"

3 – Tempo
Tempo frequency is all about timing and slowing. It is associated with the season of autumn and the element of Earth. When you think of the autumn season, you might notice that things start to slow down as the weather is in transition from summer to winter. The temperature becomes slightly cooler, and it is a time that people reap their rewards, it is harvest time. Lots of activity occurs at this time and these people love

to be active.

People with strong tempo frequency are grounded, steady, enjoy harmony and understand exactly how to perceive when something is going wrong through their senses, they are highly sensory. Tempo frequency takes the strategies from Dynamo frequency and breaks things down into chunks, tasks to be achieved on time. They love to be team players, they need connection and are reliable at getting things done, very hands-on in their approach to business. The natural question for Tempo is "When and Where?" as this frequency is also about location.

4 – Steel
Steel frequency is about systems and processes and knowing. It is associated with the season of winter and the element of metal. When you think of winter and nature activity slows down. Some animals hibernate and live off any supplies that were harvested during the autumn as they endure the harsh winter, minimizing their risk of starving to death because they planned well earlier in the year. Winter is also a time of reflection, looking back at where we have been, measuring our results and preparing for spring.

People with strong steel frequency prefer analysing with facts and figures and developing solid reliable processes that allows the business to multiply through systems. They have an acute sense for detail and are great at following and improving systems. They are introvert in nature preferring to rely on the data rather than the people. The natural question for steel is, "How?"

5 – Spirit
Spirit frequency is all about transition. Its element is water, and is the basis of all flow. It is the foundation of everything we do as individuals and as a business. It moves outside of time, and governs the transitions between the different seasons and frequencies. Everything begins and ends with water, moving through the different seasons of a cycle, essential to our existence, Spirit allows the cycle to go from creation to completion, and back to creation again.

Therefore, everyone has equal access to this frequency, and use it to move and appreciate all the other four frequencies. Therefore, it is not measured. Spirit is about gratitude, giving back, and insight. It is what drives a social enterprise. The natural question of spirit is, "Why?" the biggest question of them all.

From the four frequencies that are measured, eight profiles exist. I have just described four of them, Creator (Dynamo), Supporter (Blaze), Trader (Tempo) and Lord (Steel). Then there are four profiles that are combinations of two frequencies: Star (Dynamo and Blaze), Deal Maker (Blaze and Tempo), Accumulator (Tempo and Steel) and Mechanic (Steel and Dynamo). In all my years working with this tool, I have never encountered anyone who did not fit into one of the eight.

SUMMARY

The way to create your genius enterprise is to ensure that you and your team all focus on their core genius and leverage the genius of the collective. This ensures that everyone is doing what they love and loving what they do. As a result, productivity increases, procrastination is eliminated, morale improves, absenteeism goes down, revenues go up. No longer are job descriptions needed, but team accountabilities replace them. Projects are implemented and tasks are assigned based on your core genius. Cross functional project teams that are truly self-managed, these teams become the back-bone to the business and high performing. Project leaders report weekly to line managers which eliminates the need for performance appraisals. Projects are monitored in real time. I believe this is the new paradigm for entrepreneurs, organisational development and human resource management. It is a very organic way to do business and a game changer.

The first step on this journey is to do your profile, we also have a profile tool for children from 8 – 15 years old. I have witnessed the dynamics of families change completely when they have this understanding of each other. There are many testimonials on our website, you can check out: www.dynamicacademy.com to do your profile and find out more about how you can create your own Genius Enterprise and become a Genius Entrepreneur.

About Victoria

Victoria Jennings loves to transform organisations into Genius Enterprises. In fact, she is publishing a book about it, *Create Your Genius Enterprise*. What is a Genius Enterprise? Identifying the business owner's natural talents and strengths, and teaching them how to leverage this with the natural talents that exist within their teams, suppliers and partners.

When Victoria discovered what a game changer this was for her college IPS Institute; she utilised her expertise in adult education to share this knowledge with entrepreneurs, corporations and consultants. She did this through the creation of a second company, Dynamic Academy and designed experiential workshops to teach others the dynamic strategies to create their own Genius Enterprises. This is causing a much-needed revolution in traditional human resource management and business practices!

Early in her career, she held positions that were in direct conflict with who she was, and this made her unhappy and ill. How many people today are in a similar situation doing jobs they do not enjoy, being on the treadmill every day, going through the motions just to put a meal on the table? If Victoria had understood then what she knows now, her life would have been very different. This is what drives her, to make sure she reaches as many people as possible, so that they do not have to suffer the same fate. She wants everyone on the planet to be able to wake up on Monday morning looking forward to going to work and being paid for something they love to do. Doing what they love, and loving what they do. What a different world this would make, not only to the individuals, but to the organisations they work with as well. It's all about getting into the natural flow of life and supporting others to do the same.

Victoria has worked with small businesses across many different industries up to large corporations and universities in Australia and the United States of America. The results she achieves with her clients are outstanding; ranging from increasing revenue by 20% in six months to saving three months of salaries on a newly recruited team of 300 (equivalent of $6 million USD) by implementing dynamic strategies in their businesses that are simply not taught in main stream education.

Her extensive career in adult education has included the Technical and Further Education sector, schools, government departments and various Industry Skills Councils – all at executive level being instrumental in implementing the vocational education and training system in Australia. She has lectured at university in undergraduate and post-graduate programs in adult education, and has created her own successful multi-million dollar companies, launching her first company in 1998.

Dynamic Academy workshops create a cultural environment that honours the value everyone brings to the enterprise, and enables them to leverage that value among the team which results in all doing what they love, and loving what they do. They provide an organic way of doing business through a dynamic framework, which includes the integration of tools, processes, seasons, elements and cycles of business. The focus of all professional development is based on their talented areas – creating geniuses aligned with their passions.

The outcome is trusted enterprises with a social conscience that give back and leave a legacy – creating lots of fun along the way!

You can connect with Victoria at:
- victoria@dynamicacademy.com
- victoria@ipspeople.com
- www.dynamicacademy.com
- www.ipspeople.com
- www.facebook.com/Victoria.Jennings.904
- www.linkedin.com/in/victoriajennings1/

CHAPTER 25

TAKING AMBITIOUS ACTION: MAKING YOUR DREAM LIFE A REALITY

BY AMBER NOBLE GARLAND

Most people fail in life, not because they aim too high and miss,
but because they aim too low and hit.
~ Les Brown

"You'll only get what you've ALWAYS gotten, until you've become the person you've NEVER been." Those were the piercing words spoken by the commencement speaker when I graduated from Temple University. Despite all the hoopla, the screams from proud parents and rousing cheers from my fellow classmates, those fifteen words from the man standing at the podium were so profoundly impactful to me. So much so that they overpowered just about every other memory I have from one of the most monumental days in my life.

You see, several years prior to that day, I had dreams of eventually becoming my own boss on a full-time basis. I just could never muster up the courage to take that next step by leaving my "dream job" for the freedom of fully committing to my own success. Call it fear of the unknown or just being overly cautious about my next step. Maybe it was me being romanticized by perceived "job security." Let's face it. How many 20-something-year-olds do you know of, with an Amex corporate card without a spending limit, FREE monthly parking at an over-priced

245

Manhattan garage, a business card that could gain entry into the coolest VIP parties in the world, the ability to say Jay-Z was actually their boss (in real life) and an annual salary plus bonuses well into the six-figure range. That was my life at the time, but as someone who grew up in the inner city of Philadelphia and then relocated to a middle-class suburb a few minutes outside of the city, in no way was I raised with a silver spoon in my mouth.

I had taken the day off to participate in my college graduation, and made the trek from New York back to Philly for the festivities. One of my assistants at Def Jam was handling any work-related emergencies in my place. I was barely over 30 at that time, so I wasn't your typical college graduate. During my junior year of college in the late 90's, I was recruited out of school to become the Marketing and Promotion Director for the hot new radio station in town. I tried my best to carry half of a course load often while working 60+ hours per week, but the pressures of the job got to be too much. By the time Def Jam came calling and put me in a position to make $100,000 per year for the first time in my life, I was lured away from the radio broadcasting industry where I made approximately $45,000 per year, and completing my college studies frankly was the last thing on my mind…. or so I thought. Then life changed dramatically.

With my wedding only a year away, on the outside it seemed that everything in my world seemed to being falling into place. On the inside though, it felt like things were coming apart at the seams. Opportunities for career advancement at the record label were decreasing, and my father's health was rapidly deteriorating from the chronic illness, COPD (Chronic Obstructive Pulmonary Disease), along with the effects of multiple amputations. Life was changing right before my eyes. I was afraid of what my future would hold and scared my dad might die without ever seeing me walk down the aisle or finishing my college degree (a promise I had made to both of my parents). I didn't know exactly how I was going to do it, but I knew that I had to make bold moves fast! That day at graduation, as I walked across that stage, I reached out with my right to shake the hand of the Dean of Students and grab my diploma in my left hand. It was in that handshake that I felt a transfer of power and overwhelming sense of calm and peace come over me. It was in that very moment that I decided I would become "the person I had never been". . . the girl willing to take the leap without totally knowing if my parachute would open.

My mind was made up, and over the next few weeks I felt very different. The former sense of gloom that used to hit me each time I'd approach the Lincoln Tunnel after making a nearly two-hour drive into the Big Apple, with horns blaring and traffic backed up for miles, had disappeared. I was so driven and felt so much pressure to continue climbing the corporate ladder of success that I was stuck in my "comfort zone," that I had mastered the art of denying that in fact it was time to move on. It was no longer a question of if I was going to leave my role as a senior marketing executive, but rather how and when I'd make my exit. The entertainment business is really small, and most people held on to their highly-coveted positions for dear life, so I really didn't have someone to confide in about my plan to leave, nor did I have anyone I could model myself after.

After much prayer, reflection and good old fashioned research, I found a pathway out. I was finally committed to getting what I had never gotten, I was determined to become the person I had not yet been, and the rest was history!

Now ten years later, I have built six-figure businesses in entertainment and real estate, with a third now thriving in the Ambitious Living lifestyle brand, which houses my book authoring, speaking, training, coaching and real estate businesses. Although things were uncertain at times during my transition and got rough when I stepped out on my own, I never missed a meal or a mortgage payment on my personal home or the rental properties, I've become an award-winning three-time internationally-published author, sought-after motivational speaker, trainer, coach, mentor, wife, mom, better friend and so much more!

I want to share with you a few critically important steps that helped me tremendously in my journey toward mastering the art of my own success.

I. FIND YOUR WHO, WHAT AND WHY!

A. WHO is so essential to your life that by being more connected to them you feel a much greater sense of fulfillment, peace and overall joy?

B. WHAT will building deeper connections with your "WHO" allow you to experience?

C. WHY is becoming the bravest, boldest version of yourself that you've never been, doing something you'd never done and stepping out on your own, essential to achieving the ultimate quality of life for you and your family?

1. Had I not gotten sick and tired of constantly being asked by family and friends why I never seemed to be able to make it to holiday functions or other important events, I wouldn't have experienced that pressure I needed to help push me toward that leap. By making a stronger effort to be present at important functions with my loved ones, it allowed us to build a stronger connection. I knew why I wouldn't be able to move into the "next chapter" of my life being the type of wife I wanted to be, and still be flying all over the country for video shoots, photo shoots, awards shows, and… you name it. I was becoming worn out from ALWAYS having to be on call *around the clock!*

2. If I weren't on the verge of getting married to a really great guy and dreaming about motherhood, I might not have had a strong enough incentive to push me from the cushy job that had me working crazy 12-16 hour days. By working toward becoming a full-time entrepreneur, eliminating long days and no longer being "on-call" 24/7, I could create a deeper relationship with my fiancé. I loved having the coolest job in the world, with an office on the 28th floor of a huge skyscraper in midtown Manhattan. I felt so honored to be able to create global marketing plans and launching classic albums with iconic, Grammy Award-winning musicians like Jay-Z, LL Cool J, The Roots, Patti LaBelle, The Isley Brothers and Lionel Richie. Yet, there unexpectedly came a time in my life where helping with my disabled father's day-to-day medical care (more than I had been doing) at his small apartment in Philadelphia, became the reason WHY I need more flexibility in my day-to-day life.

3. If it had not been for my dad becoming chronically ill and eventually terminal, I may have continued to remain in a work environment that no longer served my needs. By becoming my

own boss, I would no longer be subject to the limiting rules of the personal days or sick days I'd need to take off to be by my father's side – at a time when he needed me more than he probably had in my entire life. I had vivid dreams of becoming a mom. I knew WHY someday a pint-sized human cooing, calling me mommy, taking her first steps and learning how to go to the potty by herself, would become so much cooler to me than long executive meetings with a music mogul like LA Reid on Wednesdays, or weekly marketing team 'pow wows' to discuss Rihanna's choreography, or who Mariah Carey selected as her next video director.

<TAKE AMBITIOUS ACTION>

1. Make a list of all the great things that you're looking forward to being able to do as a result of leaving that 9 to 5 grind (or 9 to midnight – as it was in my case). Share that list with your loved ones and let them know how excited you are about now being able to participate in celebrations you may have missed in the past. Tell them that you're working toward starting your own business, so you can have flexibility with your schedule and the freedom of time. This should make people close to you feel vested in helping you become successful at your new endeavor.

2. Purchase one or two packs of your favorite note cards and enough postage stamps to accompany them. Write a list of the 20 family members and friends you need to spend more time with. Send them a text message, email or voicemail letting them know you were checking in to see how they're doing and you want to double-check to make sure you have the proper mailing address for them. Then write and mail them a brief hand-written message using your notecards.

3. Make a list of all the amazing benefits you'll receive once you identify your WHY. For me the emotional rewards that I was able to envision reaping if I didn't have to travel for work as much and instead I could spend more time with my family, was a motivating factor. Imagining myself being able to be at my dad's bedside, cooking for him, changing his sheets and reading his favorite magazines to him were things that made me feel overwhelming good. Fanaticizing about a mini version

of myself tugging at my pajama pants some day because they want me to cook them some pancakes or push them faster on the swing in my backyard is something that made my heart beat faster. Writing down my WHY's motivated me in a powerful way to make these dreams become my reality.

II. FIND YOUR HOW!

There has to be a way to take this leap of faith without falling flat on your face, so you can reap the benefits of stronger connections, deeper intimacy, a more powerful presence and shorter workdays, but HOW?

1. Doing a resume audit is helpful not only when you're transitioning from one job to another, but also if taking a much bigger jump into an entirely new career. Oftentimes, people wind up in positions within their work environments, and rarely, if ever, think to update their resume or CV until they're forced to do so. Most people don't even have a bio, because they think those are exclusively for "famous" people. Not true! In fact, they find themselves in a time crunch or in a panic when an unfortunate downsizing or termination arises. You should take a deep dive into analyzing where your resume stands in terms of how relevant it is to today's business climate within your profession; just as if you were looking to be hired by your company's biggest competitor and not necessarily transitioning into the role of full-time entrepreneur. You need to understand just HOW much your professional experience and skill sets closely align with needs of a rapidly changing world full of new business models and emerging technology. A careful examination of your resume, CV and/or bio will be an exercise for you to do on an on-going annual basis.

2. Many major cities, small towns and states offer resources for startups and the small business owner. Through their offices, you can obtain a skills assessment to help you weigh how well equipped you'll be in the self-employment marketplace – being "cushioned" by the perceived safety net of working with a corporate environment by sometimes encouraging complacency. While I have always believed in voluntary continuing education, I observed over the years that many

of my former colleagues didn't always share that philosophy. I've noticed many people would pursue additional degrees or take non-credit coursework only if it was mandated. However, when you're considering stepping out on your own, you have to armor up with education and credentials that will make you competitive for the "new economy."

3. No longer will there be a supervisor or department head there to remind you that your business sector is rapidly changing or nudge you to learn the latest techniques to keep you on the cutting edge of innovation. Therefore, you should utilize all the continuing ed. resources your present employer offers while you remain there. This way you can stay current, continue to provide value while you're still there, and you can transition easier to business owner status.

<TAKE AMBITIOUS ACTION>
Determine HOW you will maximize entrepreneurship resources available to the public. You should contact the mentoring organization known as SCORE and the SBA (Small Business Administration). They provide guidance and access to financing options for both entrepreneurial novices and veteran business owners alike.

About Amber

Amber Noble Garland is a true renaissance woman – wife, mother, entrepreneur, author, speaker, trainer, business coach, mentor and civic leader.

Amber spent a decade as a marketing and promotions executive in the Radio Industry before being recruited to the global music powerhouse, Def Jam Records in 2001. There, she devoted six years to the music label founded by entertainment icon, Russell Simmons. Her role initially placed her at the right hand of the company's former President and CEO, Kevin Liles. She was promoted to the roles of Marketing Director & Product Manager for global music icons like Jay-Z, LL Cool J, The Roots, Patti LaBelle, Lionel Richie and The Isley Brothers.

Since 1996, Amber has negotiated nearly $20 million in contracts for her clients in the areas of radio, television, digital platforms, book deals, speaking engagements and brand endorsements. As a high-profile talent manager of 20 years, until her recent retirement as a day-to-day manager and transition to sought-after consultant/advisor/deal negotiator, she's played an integral part in the career development and expansion for prominent men and women. Amber has represented syndicated radio personalities, TV hosts, best-selling authors, an Emmy award-nominee, a Golden Globe award-winner, a Gracie award-winner and a world-class athlete. Over the course of two decades, a few of her notable talent management clients have included Egypt Sherrod, Idris Elba and Laila Ali.

Amber is a Realtor® and Broker-Associate, licensed in both New Jersey and Pennsylvania, who's received numerous awards for her record-breaking production and annual sales volume. She has been responsible for closing nearly $60 million in real estate transactions. Her real estate clients include modest first-time millennial homebuyers, baby boomer sellers and even a Super Bowl champion athlete. She has served as a Tech Ambassador/Instructor/Trainer for Keller Williams Realty. She's been featured nationally on the DIY Network, and has been a frequent real estate expert contributing commentary regarding housing trends on New Jersey 101.5 FM.

Amber co-wrote the national best-selling books, *Driven Success, Mastering the Art of Success* and *Keep Calm...It's Just Real Estate: Your No-Stress Guide To Buying A Home*, and she was nominated for an NAACP Image Award as a result of her contribution to the book. To commemorate the 10-year anniversary of being successfully self-employed during the U.S. economic recession, she will publish *Unapologetically Ambitious*, a memoir and "how-to" book – chronicling how she left the prestigious "dream job" and ultimately landed on her feet at a very rough time in our nation's history.

She's been a dynamic speaker for Black Enterprise's Entrepreneur's Summit and alongside Barbara Corcoran at *Inc. Magazine's* summit for female entrepreneurs, a moderator for the EPIC Conference, and an instructor/facilitator of programs held at Kean University, Seton Hall University and Princeton University.

With a strong desire to help people rise above their current life challenges and live their best lives, Amber founded the Noble Acts Of Kindness (NAOK) Foundation, a non-profit committed to improving the quality of life for disabled seniors, special-needs children (affected by developmental delay disorders such as Autism and ADHD) and families displaced from their homes due to hardship.

Amber earned a Bachelor of Arts degree in Broadcast Journalism & Mass Media from Temple University, and a certificate of completion from her studies at Harvard University's Negotiation Institute. She is a Founding Member of The Les Brown Maximum Achievement Team and was directly trained as a speaker by the living legend himself.

Amber resides in New Jersey with her 5-year-old daughter and her husband, a senior law enforcement officer.

To learn more about Amber's trainings, speaking calendar, systems for achieving unlimited success and the release date for her next book, connect with her at:

- www.UnapologeticallyAmbitious.net

CHAPTER 26

5Ws AND 2Hs OF GENUINE SUCCESS

BY DEBBIE JUNGMIN LEE

*She was afraid of these things that made her suddenly wonder who
she was, and what she was going to be in the world, and why she
was standing at that minute, seeing a light, or listening,
or staring up into the sky: alone.*
~ Carson McCullers, *The Member of the Wedding*

Everybody has a moment wondering about the above questions during
the long path of their life's journey. When that moment sparked up on
me, I was also afraid, because it sometimes involves a painful event or
experience, alone. Now I learned that success starts from questioning.
Life before questioning was a survival life not only in terms of financial
aspects but also in various aspects. If you already started questioning
yourself, you have seeds of success or extraordinary life.

The result between two directions of life; wondering about or wandering
aimlessly makes a huge difference. How to react to these questions
through my own life events was a turning point for me to awaken myself
to desire a better, more fulfilling and happy life. As William Barclay
says, "There are two great days in a person's life; the day we are born
and the day we discover why." I did not really take the time to think
about this when I had a stable and comfortable career life. I was too busy
running on the hamster's wheel, but one day, people started telling me
the same message: "Do not ever think about staying in the safe zone.
One day you have to become your true self and create your own mission

in order to have a positive impact on others. Seek a successful life by maximizing your talents so that you can help even more people."

That year, I did not quite understand why many people suddenly tried to convey the same message to me, but magically, I got started writing my first book. Still, I did not pay much attention to those voices, almost ignoring them for quite some time. However, I gradually came to realize that I had a hidden wish that was waiting to be revived and wanted to pursue the true meaning of my life. After a while, there was an event where I could listen to the same inner voice from myself. It was a surprise to me because I was not that brave person to take such a leap. Being brought up in a failed entrepreneur's family background, I always thought to myself that I should not challenge any of those risky options.

The education system I had did not really allow me to think about the alternative life either, because education normally focuses on building knowledge in subjects such as mathematics, language, economy, science and so on, in order to have a decent job in life. The brain-based cognitive ability is very necessary to get high scores in exams, enter prestigious schools and work at efficient levels. However, what my whole experience taught me – by observing many successful people and global leaders – is that non-cognitive ability and meta-cognitive ability is crucial in having a successful life. The non-cognitive ability is defined as personality, interest, attitude, perseverance, motivation, view of value, etc., and the meta-cognitive ability can be explained as "knowing about his/her own thinking." We concentrate on the marks, scores and figures so much that we often overlook these skills.

Then I began to wonder: **Why** am I here on the earth? **Who** am I really? **What** am I going to be in the world for the rest of my life?

Having a vague picture of that, I thought about who I would meet to see the blueprint of my future life. I travelled a few continents again to find world-class role models and organizations that stayed in my heart for a long time. Jack Canfield is one of those role models influencing me – with huge impact – to mold the next level of my life, because that meeting and education showed me '**how**' to become the person I desire and have a life that I have imagined. Moreover, he helped me to challenge myself to "**What+α**." If we only do what we can do comfortably, we do not grow enough. There will be definite pain and fear along the way, but challenging a higher goal makes us grow inch by inch.

I remember that when I take a classic singing lesson, all I can do is to mimic a better voice using all kinds of imagination techniques that a music teacher shows, because the vocal cord is not something tangible like other instruments. The way we learn singing is only through the imagination towards a higher, wider and richer musical voice. Amazingly, my voice gets transformed to an advanced voice while conducting this "What+α" imagination. The interesting part in this process is that my voice is stagnant if I practice alone. If you have role models and catalysts at this phase, your voice takes a leap, just as a woman gives birth to a baby even in extreme pain when she has a midwife who takes a breath with her. Not only having role models but also meeting the right partner(s), team and people is part of a bigger concept of 'who,' because I can be who I am because of them.

Some people seem to discover great 'Why,' 'Who,' and 'What,' but when there is a misalignment with 'How' – the way of being in the world, we witness that things can fall apart. It is said that authentic power lies in the soul of personality, which can guide the 'Why,' 'Who' and 'What.' Some seek false power to achieve things quickly, but waiting for '**When**' is such a delicate element in success. The first criteria most of successful start-ups share is good 'timing' according to research. There is a time "when to take an action." As Andrew Jackson said, "Take time to deliberate; but when the time for action arrives, stop thinking and go in . . ." There is another divine timing, "when to bloom." which we cannot decide but persevere until we do.

A lady I know who was devastated after the death of her husband found a job at the college cafeteria. What she could do there was to pour noodle soup for the students, but she did it diligently and wholeheartedly. One day, an oriental medical doctor of that university noticed her work and attitude. He asked her if she could help him make oriental herbal medicine in his clinic. She was hired as an assistant at the clinic. Her working attitude was steadily so sincere, that she eventually became the top manager of the whole clinic. Now, she is not lacking anything, only enjoying her life with family. 'Heartworking' adds some extra magic to the process. Thinking about '**Where**' to go is another growth strategy. No matter how small an item or idea you have, if you expand the market to the globe, it becomes a different game. And some people have a glaring dream to go to a certain country or place. Then that is where you should stand.

At last, here I have one more 'H' to add to the typical 5Ws and 1H questions because they seem incomplete to me. That is, another 'H' for '**Happify**' – a question pertaining to a 'positive purpose'. If we think about historic figures that brought tragedy to the history of mankind, they are remarkably smart to know all the 5Ws and 1H of success. They are global human resources with a strong mission (why) and identity (who), being sharply aware of what to do, how to do it, when to take actions and where to go. They even have great 'Grit' that Dr. Angela Duckworth proclaimed a key to success, having powerful motivation to accomplish their long-term goals. And they even feel happy and proud of what they do. However, they do not *happify* the world obviously, so nobody calls them successful people.

Their misbelief in the answers to these questions lead people to a miserable life. The question, "Am I *happifying* the world and myself?" is a 'must category' to be added. Finding the optimal sweetspot in the final 'H' gives us a profound dose of answers to a flourishing life. It is not accurately measurable using indicators, but it is impactful. A good friend of mine, Lin Tam, who is a VR animation start-up owner, has been pondering over what her positive life purpose would be to do this business. One day she told me that she found her true purpose: to use her creativity and energy to inspire and awaken the inner kid in people through storytelling and play. She also found her pure inner kid in her heart that she wants to keep and cherish. Now she is confident of her positive purpose to *happify* the world and herself, moving forward with all the balanced combination of the 5Ws and 2Hs. Being a *happyist* rather than a 'lobbyist' is a healthier way of reaching success.

If we miss out the final 'H' question, at one point people seem to be successful, but at another point, their lives turn out to be dreadful. According to positive psychology, experiencing positive emotions, such as joy, love, hope and gratitude, elevates the self-efficacy, creative solutions, motivation and sustainability. The distinctive trait most successful people have in common, according to my qualitative experiential research, is sound self-esteem and self-efficacy.

At what point do we call people like Nelson Mandela or Mother Teresa successful? We rather call them significant people, as they are not judged by the valuables they have but the value of themselves. Do we call Nelson Mandela a successful person when he was in prison? Or Mother Teresa in the streets of slum India? Do we describe their occupation when we introduce them, such as a politician who used to be the president of South Africa? We only call their names and they are perceived by their whole stories – not by their occupation. Success is not a 'status' but a 'story' that describes a whole long journey. They are the people who worked from their heart, not just from their brain. We notice unexpected superior outcomes when we activate our non-cognitive ability which symbolically lies in our hearts to *happify* ourselves and the world around us. We cannot be all Nelson Mandelas or Mother Teresas, but we can become ourselves with a positive purpose. If you haven't found that spot yet, then it is worthwhile searching for it. All genuinely successful people share their heart and what they have. A soul of sharing is the ultimate soul of success.

In early 2007, I lost my younger brother through suicide, partly due to the wrong and outdated definition of success. He did not even reach the point of wondering about 5Ws and 2Hs, but was only a college student. He was about to go out into the world, but instead of receiving love and support, he was pushed by parents and his 'inner society' to have immediate success in his first venture out into the world, by having a job that parents or society should feel proud of, but which he did not think he could fulfill or in which he was not even interested. There are surely other complicated reasons, but he did not share his agony with anybody else, handling it alone. Success is like a tower that we build for a long time. Everybody needs time to dig into the ground deep enough to make the foundation for the level equivalent to a skyscraper. The first phase of career life can be that foundation work in the construction as nobody can build a skyscraper or a cathedral overnight.

The parallax of success is that every life is uniquely worthy, and success cannot be measured by any one measuring stick. I literally did not know how to handle this hurt, pain, and deep sorrow in my life. After a long journey of overcoming, it was finally transformed to my passion, answers and love to my own 5Ws and 2Hs. My positive purpose is to help, awaken and walk with people who have a desire to have a fulfilling and happy life contributing to a better world, as we are all here to be leaders of our lives – but not alone.

As Carson McCullers said in her book, *The Heart is a Lonely Hunter*:

"The most fatal thing a man can do is try to stand ALONE."

About Debbie

Debbie Lee helps people and organizations with positive change and creative growth in their professional and personal life – by sharing her storytelling and transformational education. Her work does not only bring meaningful achievement, but also inner growth for the next level of life and development. She started her first career in the foreign investment field at HSBC, supporting global funds to reach their goals and then moved on to the commercial trade field, consulting with Nordic and European companies to find and unlock new global markets under the organizations of the Danish Foreign Ministry, EU Chamber of Commerce and multinational corporations.

The industries and countries she has dealt with are borderless and numerous – from lifestyle, design, food, bioscience, marine and construction to defense – by travelling to many continents. Almost 20 years of her career in the global-market-entry world gave her 'tons' of stories to tell, so that she returned to her literature instincts and became an author of: *Open Sandwich: The Nordic way of happiness; Heartworking: Time that makes us live again*; and a co-author of *Scandi-Daddy: Happier Parenting & Lifestyle* with a Danish journalist.

Along the way in her career, she met various global leaders in business, start-ups and in the political and diplomatic world on a daily basis, and observed the kind of success that gives true meaning to life. That curiosity led her to travel around the world again to learn more in the fields of positive psychology, international storytelling and transformational leadership. Now she combines all these educational elements, her hands-on career/life experiences, talents and knowledge to help people, companies and organizations live a happy and fulfilling life. She also includes spoken poetry, musical poetry and storytelling as an art in her edu-cultural stage to embrace people in a warm way. Wherever she goes, she wants to bring the soul of 'working from the heart' and the 'heartfelt relationship' between people to make humane organizations.

Debbie Lee is a graduate from Ewha Womans University in Korea. As a mom of two children, she enjoys devoting herself to inspire working moms and girls around the world who have many obstacles to overcome in pursuing their dreams, balancing work and life. She was a speaker at the Global Women Leaders forum at the ASEAN-Korea Summit and Women Economic Forum (WEF) in New Delhi.

She gives workshops, lectures, speeches, coaching and consulting as the founder and chief educator for the educational platform, Heartening School®, globally. She also delivers cultural studies and diversity education through a community-based organization, Nordic Cultural Institute® locally in Korea. All these works are possible, thanks to her dear partners who share the vision, dream and life. Her mission is to change the paradigm of success, bringing happiness, joy and growth to the society, workplaces, family and individuals. Another major purpose of Heartening School is to support children and people in need across the globe – with food, books and education – to which all the attendees of her educational program contribute together while learning.

You can connect with Debbie at:

- www.hearteningschool.com
- deb138@gmail.com
- www.facebook.com/debbie.heartening
- www.instagram.com/debbie.heartening
- www.linkedin.com/debbie-heartening

CHAPTER 27

LIFESTYLE

BY ROMAY CUPIDO

When I think about my past, I wish to shake hands with all those disasters because it brought me this acclaimed success. I decided to take hold of my dignity and have a complete attitude change – one that showed that I was in control of my life and only I was responsible for my future! My biggest inspiration was my son, whom I initially raised on my own. But I found my purpose in life and set out to achieve each goal by reaching out for the right connections that could support my ideals. Of course, you will always have negative views from friends and family, but my dreams were real to me. Even though I had many failures, and at times wondered why bad things happen to good people, it brought about the awakening that if I allow the negative to be master over me, I would never move up. I had all those life experiences and it was time that I used them as a positive advantage, and not only prove to myself that life was worth living, but that I reached for my dreams and can be an inspiration for millions to have hope. So, my purpose became "My passion to Inspire dreams." Happiness is not a dream, but a reality you can envision.

Love is a natural desire the human soul craves. But what is true love? Life is so unpredictable at times and we do not know what we want. We tend to meet the wrong people that we know are not right for us, but we pretend to give things the benefit of the doubt. What we have in common matters, and doing things that we love to do takes motivation and the right condition of the heart. What we think we want is not necessarily what we need. Giving chances and being understanding allows us time to discover the true heart of those who shows interest. If we are torn with what decisions to make, it only means that dedication is missing.

There are big differences in having a fancy for someone, having an attraction or infatuation, and falling in love. Love belongs to mature people who fully understand how they want to love, give love, and be loved. Do not compare yourself or your life ideals with others. Principles and standards should match in any relationship for respect to be its foundation. Romantic love is passion in connection that put souls in action and everything else in perspective. Love is not perfection, but a meeting of the minds. Two people must be right for each other, and in that way, they can be perfect in pleasing each other. Love is all about giving with no expectations in return. Love makes us feel good and contributes to our productivity. It leads to more than just a smile someone put on your face, it's a great partnership in mutual success.

Hope is what we do not see. It is a divine quality and our beliefs create our reality. When anything happens to uproot your life as you know it – like a loved one who loses their job, meets with an accident, gets sick or dies. Unforeseen circumstances befall us all, so we need to count the costs and prepare ourselves and our family. Sometimes it is the amazing feeling of giving your beloved family something they had always longed for, even though it was difficult or hard to afford, but your most valuable gift is your time together. If anything should happen, the family needs to be able to count on each other. The decisions we make are the choices we should be able to live with – since it could mean our survival.

Many things in life can cause setbacks, and if we are not spiritually strong to hold it together, we unravel individually. If you are part of a family or in a relationship but feel lonely, it is a sad place to be. But blaming ourselves for things that have gone wrong is a daunting place of isolation. There is power in unity and seeking help is not a shame, nor is it a weakness. It is so important to forgive ourselves and learn to understand what our current conditions are, so we can find resolve. Prayer is not a fantasy in which we hope, but divine inspiration that gives us calm. It makes us better individuals to be more tolerant and respectful of others around us. Hope is the assured expectation of that which we strive for. Hope keeps us alive, and nothing is more inspiring than to dream and reach for your goals in action that rewards your life and helps you to thrive.

Joy – If our lives are in balance, we are happier and healthier in mind and body. What we put into our mouths shows as results in our bodies. You might not see the bad effects of eating junk while you are young, but bad habits will take a toll on the body later. Good health is having a routine and goals. There is no sense in being obsessed with your body or image. It's a healthier lifestyle of correct eating and exercise that makes us beautiful. A healthy mind gives us overall strength and the ability to do more – since it makes our bodies strong. Sleep is a vital asset that contributes to good living and good feeling. If we are well-rested, we can be more focused and alert to act on opportunities and take advantage of better options for our life. We can value our time better to have more joy out of life and become a happier, healthier person – both reasonable and showing accountability for bigger responsibilities.

Setting goals and visualizing your life as if you had already achieved it. For that you need courage! It's the ability to do something that you know is difficult. It is the state of mind we are in, and having refined spiritual wholeness that contributes to the strength to see things through. It takes great courage to act and see it to its completion. But self-motivation influences our ability to do what is needed to get things done. What sense is dreaming if we do not act? You also do not go anywhere if you do not set your goals in motion. But to act, you need a plan. A well laid-out plan comes from ideas and a format you intend following. Your focused plan must have a purpose and a structure of the different goal-steps that lead to ultimate results. Successful people always share ideas, listen well to guidance and I cannot emphasize enough – read, read and read – so you take in knowledge and learn something new each day. You cannot learn appreciation. It's an evaluation that stems from the heart and recognition of a good quality. Having a lot of something doesn't mean anything unless that something has value. Dreams are for those who are willing to work hard for them.

HOW TO FIND YOUR PASSION?

Destiny is an option you allow to unfold through your choices. If you think no one is ever going to hurt you, then what reality are you living in? With friendships come envy, jealousy, insecurities, and the realisation of who is real or not? Relationships require communication, good listening skills, love and passion with time and attention for each other's needs. If you want a *Successful Business*, a *Successful Relationship* or *Family*

Life, it is all up to your *Attitude Adjustment*. Find your resolve and see things through. What better way to live than to enjoy the benefit of your rewards? The equivalence of lifestyle success is "Balance." If your desire is only to strive for money or fame but do not care to share, of what use is an Ivory Tower filled with silence? Givers shine and always receive so much more in return. We tend to think that once we are scarred, we are "Scarred for Life!" – but there is always the hope of looking beyond disaster. Love can be powerful, so who better to turn to than family? Under that protective shield, we can taste the reality of "Love Conquers All." Sometimes change is hard but it's an opportunity for ideas and direction. Change grants us willpower to see life in a different perspective and the ability to motivate us to work harder.

As a woman, we need to be more selfish! It's not what you think, so don't raise an eyebrow before you know what that means. We need to take "Time Out." We need self-attention, and please Ladies, we need maintenance. Take every single opportunity to give to yourself, because only if you give self-care are you able to give yourself to someone else. We all need love! And if you are confident within yourself, you feel free to express and share. We all wish to feel beautiful, so you deserve that valuable time from time-to-time to see that you are and feel like a beautiful woman. Being a lover is not easy if you don't feel self-worth. Go for a walk to think, go out to lunch once in a while, and beautify yourself for a date night. Every single woman needs to feel special. Allow yourself that privilege! It is sometimes good to be a little selfish and see to your own needs first, so you feel good about taking care of everyone else's needs.

THE STORY OF A FRIEND

A few years ago, a friend of ours had suffered a great loss with his wife's passing. He was lonely and with his grown children having their own lives and living all over the continent, he did not want to be a burden. Even though his wife had only just died, he responded to the interest shown by another woman. And shortly thereafter, he got married against the best interests of his heart and of what his children thought. No matter what any of us might think – if there is a marriage, it is none of our business what two adults decide, since they, in this case both people, had gone through much.

Nevertheless, he approached me one day and mentioned a book of mine he had read. There were many points that he thought applied to the condition his life was in, and he thought that he was like the character in the book who was hiding from reality. It was very hard for him to express how he felt, because he did not want to disrespect his present wife, but he could no longer bear the hurtful speech and the silent treatment. At that time, they had been living past each other for two weeks. It was difficult for him to confess his lot since he considered himself an adult, but how could I show any support or understanding if I did not know what had caused him the mental torture? I was in shock to finally learn the whole story.

As in any family, we set ground rules, and I understood since I do not like anyone to touch my personal things. But this issue came over a used towel. They both had their own personal things and during a shower he accidently used his wife's towel. So, when she used the shower and discovered that hers was soiled, she blew a nerve and went crazy. OK, I get that no one wishes to use a soiled towel, but was that a reason to go on the war path? Could she not simply raise her voice for the moment and demand that he replaced it with a fresh towel? These are small things that should not create such bad tempers. If there is respect, no couple has the right to mistreat the other, and it was not a reason to suffer for two weeks in silent treatment and a bad atmosphere. It was the smallest thing that could have been corrected immediately, if in any relationship, we consider love.

A relationship is not a competition of who wins and who is in control. Conflict cannot survive the adding of fuel to the fire without your participation. Think about how a future of stress can lead to so many health problems due to unhappy torment. Reach out to each other so you deal with emotions and feelings. Life is too short to waste on trivial things. Love is a precious gift; treasure the person you love and shower them with respect instead. Change the way you look at things and things will change for you.

Life is a mental journey. I have learned these valuable lessons through experience from being a good listener. I have to understand and practice how to be a better me, and to appreciate the other person as more important. I had decided that when my husband comes home, he should feel that his stress is left behind at his business, and I am the comfort he comes home to. I experienced enough immaturity and finally know who I am, what I need, and how I wish to love and enjoy my family life. I fought the battle with idiocy and am triumphant in my achievements. I have earned my humility and now live the reality of joy and happiness.

You can be your authentic self. Focus on what you want to produce with your life and take one hundred percent responsibility. Reflect your mirror image by acknowledging yourself for your success. Love yourself, it does wonders for the soul. Love or Fear is your only choice to make. God is the infinite intelligence who allows us to evolve and grow due to his powerful influence of love.

Staying sane in a crazy world is a huge success. Love is freedom since we do have a choice to decide the kind of life we wish to live. Do not paint a picture of someone else's life to copy. Love with passion, since love without passion is only going through the motions of life, and you never grow together as a team but grow apart with different interests. As a family, we are achieving our goals and are well on our way to living the desired lives for which we had been working so hard. As a parent, I am proud; as a wife, I am satisfied and sometimes a little overwhelmed by a man who loves me so much. I cannot describe what it feels like to wake up with someone who tells me each day, just how much he loves me.

When you are happy with the person you have become, it does not take much to appreciate the good things you already have. To inspire Love, Hope and Joy, the consciousness of life should exist within you, and that decision rests on you. I wish you joy, I wish you happiness, and I wish you all success with all my heart – since I am truly happy!

About Romay

Romay Cupido is a wife, mother, entrepreneur, and an acclaimed author of eight books. Her writing is based on life experiences – an author whose mission is to help other women lead more passionate lives. She has travelled the world and gained phenomenal cultural interest that led to her amazing zest for life, and her powerful confidence ever present. Her philosophy is to learn everything she can, and to always achieve good things with herself and better things she can share.

Originally from Cape Town, South Africa, prolific author Romay has spent her adulthood living and growing as a person while in Europe. She had come to realise her dream and put value to what was most important in life – her family.

Romay lives by the exemplary ideal that love for what you do takes passion, and the enormity of being a giver extends to all humanity. With her Poetry book, she bares her soul and shares with those whom she can relate to, and a philanthropist was born with the purpose of giving back.

Her vision is to "Inspire Dreams" while she personally reaches to achieve higher goals. Romay constantly seeks new creative challenges and accolades with her books. She is also on a mission to encourage the youth to read – to inspire creativity – with the example of her own son. She lives by the concept: healthy mind, healthy body. Good health is having routine and goals.

Even though she has always been accused of being a dreamer, it is her focus and confidence that is admirable. But she passionately thrives on living life with profound reality.

You can connect with Romay at:

- romaybooks.com
- www.twitter.com/Romay6
- www.facebook.com/Romay6

CHAPTER 28

THE WEIGHT OF IT ALL

BY NYKEISHA SANDERS

The Weight of it All

When I was in high school, I was not the athletic type. I didn't play any sports. All I did was go to dancing school and took dance lessons. Although, while dance school held my interest from the age of three all the way up until I was 16, in high school I was the chubby kid. Most people don't enjoy being the chubby kid, but it wasn't a concern to me at the time. I just lived my life happy, careless and free.

When I was about 20 years old, I was at my aunts' house and for whatever reason I decided to jump on the scale. Something had me curious to see where I stand at my weight. I got on and I didn't like the number. Boy, did I hate myself for not realizing the harm I was doing to my body. *I knew right then I had to make a change.* I started by changing my eating habits. I went from eating Snickers and drinking soda to eating broccoli and drinking lots of water. As I got healthier in my eating, it led to a workout regimen for myself. Running was my thing! Believe it or not, you would've thought I ran track in school as much as I l loved to run. I mostly ran outdoors, especially the boardwalk at the beach in the warmer months. It was so peaceful and relaxing to me.

Personally, I hated the gym; it was boring, I wasn't into weight machines or the treadmill and I realized I had all I needed to get fit. I didn't need the gym. So, besides running, I did a lot of body weight training and calisthenics right in my basement. I also used workout tapes such as Billy

Blanks' Tae Bo® and Shaun T's *Insanity*. My type of workout regimen was high-intensity training. I loved to get a sweat going and it became addictive. I knew this new routine wouldn't be easy, but there was a bigger picture ahead of me.

Passion for Helping Others

It took years of hard work, pain and suffering to get to where I am now and I am still reaching for future goals. I can now say I am thankful for what I've done for myself. I remained disciplined, dedicated and motivated. My close friends and family started to notice my changes and new habits. They were influenced by them even though my original goal wasn't to influence others. I just simply wanted to improve myself. As I continued to improve myself, others started to do the same and change their lifestyle just from my inspiration. This became a major changing point in my life. I began to train friends and family for the fun of it and they loved it, and so did I.

I realized how much of an impact I was becoming to those around me from something I decided to do for myself. Soon after, I decided to go about getting my certification for personal training and train people professionally. It was something I loved to do, so why not take it seriously and build on it. Right after I got my certification, I started working at a personal training studio. I took this opportunity to expand my knowledge and build character as a professional personal trainer.

I learned a lot working at the gym. I trained clients from 9-year-olds to 72-year-olds with different shapes/sizes and levels. I also learned how to train clients with injuries, disabilities, and limitations. A year later, I left that gym to work at a better gym with more opportunity. I started working at the new gym when it had its grand opening. Right away it felt like home. I learned more about sales techniques and marketing skills. With all the tools and skills that I've learned in the past years, I decided to go out on my own to do private training and I enjoyed every minute of it. I built my clientele quickly. I would travel to people homes and train them where they felt comfortable.

Soon after, I got a job at Jenny Craig working as a Health and Wellness Consultant – while doing private personal training on the side. Jenny Craig was a meal-planning company with "Jenny Craig's" food. The reason why I took this job was because of the opportunity to learn more about the nutritional side of things when it comes to training clients.

The Outside Doesn't Always Reflect the Inside

I want to take a step back. *Training clients is all about guiding them to the right direction to reach their goals.* Here is something I never shared with anyone before November 2016. A lot of times people believe because I'm a trainer and my body looks "amazing", that I felt amazing on the inside, but in all honesty, I didn't. I was miserable! I believed I was fat, in all reality I most certainly was not fat. No matter how many times I was told I was beautiful, fit, amazing . . . I didn't believe a thing.

I was what you call a "closet eater." A closet eater is someone who would eat carefully in-front of others, and eat the complete opposite behind closed doors. That was me. I ate like a healthy person around everyone then ate complete garbage when I was alone because I wasn't happy with myself. I got to the point where I became bulimic. I would binge eat to the point of purging. I didn't know what was wrong with me. But I did know that this was my situation at the time. Maybe I felt pressured to look a certain way to people because I had followers looking up to me. All I know was I would eat and make myself vomit. I knew it was disgusting and the wrong thing to do, but I couldn't help myself. I hid this for months - not just from other people but also from myself. I didn't want to believe what I was doing was wrong, even though I knew it was.

I wanted to continue to help others on the outside and stay hidden within myself on the inside. I began to feel weak and shameful every time I looked at myself in the mirror. If this was to ever come to light, I would hurt the people around me and I didn't want that to happen. I started to take time to myself to re-evaluate my life and my purpose. "Who am I? Why do I really want to help others?" I realized I had to help myself first. It was hard to change my bad habits, but eventually I did. I would start to meditate every day and think to myself, "How can I make a change to better myself?" The more meditation I did, the better I became as a person, mentor, leader and coach. This was one of the main reasons why I understand what my clients go through, and why I am a Fitness Coach today.

"I tell people all the time I get what they are going through, and I've been through what they are going through. My story tells it all."

I started boxing training when I was 20 years old. I did it only for the work-out benefits. I was off and on joining different boxing gyms trying it out. As the years went on, I decided I wanted to train and compete. In April of 2016, I joined a boxing gym, Freeport PAL, and fell in love. I fell in love because of how committed, motivated, and dedicated everyone was with their training and I wanted to be the same way. Also, the fact that there were professional boxers that train at the gym I knew this was the real deal and that I belonged here. People respect me even more now because of the hard work I put in as a female boxer. It takes a lot of hard work, determination, and the right mental state to want to compete and fight. I've become more disciplined and patient being a boxer, and I explain this to my clients that they aren't the only ones working hard to reach to a goal and become victorious.

I lost my first fight but won my second. I felt I was on top of the world when I won my second fight and believed that there was no stopping me now. Unfortunately, I lost my next two fights back to back. It was tragic! I was so confident in myself and with my second victory I knew I could win another fight, but then lost two fights in a row. I felt useless, worthless, and as if I wasted my time. I thought it was the end of me becoming great at anything I worked hard for. I became demotivated and wanted nothing to do with boxing.

For two weeks I stopped training and kept to myself. At times like these, I have to remember who I am and what my purpose is and why. I have to remember there were people following my lead and looking up to me. My being down on myself wouldn't be what I wanted people to see or follow. I had to get it together quick, and become an example again. I had to be an example and prove to people that when you don't succeed, it's a lesson learned and you move forward to strive to become better.

Time to Make a Change

Jenny Craig has taught me how to build as an entrepreneur. Working at Jenny Craig was not on commission, but being a Health and Wellness Consultant and having my own clients, taught me the aspect of "being my own boss." That's one thing I valued working with the company. I got the experience of transforming lives by coaching clients verbally instead of physically. Now putting the two together was a win-win. I enjoyed working with Jenny Craig, but a year into it something came over me to possibly want to start something on my own.

I met a guy named Dan on Facebook who is a Health Coach with a company called AdvoCare. Being a fitness and health coach, Dan had similar strategies to me. AdvoCare is a company that provides innovative nutritional, weight-management and sports performance products. AdvoCare also has a business opportunity through financial wellness. Hearing all the great nutritional opportunities that AdvoCare offers, including one called the *24 Day Challenge*, I couldn't be more excited to begin my journey and try the program out myself.

I felt incredible! I received so much energy, the proper recovery after workouts and I slept better. A huge accomplishment while on this challenge was that it was a great kickstart that took my workouts and training to a whole new level. After completing the *24 Day Challenge*, my goals were to keep up with high energy, look and feel great, and to continue with AdvoCare in my everyday life. Dan and I became very close and I then decided to partner with him as a Health Coach with AdvoCare.

Still working at Jenny Craig at the time, for months I wanted to quit. It had nothing to do with the company itself, but I believed I was ready to go on my own and take Personal Training full time, and start my own fitness business. Even though I felt ready to go, I hesitated. I would call up relatives and close friends of mine for advice on what they thought I should do. I received both positive and negative feedback. I became uncertain as to what decision I should make for myself. Throughout this process, I learned a lot about patience and to let things happen when the time is right, and not when I thought the time was right.

For my last few months working there, I was unhappy and not myself. I had to understand that if I wanted to make this change for myself, I had to do what I felt was best for me and just run with it. I couldn't get caught up in the negative responses or be afraid to make a change or fear the "what if's." I remember like it was yesterday. At the end of my shift I walked up to my boss and gave in my notice of resignation. Man did I feel relieved. My last day was Halloween of 2016. I never looked back! My number one reason for making this choice was because I did not believe in working a "9-5" and having a boss. I wanted to create my own and so I did.

Building my Empire

I had faith in myself and believed that whatever opportunity came my way, if I felt it would benefit me, I took it. I didn't think about failing because if I did, I would never succeed. I knew it wouldn't be easy, I knew it would take time and dedication, but I was willing to take on all challenges because I wanted victory. I now have my own Online Fitness Business called KeepFit by Keisha.

With my KeepFit by Keisha coaching program, I focus on three major points: **Body, Mind and Balance**. With the **body**, we focus on exercise and nutrition. I provide full body workouts to be performed at home, meal plans with recipes and nutritional supplements. Before we start any type of change in our lives, we can easily get distracted by our minds. We have to be ready mentally to do anything. I begin my coaching with clients by digging deep into their **mind** to understand their mental state and emotions on wanting to losing weight and why. This is probably the most powerful part of the program because it is what gets the clients motivated, and helps them understand the importance of living a healthy life. Then comes the **balance** portion. I stress to clients how important it is to have some "me time" and be able to manage their busy lives and still focus on themselves. I get a lot of clients who are unhappy with themselves because they focus on making other people happy rather than themselves, and that is something I focus on – so they can succeed on this program. With all three components, there is no such thing as failure.

Being an online fitness coach, I am able to work with people all over the world – which I love. Being able to help people online and not face-to-face is such a blessing, knowing I can change lives this way. My online program is a super-effective transformation program including full body workouts to be performed at home, meal plans, 24/7 coaching via email and messaging, coaching calls, daily tips/guidelines, a group of members on the program for interaction and encouragement from other people going through the same thing, and so much more. You will learn why dieting leads to failure, foods in your fridge that may be bad for you, how to lose 10 to 15 pounds in 28 days, and more.

I love what I do and I share my story for people to understand that it's more than just being a trainer; it's about me building an empire and motivating people to live happy, healthy and free.

About Nykeisha

Keeping fit and healthy is Nykeisha's passion! She is a highly-motivated individual with the drive and dedication to help others who want to live a healthy lifestyle. Feeling great about herself inside and out pushes her each and every day to do what she loves most. She is here to share her journey in the hope of inspiring every man and woman. She has a lot to offer and to share.

Nykeisha is a Certified Personal Trainer through the Academy of Applied Personal Training Exercise (AAPTE), an Online Fitness Coach, Health/Wellness Coach, Nutritional Advisor and Amateur Boxer. She also has her Bachelor's degree in Public Health. Her training types include cardiovascular exercises, calisthenics, high-intensity training, strength conditioning and boxing training. Nykeisha trains herself to become an example to all her followers, friends and family. It's more than just being physically fit, it's about being healthy on the inside and out. She enjoys helping people make a positive change in their lives. Her energy and enthusiasm motivate and inspire individuals to become better people each day forward. Her desire is to influence as many people as possible all over the world and push them to be the best they can be.

Nykeisha remembers while working as a trainer at the gym, she had a few encounters with some male clients not wanting to work with her because she was a female trainer. Quickly, she realized in this world we live in, it's harder for a woman in most positions to achieve success just by being a woman. While some people believe females are not capable of doing a job just as well as a man could, Nykeisha has proven that she is just as great as any other male or female as a professional fitness trainer. She is committed, hard working, and a high achiever – setting herself a higher standard to show she is the real deal.

When she's not training clients, Nykeisha enjoys spending time with her family. She loves to travel and take as many adventure trips as she can. She enjoys meeting like-minded people when networking and connecting at social gathering and events – which she does pretty often. She spends a lot of quality time reading, whether it's educational or recreational books. She likes to keep her mind busy and strives to learn something new every day.

Throughout her coaching program, there are many ways to be educated on living a healthy life. Being a strong and healthy female conveys inspiration in others. No matter your age, gender or health status, there is always a way to look and feel healthy. All you have to do is make that commitment and reach your goal.

To learn more about how you can get started on your Transformation, please reach out to Nykeisha:

- Website: https://keepfitbykeisha.com
- Email: nykeishasanders@gmail.com
- Facebook: fb.com/keepfitbykeisha
- LinkedIn: Nykeisha Sanders

CHAPTER 29

MASTERING SUCCESS WITH HORSE SENSE

BY LAURA J. GABBARD

One look and I knew he was hurting. After almost thirty years of marriage, I knew the man like the back of my hand. He blew off my inquiry, saying it was just a headache from too much sun. It was hot and he'd been out baling all day. I heard his words, but my gut told me to keep a wary eye out.

The battle was on over the next forty-eight hours, as he fought to right his ship and convince himself he was fine, and I, knowing otherwise, tried to convince him we needed help. He's a stubborn man, but when it became impossible for him to button his shirt, he finally conceded. For the first time, I saw fear in his eyes as he willed his fingers to work and they refused him.

Just a few hours later, the ER Doctor plopped down on the stool and said, "Well, you have a brain tumor," like he said it every day. "We're going to have to do surgery." And just like that, our life was turned upside-down.

We looked to those in white coats around us – the ones most obviously equipped to help us deal with the nightmare that we were in. They stood side-by-side, like so many fence posts in the yard, with the same look on their faces and the same words in their mouths. They may as well have been shouting, "We can't help you! You're going to die!" We saw the faces of our loved ones, afraid and at a loss to know how to help, then we looked to each other and drew strength from our own historical ability to stick together and survive. We'd been through some really tough stuff before. *Surely, we could do it again.*

Though they told us they had no cure, they still wanted us to do things their way, even though radiation and chemotherapy for the rest of the short life he had left would buy us a few months at best. It wasn't good enough. Then we got lucky. A bit of divine timing and a call from my sister, led us to a naturopathic doctor who said she could help. This was an easy step for me, as I'd been using a Holistic Approach to health and maintenance with my horses for years. They were thriving, and yet my family had been a hard sell, Reid being the most resistant.

We ultimately decided to walk away from a traditional treatment and go Alternative. Our friends and family freaked, or most of them did, indicating that we were out of our flippin' minds. We really had nothing to lose though. If what the doctors said was true, he'd be dead inside of a year with or without their help. This new doctor was the only doctor we'd seen who shared our hope of recovery.

The Holistic Approach to medicine really means simply that the goal is to treat the patient as a whole being, consisting of the body, mind, emotions and spirit, rather than focusing on a disease or damaged part. The approach gives the being what it needs to heal and restore itself, which is what it does every day anyway, unless it becomes compromised.

So, we adopted this approach wholeheartedly. With the help of his new doctor, we started creating a healing atmosphere. I cleaned up his diet and fueled his body with the best food I could find. I cleared the house and his surroundings from all toxic and chemical exposures. I helped him face his fear and learn to not let it control him. I coached him on the power of his words and attitudes and taught him how to use that to work with his healing process rather than against it. I protected his space as best I could from outside influences that had a negative impact. And I celebrated his tiny successes and encouraged him to be proactive and take responsibility for his own recovery.

How did I do all that? I asked myself the same question. All I can say is that you don't know what you're capable of until you have to do it... and that I had been well-prepared by my own life's experiences and interests. My mom told me, "Honey, it's like you've been preparing for this your whole life." It's funny, but I learned most of what I needed to do for Reid from my horses, especially one named Jack.

Jack was my four-legged equivalent of Reid. A grey Polish Arabian with attitude. Talented, tough, and hard-headed, he gave me plenty of grief over the years, but also some of my greatest triumphs. His personality mirrored Reid's and when I finally got dialed into his frequency and figured out what made Jack tick, my marriage got better as I used the same techniques on my husband. Looking back, I know there is no coincidence that I went through a health crisis with Jack that paralleled my experience with Reid. It was uncanny, and I didn't make the connection for a long time, but I had already been through a truncated version of Reid's illness with Jack. I treated them the same way, used the same words with them, and fought with everything I had to save their lives. Jack's ordeal was like a trial run for the big challenge just a few years later.

Even though I knew what to do for Reid, it wasn't easy. It was an around-the-clock job as months turned into years. Riding the highs and lows, constantly on-guard against the real threat — depression. It is very easy for a person who is chronically or terminally ill to slip into a downward spiral. In fact, it may be an even bigger problem than the disease. I quickly learned to recognize the signs and take the necessary measures to get him turned back around.

Sometimes he just needed to have a pity party and get it out of his system, I'd tell him, "You wanna feel sorry for yourself that's fine, you've got 24 hours to get it over with." He always needed something to look forward to, so we lived our lives six months at a time, from Christmas to the big summer BBQ when we celebrated his survivorship. Getting him involved in something bigger than himself also worked to pull him out of a funk – a project or something charitable. Sick people can become very self-absorbed. But many times, I would just have to make him mad – get him back in the fight, play it tough, give him a good square kick in the hind parts. And the real secret? I never treated him like he was sick. I helped him do what he couldn't, but I didn't coddle or pity him. If he was going to recover, he had to act the part and believe it was possible. His doctor's first instructions, "I want you to live like you are already healed."

I was a good caregiver and it showed in my patient, he continued to beat the odds year after year. But I really sucked at taking care of myself. I never asked for help, even though there were those willing to help me. *It's just easier for me to do everything so it gets done right.* I didn't take a break when I needed one. I'm tough, and I do what needs to be done, no matter what it costs me, including some of the things I needed the most to survive this experience. The one thing that has always brought me joy and been my therapy since I was a girl was right at my fingertips, always available, and I left them standing out in the corral. The most I did was throw hay over the fence twice a day. Why? I don't know. They said my husband was dying, and I guess I didn't feel like I deserved to have any joy myself. To this day, it is my one regret.

Reid fought for his life for almost five years, and I fought right beside him every step of the way, sometimes harder than he did. I watched him rally. I watched him slide. I watched as the battle raged inside him as he tried to make sense of his new life. He could not find himself worthy of the all the love he was shown, and he could not believe himself worthy of a miraculous cure when he felt like such a burden on the family and me. I watched him learn and grow in amazing ways, knowing it was all a journey he had to take. I could not live it for him or make it less painful or hard. I could not make him live, no matter how much I wanted it to be so.

He was an amazing man and his story is an inspiring tale of going against the flow in search of something better – one that I captured almost every detail of in my book, *My Toughest One.*

He passed away unexpectedly in 2015, and when he did, I was left with the shell of who I once was. Barely alive in some ways. I hadn't realized the toll his journey had taken on me.

I always knew I would go on without him, I had learned so much over the last five years, and God surely didn't put me through all that for nothing. I felt He'd been preparing me for something big. *Helping others, maybe?* I didn't know what, but I was tired, really tired, so very tired. I didn't even really know how tired I was. My bucket was empty, except for the generous donations from my grandkids. Bless them.

The grieving process is exhausting and just that – a process that is different for everyone. A harsh reality for a bone-weary widow. After a whole year focused on restoring my own body, mind, and soul, I started poking my head up and looking around. What am I going to do with the rest of my life? I began searching.

April found me at a retreat in Santa Barbara, CA, with the Canfield Group. There, I dusted off a life-long dream of owning property in Northern Washington. I didn't know how I was going to do it; I just knew it was going to happen. And in September, I was signing papers on my dream ranch. *Where there's a will there's a way, they say. It's so true.* I had found my power and purpose.

As I sit up here in God's country, surrounded by timber, mountains, and wildlife, where the stars are so bright at night you think you can touch them, I can't help but smile. *I have come home.* I want to cry as I watch the horses racing across the giant pasture. It's a happy cry, as I've always wanted this for them – the chance to be horses, to roam and run and be the way God made them. They love it, too, and usually remember to thank me.

My body is getting stronger, and the air is so clean my mind is getting clearer and more focused. My plans are getting bigger, and as I ready myself for guests at ReBoot Ranch Retreat, I feel a sense of wholeness. I know the importance of what I can offer them. I know the power of time – away from the stresses of life and spent in the presence of some of the best therapists on the planet – Junior, Sasha, Oscar, Jen, Cowboy and Henri, the resident ass and the butt of all our jokes (but probably the wisest one here). I know what happens when we feed our brains and bodies with good fuel. I know what's possible when we learn the tools and strategies to help improve our current situation. It's nothing short of a chance to find themselves again and reboot their life.

These are things that kept my husband alive four years longer than the doctors expected, and the things I wish I had done more of for myself when I was in such high demand and didn't think I had the time. I know I could have done even more for Reid if I had taken better care of me, but now I'm fueled and ready to help others become master of their own lives and stay healthy to enjoy all of their success.

Here are seven things for you to take to heart if you are facing a health crisis or caring for someone who is doing so:

1. You are able.
2. You always have choices.
3. Fear paralyzes, face it down.
4. Take 100% responsibility for your recovery.
5. Feed your body, mind and spirit only the best.
6. Believe in the body's ability to heal.
7. Show gratitude and find joy in your journey

I believe I have been given the tremendous gift of a new start and believe that *within every adversity there are seeds of a new beginning.*

About Laura

After helping her husband beat the odds and astound doctors with five years of life beyond what they predicted, Laura knew that she had to share the secrets of her success with caregivers and others who had suffered a loss or health crisis. She took a year to fully grieve her loss, shared the intimate details of their amazing journey in the book, *My Toughest One*, and then bought a ranch in Washington and launched ReBoot Ranch Retreat. This is a place where others can reboot their health, reclaim their creativity and purpose, and reset their life with the cognitive and behavioral tools that sustained her and Reid through their difficult journey, with the help of her horses.

Born horse-crazy and lucky to have been raised in the country, she's been surrounded by four-legged companions her entire life – many with special needs. Laura always had a big heart for animals and an uncanny ability to nurture and heal, which she says she inherited from her grandmother. The small farm where she started her family seemed to attract what her husband called the blind, crippled, and crazy. They always had a unique collection of critters that needed help re-establishing their health.

She became interested in a more holistic approach to horse health and training while teaching her two daughters to ride. In 2000, she and an amazing group of kids called the Red-Hot Riders 4-H Club introduced Natural Horsemanship at the Central Washington State Fair. The event attracted attention across the United States, following an article in *The Trail Less Travelled* Magazine.

For ten years, they travelled and offered demonstrations to teach other kids how to really have fun with their horses. Her philosophy of teaching youth how to think like a horse empowers them in miraculous ways. When a child can influence the behavior of a thousand-pound animal and create a relationship based on trust and communication where the horse would rather be with them than anywhere else, it's a beautiful thing and it increases their safety and self-esteem in profound ways.

Laura is a visionary with a knack for creatively solving relationship problems and health issues. She is also an artist, published illustrator and writer, and has a fondness for painting cowboy boots which she says is surprisingly very therapeutic.

You may contact her at:
* rebootranchretreat@aol.com

Or visit
* rebootranchretreat.com

CHAPTER 30

CREATING A MIRACLE LIFE

BY VINCE KRAMER

Success is not the key to happiness. Happiness is the key to success.
If you love what you are doing, you will be successful.
~ Herman Cain

Despite popular belief, success isn't a one-size-fits-all. It is different for you than anyone else, because you are uniquely different from everyone in the world. You are unique in what excites you, brings you happiness and what you want in your life. What makes me passionate and is purposeful for me might not be, and probably isn't, the same for you. You have a combination of talents, gifts and desires no one else has. Because of that, success and a Miracle Life will look different to you than to me, your neighbor, your mentor and even your spouse.

When you were young, you were taught by your parents, teachers and society what success looks like. You learned through your perception of the circumstances around you what brought praise and made you feel loved, and you developed a belief that more of those actions or things would make you happier. Believing you would be happy, you tailored your actions to receive praise, love and approval from those closest to you.

As you got older, the tendency was to base your definition of success on what you saw others experiencing around you or even by what you were told success should look like. If others seem happy, we have been taught that what they have is responsible for that happiness. We all want to be happy, so we strive for what others seem to have, believing that will bring the happiness we desire. You also have been told throughout your life by "those who know better than you" what you should want in life. In both cases, you end up looking for happiness and success from the world around you.

From five to twelve years old, I was highly influenced by my grandfather. He pushed me to always be better than everyone else. He lectured me about "amounting-to-nothing" if I didn't get good grades, a good job and make lots of money. He stressed almost abusively that I had to be better than everyone else, or I would never be good enough. He was a major factor in how I lived the next thirty-five years of my life. I learned well and accomplished everything I set out to do. I was living life by his rules and those of others I believed were successful. I wanted things in my life that many of the significant people in my life, society and television told me would make me happy and successful. I'm sure you know what I mean; if you have this car, this size of house, this many children, hold this job, go to that school, etc., etc. . . . the list goes on and on. I didn't feel successful, so I kept looking for the next thing that would make me happy. I was being guided by beliefs, habits and patterns that I wasn't aware were there. I was living life by others' rules and on autopilot.

For much of the first fifty years of my life, I lived on that autopilot. Don't get me wrong, I had everything that I thought I wanted: a beautiful wife, a dream job flying for a major airline and an incredible house in the mountains of Colorado. By society's standards, I had it all. In fact, by my standards, I believed I was happy and content. I had followed all the rules and was living what everyone told me was the perfect life. But there was always something missing. And then . . . I had what I call a "crisis awakening." Actually, it was more like a "triple" crisis awakening. In other words, something happened in my life that jolted me into awareness, that there was something missing in my life. The three events were a loss of a friend and fellow pilot on 9/11, losing a six- figure annual pension, and taking a 60% pay cut when my employer declared bankruptcy, and the most devastating, my wife of 21 years telling me she wasn't happy and the only way she could be happy was by getting a divorce.

We all have these awakening moments. They are opportunities throughout our lives to look at life from a different perspective. Some of them we choose consciously, others come from some sort of crisis. These crisis moments can range from a bumped knee when we are angry to a life-threatening bout with cancer. As I look back, each of the three events was an opportunity for me to open my eyes and realize that, "I wasn't really living life, it was living me." The divorce finally got my attention. I had lived my life exactly the way I was told would bring "happiness ever after." Where was it?

Before the divorce was final, I started my search to find what was missing. During a Jack Canfield workshop, I learned exactly what was missing. . . it was me. In that very moment, I decided to live my life on purpose and by my design. I dedicated my life to learning everything I could about creating and living a Miracle Life and sharing it with the world. It has been a challenging journey. I have learned from mentors like Jack, Joe Dispenza, John Maxwell and many more, attended some of the most acclaimed workshops and seminars, read hundreds of books, and most importantly, "done my work" and continue to daily. I searched for answers to happiness and success. I found many answers and continue to uncover more and more.

So, what makes you happy? In your uniqueness, what brings joy to your life? What does success look like to you? What would be a Miracle Life? When you can answer these questions, you can design your Miracle Life! You aren't going to find the answers in a book, from a guru or by emulating your mentor. You are the only one that can answer these questions for you. When you uncover your unique answer to these questions, you are on your path to a Miracle Life – a life of success, happiness and fulfillment. In your self-discovery, you will find empowerment. If you don't take the time to examine your life, life is living you.

It is essential for you to have a unique "blueprint" of your Miracle Life and the "roadmap" to living it. Knowing what you really want and how to create it will change the way you live for the rest of your life. Through my studies and personal work, I learned how and why we create the lives we do. I was astonished that there is so much available to assist us on the journey. Unfortunately, the information and techniques are scattered here and there. I wanted to have all of it available in one place and I developed a process, The Miracle Life Method, to build a blueprint and create a roadmap for your own journey to self-discovery, empowerment, success and happiness. In my online program and live workshop, I share how to create life by your design based on C.R.E.A.T.E. The acronym stands for **Conscious, Reframe, Embrace, Attune, Transform** and **Empower**. I can't share C.R.E.A.T.E. entirely in this chapter, but I want to share an important principle in mastering the law of success.

To create the life of your design, the life you say you want, to find true success, there are three things that you must know:
1) What you really want
2) How you create
3) What can stop you or slow you down from getting what you say you want

You Have To Know What You Really Want

Knowing what you really want begins with becoming **conscious** of who you are. It is going beyond what others expect you to be or what you want others to believe you are. To know who you are, it is essential to know exactly where you are in this very moment. There are many clues to where you are in every moment. How you talk to yourself and allow others to talk to you provide insight. Your beliefs and thoughts will bring more clarity. A self-inventory of what brings joy in your life, the people in your life, what you enjoy doing and where you want to be, will assist in your self-discovery of the real you. Your uniqueness comes from the combinations of gifts and talents that only you bring to the world.

The next step is to **embrace** who you are. When you embrace who you are and that you have much to offer, you can move forward in uncovering why you are here and what you want to share with the world. You will know why you are here when you experience: joy and contentment, the things you want on your bucket list, the type of people you want around you and sharing your unique gifts and talents with others. These are the things that you really want and when you are intimately familiar with them, you can design your Miracle Life. You can consciously choose the life you desire and know what you really want.

You Have To Know How You Create

By understanding how you create, you will understand the part that you play in it and can actively create what you want. In the early 1900's, Albert Einstein, Max Planck and several other scientists established the foundation of Quantum Physics, the science of energy. One of the many important discoveries is that the observer creates reality. In other words, what we think and our perception of the circumstances around us create our reality. I go much deeper into this concept in one of my workshops, but know that you are constantly creating with each thought, even if you aren't aware you are thinking. "As you think, so you become" sums it all up.

Experts estimate that the mind thinks between 60,000 – 80,000 thoughts a day. As many as 98 percent of them are exactly the same as we had the day before, and most of these thoughts you have day after day. You are thinking constantly either consciously or unconsciously and are constantly creating with the thoughts you give attention. Your beliefs shape your thoughts and perception of the circumstances in your life. These beliefs include ones that were programmed into you before birth, ones you formed as a child and still others from society, school and religion. The good news, in knowing and understanding the thoughts, beliefs and habits of the past, you can go beyond the current limits of your mind, beyond conventional thinking and outdated beliefs and choose thoughts and beliefs that support you in living a Miracle Life.

Your predominant habits of thinking shape your actions and generate all your results. To master the art of success, you must **transform** your mind and consciously think thoughts that **empower** you to create what you really want. **Transforming** your mind entails being aware in the moment and thinking thoughts consciously and on purpose. When you know what you want as the observer, you can think thoughts that create that reality. When your thinking and actions match what you want, you **attune** your energy to the things you want and in turn attract them. Your thoughts must be "from" being or having what you want already, not from a place of "if" you have it. As you continue to think these attuned thoughts, they become a belief, which in turn, becomes a habit.

As you develop these beliefs and habits and align your energy, you **empower** yourself to live your Miracle Life. In turn, you **empower** others to live their Miracle Life.

You Have To Know What Can Stop You Or Slow You Down From Getting What You Say You Want

In our observer-created reality, only you can keep you from getting what you want. Now that you know you are constantly creating with your thoughts and aligning to them, you can understand what stops you from getting what you say you want; either your thoughts aren't about what you want or you aren't **attuned** to them. It is that easy and that difficult.

It is important to be aware of your thoughts. We have the tendency to think thoughts from a place of lack or from a place we don't have what we want and that is what we create—more lack. You must think about what you do want and not about what you don't. For example, you want to make more money. If you are thinking I don't have enough money to have the house I want, your thought is about not having the house that you want and that is what you will create, not enough money. When you **reframe** and think about the new higher paying job that you want and put your attention on it, that is what you will create, the higher paying job.

Your thoughts come from your beliefs and your beliefs from your thoughts. A belief is a thought you think over and over. Your beliefs are a choice and you can choose ones that support you. When you believe a belief until it is an automatic part of your behavior, it becomes a habit. Most of your beliefs were formed before you were two years old and based on your perceptions and observation of the people around you. You became what you are based on your experiences of others. These thoughts, beliefs and habits become automatic, and if you aren't aware of them surfacing, you react to life and make decisions based on the perceptions of a two-year-old. You can't create a new life when living from the perspectives of the old one. In other words, you will create more of the same instead of your Miracle Life. The good news, your beliefs can be **transformed**. You can choose beliefs that **empower** you by **reframing** your perception of the circumstances you experienced.

You must be aware of all you are. Through your life, you have been discovering and developing parts of yourself that will help you create your Miracle Life. The tendency is to accept parts of you that you believe are good and judge the parts of you that you think are bad. It takes every part of you to create the life you want. The Swedish psychologist Carl

Jung termed the parts of ourselves we don't accept as shadows. We bury these parts of us deep inside and ignore them instead of seeing the gift in them. You must learn to accept every part of you to create the life of your desire. If you try to keep that part of you under the surface, sooner or later it will pop up and sabotage your dream of a Miracle Life.

You are a powerful creator. A Miracle Life of success and happiness is only a thought away.

About Vince

Like you, transformation and human potential expert, Vince Kramer, has seen personal growth training take many different forms over three decades. No matter the form, people want results and support. It is Vince's passion to partner with individuals, parents and groups in finding lasting empowerment, purpose and passion – in creating businesses, relationships and lives by their design.

As a Speaker, Trainer, Author, and Coach, Vince brings a unique combination of experience, education and research, in presenting keynotes, workshops and online training in finding happiness and success in living life by your design. Through extensive research and study in leading-edge science, he has developed specific methodologies and results-oriented activities to produce breakthrough results in self-discovery and self-empowerment.

He passionately believes everyone is unique and the creator of their own life. This passion combined with 30 years' experience as a corporate leader, entrepreneur and military officer gives him a unique perspective on bringing passion and purpose to every aspect of your life. It is his desire to inspire and empower you to find success and happiness by designing and creating a life fueled by your desires.

Vince's greatest strengths are his ability to connect and to answer a question in a way that anyone can not only understand the answer, but grasp the entire concept. He absolutely loves sharing life-transforming materials with his audiences, and making a difference in even just one life brings him tremendous joy.

Vince is the Chairman of Spirit Wind Inc., the parent company of Imagine Miracles and the Sophia Retreat Center in Dolores, Colorado. He founded Imagine Miracles, which trains people of all walks of life how to discover, design and create their Miracle Life. Vince wrote and produced the *Miracle Life Method*, an online training program and associated workshop based on the C.R.E.AT.E. model. His other programs include Discovering Your Passion and Purpose, A 21-Day Guided Journey to Self-Discovery and Empowerment online program and workshop, and Discovering Your Beliefs.

Vince and his wife, Mary, are the owner/operators of the Sophia Retreat and Event Center in Dolores, Colorado. The center provides an intimate all-inclusive environment that supports facilitators and their clients in achieving maximum results. The center is the home of the Imagine Miracle's workshops and is open to all groups and organizations desiring a place that assists them in providing a first-class heart-based experience.

Vince earned his Engineering degree at Southern Illinois University and a Master of Science degree in Training and Development from Lesley University. A graduate of Air Force Officer and Pilot Training, he is currently an Airbus Captain with a major airline. Vince was trained and mentored by some of the biggest names in the transformation and personal growth industry. The list includes, but is not limited to, Jack Canfield, John Maxwell, and Joe Dispenza.

Vince lives with Mary, his wife and business partner in Dolores, Colorado. When not sharing their passions, Vince and Mary love to travel. Vince can be reached at:
- imaginemiracles.com

or
- sophiaretreatcenter.com.

CHAPTER 31

HOW I MADE MY DREAMS COME TRUE

BY RAFAEL VASCONCELOS

I believe that anyone can achieve their dreams if they are willing to work, grow and change. There are no shortcuts. We will all have to go through a process that will allow us to grow at all levels. We will grow at the physical, emotional, intellectual and spiritual levels.

I believe that we are all born with great potential. But we will only put it into action, when we have planned to achieve something. For most people, it is difficult to get started, or be persistent enough to achieve their dreams. On the road to success, many things happen and we often get out of the way. When we find difficulties, we often feel like giving up. But we have to understand that if we want to accomplish anything, giving up is not an option.

MY HISTORY

I was born on an island in the middle of the Atlantic Ocean, called Madeira, that belongs to Portugal, and is considered by many in Europe as the Atlantic pearl. My father was a cop and my mother was a teacher. We were a middle-class family. I had seven brothers, and every month, it was a financial challenge for my parents to pay the bills. All my childhood I watched my parents working hard to support the family.

My mother for many years worked twelve hours a day teaching. My

299

father worked as a police officer, doing many extra hours to increase family income. My mother's dream was for all the children to have a college degree so they could have a career and get a job more easily. My mother used to say, "... today, we can have money and tomorrow we can lose it, but knowledge is never lost."

My father had a totally different purpose; he wanted every child to have his own house. So, even with the low pay of a police officer and ten people at home, he saved a lot, so he could invest in a piece of land and gradually build houses for his children. I learned from my mother, that if we want to achieve our dreams, we have to be fighters. Although she did not talk much about it, I saw her example. She always said: "You will have to study and learn until you die."

My life was so influenced by my mother that the desire to read daily and to continue my education began when I was a little boy. My father had an entrepreneurial spirit. He wanted to leave eight family homes, one for each child. Unfortunately, he passed away very early. However, he left 5 houses.

From my father, I learned that we have to be entrepreneurs, have a giant dream, save, invest and work for what we want. I learned from my parents some basic principles to become a person of principles and values. I understood that this was the basis for the realization of any lasting goal in this life.

MY DREAMS

When I was 11, I practiced table tennis and I had a dream of becoming champion of Portugal in this sport. After a few years, I managed to realize this dream. Later, when I was 25, I had the dream of becoming a successful businessman and also becoming a millionaire. Several years later, I was able to achieve this dream too.

MY METHODOLOGY

Whether I was practicing sports or as an entrepreneur, I wish someone had introduced me to a method to achieve the results I wanted. The method I present here is the result of more than 30 years of practice and reading many books. It's a tried-and-tested method that worked for me and will work for you, the reader. You just have to put it into practice. This methodology I call "The Methodology for Success" is composed of five parts:

1. Definition of the current situation
2. The dream
3. Preparation and choice of vehicle
4. The road to success
5. Results

1. Definition of the Current Situation

The definition of our situation is important, not to feel blocked or to give up, but to know that in order to reach our dreams, we will have to go up several steps. There will be so many more steps depending on how far we are from it.

But a great walk always starts with the first step.
Why we are in the current situation?

We are in the situation that we are, due to the thoughts and actions of our past. Sometimes, if we have never had success in the past, we believe that we could never succeed in the future. Starting something new or having a big dream is always a difficult job, because we often doubt ourselves.

Our mind will give us a rational explanation that will make us feel good, but deep down in our heart, we do not feel really good. We tend to live in our comfort zone and do nothing. Often this area does not have great comfort. If we have been very successful in the past and today for some reason we are no longer living that success, we often live in the past. It's another comfort zone.

It does not matter your current situation, we have to understand that life is like a river, water has to be in motion, so that our life does not become stagnant.

We need to have purpose and meaning in life.

It is important that we have purpose and meaning in our lives. With this, we will have a much happier life. If we are alive, we have a mission. We are all born with talents, our purpose is to put these talents at the service of others and make a positive difference in their lives.

2. The Dream

When we have a great dream, if we connect with our heart we will be inspired and our actions will be more effective. The dream is almost as if we feel a calling within us. Sometimes we can start something at the invitation of someone else. But it will be only our dream if we feel it inside ourselves. It cannot be another person's dream, it must be our dream. It is like a "fire" that is born within us.

The Blocks

When the dream appears, the blocks usually appear. Our fears, our past defeats and the situation we face today can be a challenge. We begin our internal struggles. The people around us usually do not help us. They will criticize us, they will laugh at us, and they will say that it is impossible or that we are not realistic. If we connect with this – with our fears and with our low self-esteem – it becomes easy to give up.

It is our mind that creates our barriers. They do not exist, but they look very real. We all go through this. Our mind will comfort us and will tell us that it really is impossible and that is why it is not even worth starting. Denial is the easiest. Our reality is created by us. So, if we do not like our current reality, we have the ability to change it.

The Vision

When our vision becomes clear, our ability to overcome our fears and not to listen to the destructive criticism of others increases.

Follow Your Heart

Deep down in our heart is what we really want to do. When we connect with it, we understand what we want to accomplish. There are no barriers there!

3. Preparation and Choice of Vehicle

We really have to believe that we will achieve our dreams. What helps us to believe is the visualization of the dream. To visualize the dream every day, it is essential for it to be well-engraved in our subconscious. This visualization must be accompanied with our emotion. It is on an emotional level that we are going to connect with what we really want. This feeling will awaken in us an inner fire that will inspire us.

Inspiration is different from motivation. Motivation we can have today but not have tomorrow. The human being is an emotional being, so it is normal some days to be more motivated and others less. Inspiration goes further. It is an inner fire that does not stop, and when you are not working towards your dreams, you feel that something is missing and you start to become uncomfortable.

Believe It

Believing is the key to move towards what we want. Usually, it is through small victories that we gain this confidence. If our spiritual vision of life is developed, you will feel much more confident; you will be guided through a superior force, the Faith.

The Appointment

Without discipline and commitment, we will not be able to reach our goals. Here it is important to have the spirit of sacrifice. We must sacrifice our present well-being for a greater good in the future. Commitment is that it helps us overcome our self-indulgence. The human being is self-indulgent by nature and if he does not have discipline and commitment, he will choose the easiest path and usually it´s not the path that leads to his dreams.

Choice of Vehicle

The right choice of vehicle is fundamental to reach our dreams. We have to look until we find it. We can only find it if we have our dream clear in our mind. If we want to be a millionaire, for example, and we are employed in a coffee shop, with this vehicle we will never reach the dream. We should seek to find who are the people who have what we want, and seek to see what they have done to achieve those results.

The speed with which we come to our dreams depends very much on the vehicle we have chosen, and the size of the dream.

4. The Road to Success

When we begin a journey into our dreams, many things will happen. We must always be challenging ourselves, because we will be doing new things outside of our comfort zone. Here it is important to always keep our focus on our dreams so that we do not get lost. Humility must accompany us, not only in this journey, but throughout life; it will always lead us to improve.

The Labyrinth

When we start our walk, we will not be able to see it all the way. But this is normal. The important thing is to walk in the direction of what we want. We must always walk with a spirit of learning and overcoming. It is the path that leads us to our dreams.

The Process

From an early age, I committed myself to personal and professional excellence. If you commit to excellence, it does not mean that we already know everything, or that we will not make a mistake. It means that we will keep ourselves humble and learn every day, not making the same mistake twice. It will lift us up, whenever we fall.

The Great Test

We will have many challenges to overcome along the way, but there will be at least one which will test us at all levels – mental, physical, emotional and spiritual. So, when that happens to us, we have to understand that it is for us to grow and not to give up.

Giving Up is Not an Option

Staying on the path of our dreams for several years is one of the great tests that we will have to pass, the so-called 'proof-of-time' test.

Having a dream deeply engraved in your subconscious and one that is already a part of it, is essential. For me, this was one of the reasons that never gave me peace while I did not realize it. If you associate with positive people who also wanted to fulfill their dreams, it will help your walk a lot. It makes it easier. You stop being the only "crazy"; there is someone else to share the journey. When we are on a team, that feels good, we do not even notice the way.

What we are today is very much influenced by the people around us and by the books we read.

5. Results

We have to understand that more important than the results we obtain, it is the person we have become that counts. When we realize our dreams, we gain a new perspective all the way. Here we understand better the situations of how we started, the way we prepared, validated the vehicle we chose and our growth process on the walk.

We defeated our negative and limiting beliefs. We showed ourselves that we are capable, when many times, nobody believed in us. On the way to results, we often attach ourselves to situations. I have learned that to achieve the results, you have to overcome attachment.

When we reach our dreams, we gain new confidence to continue and find a new dream. Life is only worthy when we are on the path to success.

Live the Dream

When we reach our dream, we feel an inner peace that we have difficulty describing. It is a feeling that we have arrived. It is something that goes beyond our emotional part and enters the spiritual part. That gives us a lot of peace.

It is our moment of truth. For it became a reality that until very recently was only an idea. It is a moment that we are no longer "crazy" and often we become visionaries. We feel that we deserve the best of this life. More than money, we feel free.

Whenever we realize our goals, we feel a lot of internal power. We feel we can accomplish anything!

The Search for a New Dream

When we realize a dream, it means that it is time to start working on another one. To be on the road to success, we always have to work to achieve a dream. As long as we live, we have a mission. We will only do it if we keep on the road to success. I think we are happier when we have a reason to get up every day and take another step towards our dreams.

THE LEGACY

On the way to our dreams, we will impact many people with our example. Reaching our dreams, we can also share our story and inspire others to achieve their dreams. Our life becomes a legacy because of the positive impact we have on the lives of others.

ADDENDUM

When we hear the story that someone has achieved their dream, our belief increases and mental barriers disappear. People feel more inspired and work harder for their dreams. My hope is this chapter has helped to inspire you to take the first step in realizing your dreams and knowing that you have what it takes to make it happen. So, Dare to Dream, Dream Big and Follow these simple steps to be on your way!

Author's note: The information in this chapter is based on my book, *The Methodology for Success.* ~ R.A.M.

About Rafael

Rafael Alexandre Magalhães de Vasconcelos is the Founder of the Vasconcelos Group and also the Vasconcelos International Group. He is an International Leadership Trainer. Rafael is passionate about helping people reaching their goals. Through his success in different areas of his life, he has learned practical ways to help other people achieve their dreams as well.

Rafael received a Bachelor's and Master's degree in Systems Engineering and Computer Science, University of Minho, Portugal and did post-graduate work in Engineering and Technology Management at the Instituto Superior Técnico, Portugal. He also attended a Technology Marketing Course at the University of Texas, USA.

Rafael travels the world speaking to audiences of eager listeners on the subjects of leadership, motivation and personal development. He is a much sought-after International Coach and Author. When Rafael is not running his businesses, or seeking to inspire and teach people how to achieve their dreams for success, he enjoys spending time with his Family.

To learn more, check out his book, *The Methodology for Success*, visit:

- Website: www.rafaelvasconcelosweb.com.br
- Email: autor@rafaelvasconcelosweb.com.br
- Facebook: @RafaelVasconcelosWeb
- LinkedIn: br.linkedin.com/in/rafaelvasconcelosweb

CHAPTER 32

BREAKING BOOTCAMP

BY ANGEL SHAW

FIGHTING FOR SURVIVAL

If the average person were to view this scene, it would be a hybrid melding of a "Big Brother" reality show vlog crossed with a soliloquy from a tormented creature from *Lord of the Rings*. However, if any cookie-cutter 'psychology-wannabe' was also witnessing this, they would claim, "Here is a classic case of a person with a broken mind," and then commence listing a cornucopia of potential disorders along with a cocktail of pharma to fix it.

I was sitting in the dark confines of a closed-door clothes wardrobe, in a wee cottage, in the Highlands of Scotland, regrouping . . . . Ding! Ding! In one corner of my mind Combat Barbie, in the other the Irish Lace Banshee, fighting for the prize and title to the delicate threads of my sanity and... soul? I hesitated, dare I exercise the possibility I possessed either?

My left hand was gently massaging the throbbing pain of my bloody and bruised knuckles on my right hand, mentally recapping the early morning assault.

"Wake up... Wake up... For fek sakes woman, wake up!" my husband was shouting, dragging me out of another violent night terror. I swung a wide right hook and grazed his left shoulder and straight into the headboard. It was an instant reality check. My eyes flashed wildly.

SIT REP! It took a second to let my conscious mind acknowledge my location and his identity.

"Christ woman! What the hell is wrong with you?" he cussed, in his heavy Scots accent. My eyes welled in tears, my jaw clenched in stubborn pride.

"Nothing.... it was just a stupid dream." I snapped, as I wiped the sweat from my face. I was soaked in sweat again. He was right ... what the hell was wrong with me?

"Sorry cara." I whispered.

"You need to go see a doctor, or something. These dreams are getting outta hand."

A chainsaw could have cut through the tension in our bedroom that moment. I laid there in silence as I watched him aggressively get dressed and stomp down the stairs to the kitchen. I waited until I heard the front door close and his Peugeot engine fire up. He was gone for the day. I turned off the side lamp on the nightstand, and then crawled inside my vertical wooden womb.

I would shut myself in that wardrobe to get grounded, stifle my crying and contemplate cutting the delicate thread of life. However, guilt is a powerful intervention, and had it not been for my 13-year-old daughter, I think this story would never have been told. I'd sleep most of the day, forcing myself to get up, make her lunch, help with her homeschooling and feign as though I was normal.

I pulled my knees close to my chest and begged, "Please God. Please God. Please God... what do I do? I really can't take this much longer." Tears streamed down my face. My heart was breaking and my head felt like it was being crushed in a vice.

"Knock that shit off, you're being a pussy." I scolded myself aloud. "You need to man the fek up right now, soldier."

I sat there, took several deep breaths, hiccupped one last sob, regrouped and organized my mind. Someone said once, "I was too Army for the

Army." I fought tooth and nail to prove that as a woman I could be equal to or even better than my military brothers. I earned my wings at the Canadian Airborne Cadre. Even in my worst pain I wouldn't surrender. I was lean. I was cocky. I was Celt-bred. . . . Now look at me!

I was a damn mess, running from some inner cerebral combat and entangled in self-sabotaging dialogue. I had lost control of my emotions, and unable to figure out my issues.

RECONNAISSANCE

I elected early retirement after ten years Regular Force as an NCM in the Logistics Corps. There was this continuous playback recording of the last conversation with my senior officer haunting me.

"Corporal, is this right? You are submitting your release for the early retirement Forces Reduction Plan?"

"Yes, Sir."

"Why? You are number 2 on the promotion board. You are at the halfway point of your career. Your pension isn't going to be worth much."

"Yes, Sir, I understand. I have come to the conclusion that I have children, and I don't feel its right to have somebody else raise them. My marriage is rocky and I feel it is in my family's best interest that I leave my military life, be a mom and pursue a new career."

"You do realize when you got in the military, we were your family."

"Yes, Sir, but I had children and now that's my priority."

He was right. I left home early. I barely passed high school. I was struggling working three part-time jobs to pay my rent and utilities. . . There were times I didn't eat. The military provided a roof over my head, a bed, clothed me, fed me three meals a day, gave me structure, discipline, honor, security, taught me teamwork, and defined a new family.

"And you, leaving the security of a government job, is in their best interest? What are you going to do?"

"Well, Sir, I have six months accumulated leave and a full-year severance package. First, I need to re-establish my place as a Mom and I'll figure it out."

"Where did you say you were going to go?"

"I'm heading out west to Alberta. I have my horse and I'd really like to get back to my passion, training horses." He looked at me with the eyes of a king who sees a bona fide fool speaking lunacy in his court.

"You know statistically 90% of people who get out comeback after a year. It isn't easy out there. If you wait too long, you'll have to redo Basic."

"Yes, Sir. I understand, Sir."

"It will take time re-conditioning to a civilian life."

"I'm good, Sir." I paused. His words seeded into my preconditioned military mind to germinate.

Was I good? I used my paid leave time to do as I said, re-establish my role as a mum. That venture was unadulterated hell. Little people, elementary school children, are not soldiers and don't respond well to direct orders barked at them. There were several shouting matches. It did not take long to convince myself I was not "Mommy Material." I was grateful when they were in school full time. I needed to find me. I needed to find the person I was before Bootcamp.

I turned first to the obvious occupations service sectors like Security and Emergency Medical Tech. I then fell back to trades that matched my MOC in Logistics like Heavy Equipment operator and Long-haul Transport trucker. There was the cherry high of a new job, but after six months I would feel empty and I'd slip back into depression. I couldn't fit in and I didn't know why.

The idea came to me that maybe if I left those careers completely, I might have a chance to find something more inspiring that gave me a sense of purpose.

I remembered I loved Art in school and signed up for 3-D Animation in college. I thought networking would help. In my heart, I realized I was empty because I had no one who could relate, so in the evenings I used internet chat rooms to try find military friends anywhere in the world. I was at times perceived slightly eccentric. One night I had a dream I was moving to Scotland and that idea nagged me constantly. Then one day I met a man who said he was from Scotland and we evolved into an online romance. After seven months, I cashed out my small pension, sold my home, my horse, shipped my furnishings to Scotland and got handfasted. I was free. Or was I simply running?

We were living in a very idyllic setting in the highlands. I got hired by the Estate of Stuart–Fotheringham, and I actually rather enjoyed the trust bestowed upon me to tend to this dignitary, his family and his holiday cottages. The dreams, depression and anxiety stopped. Then it happened, something was triggered and my ghosts found me. One day my husband left for work fine and by that afternoon he was injured on the job and couldn't work. The money ran out, so I returned to Canada to work in the one place I knew where money could be made, and that was oilfield trucking. It didn't take long and I was in another failed marriage starting from nothing.

My life was truly a game of snakes and ladders—constant highs and lows. I turned to self-help books to try change my way of thinking. There were good days where I was in a euphoric state of gratitude, then some were so low I found myself sitting once again in a corner, emotionally broken and entertaining suicidal thoughts again.

One day, by fate I met a young woman whose mum was a Safety Officer. She helped me get my courses and even before I had my diploma in hand, was offered a job up north in an oilfield camp. When I got there, I thought I was in heaven. It was like I was back in the service. I had barracks; I was in a chow line eating in a mess hall; I was in a locked down compound with security guards doing patrols with dogs. The best thing was I had a room with a real bed and climate control, fresh towels and housekeeping, no worries about explosives or gunfire or mindgame inspections.

Then my first epiphany came!

During basic training, instructors intentionally strip you of your previous identity, your individuality, your ego and free will. Once they have you down to your raw core and vulnerable, they rebuild you.

When you were asked a direct question, you were expected to reply, "Yes, Sir" or "No, Sir." Defer from the script and you were severely reminded, "You are not paid to F***ing think."

We had it ingrained that a platoon was unified. If one failed, we all failed. We were only as strong as our weakest. Regardless of the situation, repetitive corrective training was enforced until there was no thinking. We learned to watch out for one another, and bring everyone up to par. Camaraderie was established through our intensive training and into battle. You eat, breathe, sleep, live, love and die besides one another. Each day bleeds to the next, but the comfort is the buddy beside you is going through the same thing.

As a Safety Officer, I felt like I had a platoon again. I encouraged teamwork and watching out for one another's six. The crews could count on me to follow through and we cultivated relationships built on trust and empathy. Like a leader, I developed lesson plans, instructed and mentored. I was embraced in their comradery, as "one of the boys" again. These were the key components I was missing to allow **me** to function in a civilian world. I made the stupid mistake of going out on my own, completely solo. Damn my ego. Then the second epiphany struck.

People are naturally gregarious. We need connection, kinship, camaraderie, "The Platoon." The Military's core mission through our basic training, all our unit exercises in the field, the specialized courses, was to have us perform like a sophisticated machine with loyalty and integrity. That is how they get their financial investment in return. However, in my opinion, they also did a huge disservice in convincing us that without them we could not adapt. That means for those who have received a discharge or retired, you feel your shelf life expired; decommissioned like a 1954 pattern old 'diesel deuce.'

I believe that I can break the Bootcamp's imprinting methods. Instead of being a recruiting officer for the military, I would be a civilian recruiter. If I could help mentor and have some intervention in lessening the statistics from Veteran's affairs, those 20 suicides per day, I would have purpose.

Through the various coaching certifications and near completion of my Transpersonal Counseling diploma, I have some guidelines to help you with the transition.

FIVE STRATEGIES TO HELP YOU RIGHT NOW!

#1. Reality check

You are no longer in the service. No matter how tough you think you are, that isolation wreaks havoc in your head, there are no medals for that.

- Make a plan just like you do a route card for a convoy move.
- Start with looking for support groups in your area before your release or very   shortly after.
- Utilize websites such as: militarysupportgroups.org or go to your parish.

#2. Connect

When all you know is how to function in a platoon environment, seek out a new platoon. What I discovered one day while speaking with civilian construction and oilfield personnel who were under the camp environment alongside the military in the Middle East, they suffered from the same sense of abandonment when they returned to their lives back home. They felt like intruders to their family unit. They missed the community and sense of security of the troops. They really are no different to us.

#3. Volunteer

By giving your time to help others, you in turn help yourself. When we have purpose, we feel significant. There is a sense of community and camaraderie working with others for a cause. For myself, it was organizations like Army Cadets, doing security for music festivals and assisting with a Horse-therapy program at the Women's Correctional Healing Lodge. Remember who you were and what you loved. For example, if you like animals, volunteer at the adoption center for the SPCA.

#4. Communicate

There are four main types of communication:

- Verbal – this is done in speeches, coaching, teaching and YouTube Vlogs
- Non-verbal – which is body language which will support or conflict your verbal
- Written communication – as in blogging, email lists, poems, writing a book
- Visual – like the arts, painting, dance, film production and even landscaping

These outlets are imperative to releasing the past and reintroducing your creative self. Reflect upon your favorite subject in school and revisit that subject perhaps even rekindle your interest.

#5. GROW!!

If you honestly want to find a quality of life, enroll in an online group study program, which will teach you a systematic digestible approach to your reintroduction to a civilian life. This is a format similar to basic training—using building blocks on each lesson but **without the drama or trauma**. Build *esprit de corps* with a new platoon that allows you to exercise your individuality with courage and pride. Participate with fellow veterans as you share your wins and consciously choose to evolve to that greater version of yourself.

If I have only one thing to imprint in your head, let it be this; this is just an end to one chapter of your life not your whole book it's time to write something amazing and under your rules now.

P.S. Always remember, somebody does genuinely care.

Peace. Out. . .

About Angel

Angel Shaw was born in rural Saskatchewan, Canada, ranch-raised with an extensive military family history. She herself is a decorated military veteran from the Canadian Armed Forces who has continued to be involved in the public sector since military retirement including a K-9 security unit – she currently still works as a Safety Officer on international projects.

Angel scored exceptionally high in aptitude testing for communication and leadership, and seemed to instinctively gravitate to those roles, as she found herself being a mentor, coach or manager throughout her various employment opportunities – such as a riding coach, personal fitness trainer and Field Lead investigator.

After surviving a house fire and sustaining a huge setback due to a couple of accidents, her mission is to inspire and empower people after traumatic events to grow beyond self-limiting ideas to rise like a Phoenix from the ashes of the pyre. Angel elected to honor her skill set and pursue coaching as a career and focus on PTG (Post Traumatic Growth) for those who have non-clinical maladies. She also wants to assist fellow Veterans in their transition into a civilian mindset with peace and confidence.

Angel is in progress of completing her degree in Philosophy with an emphasis in Transpersonal Counseling. She offers coaching services, consulting and workshops, and is available for speaking engagements.

To contact her, please use:
* angelshaw.com

CHAPTER 33

AWAKEN YOUR INNER GENIUS™
—SUCCESS IS A STATE OF BEING

BY SOPHIA STAVRON

People are always asking me to help show them how to be happier and healthier in their lives. . . How to deal with the daily stress and anxiety . . . How to get unstuck from a situation or relationship. 'What's my purpose?' is a common question. How do I tap into my intuition and start becoming more spiritual? Or how to get clarity about the goals they want to achieve in their life. And that's just a few of many questions I've received over the last couple of decades. You are not alone if you have ever asked these very common questions. I am known for creating immediate transformation and long-lasting results with my clients. Which leads me to the question that I'm routinely asked by people I've worked with or would like to work with me, "How did you become a master of knowing exactly what to do in the moment dealing with all types of situations and issues?" Simple answer! I practice BEING in the moment and LISTENING to my inner world.

I played in my first band right before the age of two. And not just any band because as you will clearly see in a moment, I was committed to success and had a passion for music at an early age. I performed and sang with America's biggest band, "The Lawrence Welk Show!" Yes, it's true! Every Saturday night around 6 p.m., I would head from the living room where the television was located, to the kitchen where I stored my instruments. Thankfully for me, all my instruments were stored on cabinets near the floor. Like clockwork, my mother would start to chase after me knowing that I was about to change her perfectly organized cabinets into chaos with pots and pan laying all over the kitchen floor. I rummaged through my mother's pots, pans, and other cooking utensils to find the instrument I was in the mood to perform with.

Side note...I am a firstborn American to Greek immigrant parents. Part of being Greek means we take our food seriously, and what we cook our food in matters as well. With that said, knowing that my mother will do her best to maintain perfection in the kitchen and keep her tools to cook with in perfect shape, I needed to grab my band instrument FAST! This is where I learned perseverance, being focused, having clarity of your goal, setting an intention, and getting the end result with the right attitude. After quickly grabbing my violin, I would run back to the living room. My father was always waiting with his big smile and my younger sister sitting next to him on the couch as my audience and biggest fans for my Saturday night gig.

I usually played with the Lawrence Welk Band as a confident violinist. Emotionally, I had an incredible amount of joy turning the vegetable strainer that I had attached a rubber band over the top with as my violin and used a wooden stick as my bow. I knew intuitively that I was meant to play violin in an orchestra. So, by the age of three, I relentlessly started asking my parents to buy a violin for me.

I never gave up on my dream to play violin in an orchestra and never stopped listening to my inner voice that led me to express myself creatively. Finally, after moving into a new house at the age of five, my parents realized that my dream was no longer childish – thanks to the piano teacher who lived three houses down from our new house. She recognized my talent and how passionate I was about playing the violin, so that she gave my parents the contact information to one of the best violin teachers in Lincoln, Nebraska. I started studying the violin with the Suzuki method at age 8, then became first chair violinist as soon I entered 7th grade. Last orchestra I played in was the University of Nebraska–Lincoln Orchestra. And that was the early string of successes in my life.

I believe you can achieve an endless list of successes in life and not only of the financial kind. Take a moment to reflect on our own life. Something as simple as listening to your intuition can guide you to your next HUGE career, healthy and loving relationship, better parenting, better financial decisions, better nutrition and health, and most importantly, a better relationship with your Self. Becoming more conscious and aware of your mind, body, and spirit connection will lead you to your own string of successes.

Currently, there is a vast amount of research that scientifically and medically has proven how powerful the mind, body and spirit connection can be. I spoke to one of the top neurologists in Cleveland Clinic – Miami a year ago in March 2016. I asked her if I could really control my body with my thoughts and emotions? I tell my clients it's possible, and I have my own long list of case studies over the last 25 years that prove your thoughts and emotions can really control your body or at least manipulate or manifest in your body. The neurologist firmly replied, "Yes! Your mind is VERY powerful! I have seen incredible cases where patients created their own symptoms." I am grateful this intelligent doctor is helping people understand the power of the mind and what the thoughts we choose to create can alter in our physical body and overall health.

My own awareness of how powerful our minds can be was revealed to me very early in life. I started meditating at the age of 6, while on vacation in Greece for the summer, visiting all my relatives. I needed some peace from all the different emotions I was feeling and the energy I was feeling from others. On this trip, I also experienced the death of my Grandfather, and witnessed my father cry and mourn for the first time (due to his father's passing). This is when I taught myself and my sister meditation!

My sister and I found a beautiful rock to sit on located on one of our favorite beaches at that time. We closed our eyes as we faced the sun and just tried to feel the waves of the ocean and think of nothing. We didn't know back then what we were trying to do is connect with God, nature and our inner world. But we did, as young children, feel an inner presence of peace and love. From that moment on, I have been practicing and teaching meditation.

Success comes from being in alignment with your inner world, what makes you light up with happiness, listening to your intuition, and creating sacred space within and in your outer surroundings. All of this is accomplished in the presence of unconditional love. Simply put, by living from the inside out, the end result will be success.

Personally, it feels so natural and easy for me to connect with my client's heart space by being a conduit of divine intelligence to help guide them to the answers that they are searching for, that resides within. This feeling of ease and my uncanny ability to navigate through another person's inner world is something that I realized as a young child to be my spiritual gift. As an adult, teaching self-love and helping people who are searching for better health in all aspects of their life through the mind, body and spirit connection is my passion!

With that said, I believe we all hold the opportunity for being a lighthouse to help others on their own journey and life lessons. Finding words to describe this powerful approach to health, success, navigating through the inner world and how I serve people on their journey, finally fell into my lap during one of my meditations a few years ago. . . Awaken Your Inner Genius™. This approach to health and success organically appeared because of my results-based, transformational work with clients that I do by using the Stavron Method™ which is time tested and proven successful.

What does Awaken Your Inner Genius™ look like?

- Letting go of using just your mind to figure out how to navigate your life… this is a time to embrace the messages speaking to you from your HEART.
- Creating space for meditative or contemplative awareness, presence, and pure consciousness.
- Listening to what makes you happy and actually doing it instead of thinking about it.
- Releasing the past and live in the moment.
- Acknowledging your thoughts and feeling your emotions instead of not dealing with them.
- Paying attention to your body—pain happens as a means of communication that something is off balance.
- Moving forward with courage and strong intentions while being patient with the arrival of the results.
- Rising into a place of total fearlessness.
- Seeing other people through eyes of kindness, compassion and non-judgement.

- You are not hiding behind past self-sabotaging patterns anymore.
- You are consciously choosing to be FREE from the past, free from constrictions.
- Any attempt to hold on to old beliefs and limiting patterns will not work anymore.
- Accepting that every experience makes you stronger – and wiser.
- Living your truth without any apologies.
- Allowing the energy of unconditional love and your authentic Self to shine brightly through you!
- Embracing this new chapter in your life!

And how can you Awaken YOUR Inner Genius™?

Let me show you a short version. There are three affirmations I have intuitively used for years which recently I discovered are very divine in nature. Saying these affirmations daily will help shift your mind, open your heart, and empower you into action. Try it out now! Repeat the affirmations below three times in a row to really feel the shift of your energy within.

To take your transformation to a deeper level, try repeating these affirmations in front of the mirror! Yes, you might have a fleeting moment thinking you're a 'dork' talking to yourself in front of the mirror. Not to worry, because many of my clients in the past have had the same thought, and not only did they survive, they also found out something about themselves they were not aware of, and you might too. It's hard to look at yourself and declare, "I am love!" when your self-talk is anything but loving.

- I am Light…this is divine intelligence.
- I am Love…this is divine heart.
- I am Powerful…this is divine action.

In order to make a significant shift in mindset and start living the best version of yourself from your powerhouse, daily rituals are put in place to help support your transformation. I have much more information located on my website, www.SophiaStavron.com that expands on more ways you can Awaken Your Inner Genius™.

- You are unique yet made of the same stuff that connects all humans.
- Your mind creates, so be conscious and use it wisely.
- Your emotions heal, so stay connected and nurture them.
- Your body needs to be purified and nurtured.
- Your space affects you, so be aware of your surroundings.

I live my life being in service to others, and continue to do so by using my divine gifts. But what would happen if I was not aware of my own purpose in life? What if I had no idea what gift I came into this life with, and never pursued the answer? I asked these questions of my own self a couple of years ago, and came to the conclusion that it would be a 'tad' selfish for me to continue working one-on-one with clients when I could be sharing my divine gifts with millions instead of thousands of people and make a more dramatic impact on the world. And here's where your state of BEING comes into play. Be the best version of you!

Success is easily found when you operate from YOUR Inner Genius™!

About Sophia

Sophia Stavron is the Founder and CEO of StavroHedi, LLC with co-founder and sister, Dr. Vickie Stavron Zahedi, in Dallas, TX. StavroHedi in Greek means crossed hands. It's Sophia's belief that we get through life successfully by lending a helping hand to others and empowering ourselves. She honors her parents who are Greek immigrants through the legacy she leaves with her work.

From Celebrity Esthetician hiding her powerful spiritual gifts to piquing the curiosity internationally of doctors, researchers, professors and healthcare practitioners at the Neuroscience conference in London, U.K. in September 2016 with her eyebrow-raising abstract, "Stop Dementia In Its Tracks With Alternative Healing Modalities" – revealing her scientifically-proven work done with her father, she is always evolving!

Known as the approachable, compassionate solutions provider, she helps committed executives, entrepreneurs, and athletes produce powerful results through a proprietary approach to transformation, so they can experience extraordinary results and abundance in their business, life, health, and spiritual practice.

After working with peak performers over the last 25 years, she discovered all results in life are manifested from the health of the mind, body and spirit system. Essentially, the quality of results is directly related to the quality of your spiritual, mental, emotional, physical and environmental systems. She shows you how to live a better version of your Self with enhanced awareness. When you shift the limiting beliefs and blocks within each one of these systems, and align all of them in the same direction, then you can achieve uncommon and unique breakthroughs and results.

Sophia is a provocative, inspiring author, sought-after international speaker, powerful and gifted intuitive, who integrates humor and fun while creating shifts in your mindset, mental health, and spiritual well-being.

Sophia is an Executive Producer in the documentary short film, "The Soul of Success: The Jack Canfield Story" about the life and legend of Jack Canfield, a Best-Selling Author®, originator of the Chicken Soup for the Soul series and the most recognized success coach in the world. She is also an Executive Producer in the documentary short film, "Real Heroes: The Rudy Story" about the man who inspired the movie, Rudy – Rudy Ruettiger. (Both films with Five-time Emmy Award Winning Director, Producer and Filmmaker, Nick Nanton.)

In addition, Sophia is an Executive Producer of the movie, "Amy's Victory Dance", with Director and Emmy-nominated choreographer, Brian Thomas: The movie is a documentary film that chronicles dancer Amy Jordan's triumphant return to the stage – after her 2009 near-death accident.

Other Credits:

- Filming Producer Assistant of Fonya Naomi Mondell for Bob Schneider Live at the Paramount Theatre DVD.
- Sophia has appeared on WFAA prime time news in Dallas.
- Interviewed by Brian Tracy for *The Brian Tracy TV Show* airing on ABC, NBC, CBS and FOX affiliates.
- Co-Author with James Malinchak, featured on the hit ABC TV show, *Secret Millionaire*.
- Personally trained and certified by Jack Canfield as a Certified Success Principles and Certified Canfield Methodology trainer.
- Pranic Healing Practitioner, Psychotherapist, and Arhatic Yoga Practitioner trained by Master Stephen Co.
- Meditation and Mindfulness Teacher.
- Music composer, producer and performer.
- Past President and Director of non-profit 501(c)(3) Sophia's Creative Learning Center for the guidance and development of children under the age of 13 years old.

You can connect with Sophia through her website: www.SophiaStavron.com

CHAPTER 34

RENEW YOUR MIND

BY VILMAR D. BORGES

Do not conform to the pattern of this world, but be transformed
by the renewing of your mind.
~ Romans 12:2 NIV

Do you ever feel like you are limited by the pattern of this world? I am in the construction industry for almost 20 years, and for the last 14 years I have my own company providing high-end interior trim work. One day, I was having lunch with a few guys from other companies in this project and some of the guys were complain about the economy, the weather, the bills they had to pay, the traffic and how things never change. As I was watching them trying to see what was wrong with that picture, when suddenly Romans 12:2 hit me like lighting striking a tree. I have read that passage a couple of times but never realized how true that was. If I was going to live my full potential and impact the lives of others, I need a change. Even though I've met great people and like what I do, I felt like that I didn't' belong there.

So many people are not living their full potential because of the condition of their minds. They become so well-adjusted to the pattern of this world that they fit into it without realizing. What does 'the pattern of this world' mean? It means live an ordinary life, you go to work, get paid, pay your bills and do what everybody else is doing: buying things that you don't need with money that you don't have to impress people that you don't even like. They constantly dwell on negativity from the media, from what people say about them or even self-doubt and not knowing that their problem is simply the fact that their thoughts are out of control. Some people focus more on what they don't have, instead of been grateful with what they do have and doing something with it (what they do have), to reach new levels in their lives. Some people just settle for good enough and sabotage their lives from living a life of more than enough—they settle because they are limiting themselves by self-defeating thoughts.

The problem is not the economy, the weather, the traffic or whatever we decided to place blame on, the problem is what you allow to take control of your mind. Then I realized that I had to renew my mind every day in order to change my life, I didn't want to live like that anymore. I know we are created for greatness, we all have unique gifts and talents, and if we don't allow those self-defeating thoughts to steal our joy, happiness or future, we can accomplish anything if we put our minds into it. I am going to share with you three steps that for the last 12 months has helped me accomplish more than I can ever imagine, which I call **TAG**: **T**hink, **A**ct and **G**row, and I believe that it can help you too.

Step 1: Think

Think about what success really means to you, what is your definition of success? Fame, wealth, a nice house or an exotic car? There are a lot of people who are successful in this world in a lot of different areas of life. They've accomplished their financial goals but it doesn't mean they are successful in their relationships – you see that a lot in show business. In sports, you see athletes that are very successful, but they had struggled in school. As you can see there are many different areas in life to think about how to succeed. My definition of success would be: to do everything to the best of my ability and with excellence, in order to produce results that will add value to others without expecting anything in return. I also think being successful isn't just about what you make happen for yourself, it's about the person you will become, and what you can do to impact the life of others.

Now think about what happiness really means to you. I used to compare myself with others and think, "If I had that kind of car, house or money, I would be happy." I used to spend more time complaining about the things that I didn't have than being thankful for what I had, and focusing in on what I wanted. So many people are the same way – waiting for things to happen by chance in order to be happy. Happiness is a state of mind, it's a choice – you can choose to be happy wherever you are with whatever you have. You have to understand that our lives are the reflection of our thoughts, and everything that has ever happened to you is the physical manifestation of whatever you allowed to enter your mind, good or bad.

If you choose to be happy, things will start to change for you, and that's why we have to take control of every thought so you can change your life by renewing your mind. Change the way you think by allowing your mind to be renewed, and stop the comparison to others that blocks you from being the best that you can be. Now, I want you to think about the kind of thoughts you have allowed to invade your mind. What have you been thinking about? Remember that happiness equals success – not the other way around; you don't have to be successful first in order to be happy, you have to choose to be happy first, then everything else falls into place.

Everything that has been built started with a thought, an idea which was transferred onto a piece of paper and now what was ink on a paper becomes a house, a cell phone, a car, etc.; it is the physical manifestation of a thought. Have you ever heard that expression. . . "to take a step of faith?" or. . . "I hope my dream comes true?" What is faith? What is hope?

Some definitions of faith and hope are:
-- *Faith*: (noun) – strong or unshakeable belief in something, especially without proof or evidence;
-- *Hope*: (noun) – the feeling that what is wanted can be had or that events will turn out for the best.
-- *Hope*: (verb) – to look forward to with desire and reasonable confidence.

Wow! You see, whatever you think of yourself or what you can do, if you have an unshakable believe so strong that you can feel what is wanted can be had, you will accomplish anything you want, but you have to take action – which leads us to the letter **A** in our acronym **TAG**: Act.

Step 2: Act
In order to continue advancing in life you have to be grateful for everything you have. That is the first action when you wake up; it's so powerful that once you create that habit, you will see the changes all

around you throughout the day. Take responsibility for everything that has ever happened to you and ask yourself: how can I improve? What can I do to make myself better and help others? And you have to act on that thought while it is fresh and you are inspired to change or improve; the faster you act on it, the more likely you are to follow it through.

For instance: If you want new clothes, take action and get rid of all the old and out of style clothes that don't even fit you anymore that were in your closet for so long. It's the same way with our health, spiritual or professional lives – you have to get rid of the old thoughts, habits and make room for the new, it's time to let all of that go. Get rid of comparisons too, you don't have to prove anything to anybody, you aren't here to impress others, it's a distraction that makes your mind drift away from your goals. Take a close look at all the people that you associate with. Are they lifting you up or are they pushing you down? Are they cheering you on or are they criticizing you? Someone once said, "If you are the smartest one among your friends, you need new friends."

Take action by changing your environment, you can't hang out with those who had settled for good enough. If that includes some longtime friends or even family members, so be it. Turn off the TV and stop feeding your mind with negativity. I've heard someone once said that you can always make more money, but you can never buy more time. Without the TV, you will reconnect with your family, spouse and kids, and you'll be able to invest more time in personal growth. Sign up for that class that will promote you to a new level in your company… and so on.
Always walk the extra mile, do more than you're paid for even if nobody notices; do it for you. If you don't get the promotion that you deserve, it is time to move on.

Create a habit to read at least ten pages of a good book each day; if it is personal development, leadership or whatever industry you are in, it will help you to become a 'better you' and it will give you an edge over others who have settled for good enough. Want to get fit? Take action for your health by changing your eating habits and starting to exercise; I used to eat very poorly throughout the day – sometimes not even stopping for lunch, and when I got back home at night, I used to eat like a starved animal, my cholesterol was very high and some nights I didn't rest well. Since I have changed my eating habits and started to work out at least 30 minutes a day, my cholesterol went back to normal, I've lost ten pounds and now I have six packs, okay, four packs, but I am still working on it. Every little action that you take every day will compound over time and produce the results that you want, and you'll see things changing for the better. So, be grateful, do more than is expected from you, don't stop learning and take good care of your body and all these will lead you to growth.

Step 3: Grow

Growth doesn't happen overnight. You have to have a plan and you have to be intentional and patient. See how farmers wait patiently for the crops to grow? There is a time to sow, to water and to wait. For a period of time, the farmer doesn't see anything happening, he's watering day after day but nothing seems to happen, but this is the time that he'll have to take really good care of it, because all the weeds start to grow in. And if he doesn't remove them, they will grow, suffocate and eventually kill the crop. It's the same with your life. You had a dream and you took action, but the waiting time seems like it never ends, and the "weeds" of life: self-doubt, "I-don't-feel-like," criticism, naysayers, closed doors, all of it can "suffocate" your plans to grow.

You have to understand that not everyone is going to cheer you on, and as you grow and increase, some of your friends, family or co-workers will get jealous and will start finding fault in you. Don't be surprised if the ones closest to you try to discredit you, because some people simply can't handle your success, you're the reflection of what they could be but they are not. Don't lose focus trying to please everyone around you, remember you are created for greatness. You can't always control your circumstances, but you can control your response. Remember that: "Life is 10% what happens to you, and 90% how you respond."

As you wait and grow, don't be discouraged – have faith, be hopeful and positive. Have a good attitude towards everything, peruse what you love, expect great things, look for ways to help others succeed and you might be closer to your breakthrough than you think.

About Vilmar

Vilmar D. Borges was born and raised in Curitiba, the capital of Parana State in southern Brazil. In his senior year in high school, he got a full-time job and eventually dropped out of the school to financially support his single mom. After five years, he got fired and went on to work as a field supervisor for a Canon copiers authorized dealer, and later on as a sales manager for a 3M dealer. He then took a yearlong marketing and advertising program before he opened his own business.

In 1997, he came to the U.S.A. following a long-time dream to become a film maker, but it didn't happen until 2008 when he graduated from Palm Beach Film School in South Florida. He was the director of photography for one of his classmate's short film called *Refuge of Dragonflies* which won 4 awards. Using the principles of how to communicate efficiently and connect with people, skills that he learned back home, he had an edge over other contractors in the construction industry.

A couple years ago, he realized that there was more to life than just going to work, getting paid and paying bills. In a search for something else, he came across some quotes and teachings of some well-known speakers and personal development teachers, and was inspired to accomplish more in life and to help others do the same. Today, he is a certified Coach, Teacher and Speaker with the John Maxwell Team, and has attended many other seminars with great mentors and speakers like Darren Hardy and Jack Canfield. Since then he has been using three principles which he likes to call TAG: Think, Act and Grow, which has helped him accomplish more and live a happier life.

You can find more about Vilmar D. Borges at:

- www.vilmarborges.com

CHAPTER 35

SUCCESS IN THE PALM OF YOUR HAND
HOW TO ACHIEVE MORE, IN LESS TIME – USING TECHNOLOGY TO HELP YOU REACH YOUR GOALS

BY DEB SHAPIRO

As a lifelong entrepreneur, I've lived and experienced much of what Jack Canfield teaches. From an early age, I was taught to **"Believe in Myself"** and by doing so, I could reach any **"Goal."** Having this confidence allowed me to always **"Ask"**, never fearing a no answer. Not being afraid to **"Ask"** has shaped much of my life.

Another "constant" in my life has been *always* striving to **"Improve."** No matter what area of my life I wanted to improve upon, I've reached out to others, with Jack Canfield being one of my favorite teachers. So naturally, after I sold my business of 34 years, and wanted to **"Plan"** the rest of my life, I used Jack's *The Success Principles* as my guide. I had not yet reached all my goals, and I was determined to really get it right *this time!*

As I delved into *The Success Principles*, I started wondering *why*, if I've diligently *read, listened, journaled,* and *repeated affirmations,* am I still not where I want to be? What am I doing *wrong* or not doing *right*? And because you are reading this book, I suspect you may be asking yourself the same question.

I've decided we're not doing anything *wrong*. What we're missing is a *process, framework* or *roadmap* to guide us through the multitude of valuable information the *Success* world has to offer. We get "bogged down" in the mountains of "actions" we need to incorporate into our daily lives in order to achieve our goals. Achieving goals requires concentrated *awareness*, dedicated *discipline*, and *repetition*. We have *better* than good intentions. However, it's *time, structure* or a *system* that's missing. And, there is a no better time than "now" to "fix" this problem!

When I open a new book on *Success*, it's like the first day of school! Anything is possible! I read each chapter, and diligently take "notes." Even though I'm extraordinarily organized, I always end up with stacks of "pages" and don't ever refer back to them, because I'm onto the *next* chapter, concept or principle. *And* the daily "to do" actions from each chapter keep piling up!

One day, after trying to quietly meditate at home, I found myself constantly interrupted by leaf blowers, hedge trimmers and lawn mowers. It was impossible to stay focused. So, I decided to go for a walk. Suddenly I thought "what if I tried meditating and walking for exercise, at the same time?"

I quickly found *one* Walking/Meditation App on my phone, and soon my whole world changed! As a matter of fact, the concept for this chapter came to me the very first time I combined walking and meditating.

**It was during my first walking meditation experience
that an idea was formed.**

What if, instead of our mobile phones being a distraction (as they many times are), we use them as a "tool" to help us achieve our personal *Success* goals, by incorporating those "goals" or "actions' into our daily lives?

So..."Success in the Palm of Your Hand", was born!

My first experiment was using the calendar on my cell phone to incorporate "action" words, that correlated with my current personal Success goals, into my daily life. This alleviated the need to *read* each "action" several times daily. As an example, I took "actions" from the first chapter of Jack Canfields, *The Principles of Success*™ and set them up as activities in my cell phone calendar. (One every hour, with "*reminders*" on the half hour.)

    9:00 Take Responsibility.
  10:00 No Blaming.
  11:00 No Complaining.
  12:00 Face Facts Quickly.
   1:00 Pay Attention to Results.
   2:00 What Can I Do Better?
   3:00 Am I Limiting Myself?

I set up these daily "actions" for one week. And importantly, didn't go beyond 3:00. Even though the phone calendar is a great "tool", it's important to give ourselves a phone "break" everyday.

As we all know, repetition is the key to real learning. Not only did *I see and read* "actions" on my phone twice hourly, I was also *reminded* of "actions" on my Fit Bit watch, and on my computer Google Email and Calendar, each time I opened them. So, I was reading four repetitions of *each* of my personal "actions" in my plan:

- On my phone calendar
- On my Fit Bit watch
- On my Google Calendar
- On my *unread* emails list

I was totally amazed at how effective this simple practice was. My mind could be a million miles away, and the "reminders" reset my focus on the "action" at hand. These "actions" stayed in my mind, and were transmitted to my "inner self/guidance system" all day long.

READING, WRITING, RECORDING AND LISTENING

I discovered this process when working Principle #2 in *The Success Principles*. It's very simple to implement, and *extremely* effective!

After reading Principle #2*, I listed in *writing*, all questions from "Be Clear Why You're Here."

1. What do I truly "love" to do?*
2. What am I "good" at?*
3. What is "important" to me?*

After completing a written list, I used a voice recorder App on my phone to record the questions, pausing 10 seconds between each. I found that *writing* the questions, *saying* the question out loud, and then *listening* to the question, pausing the recorder after each, I gave myself time I needed to *think* about the answer and finally *write* the answer. It's the power of repetition and technology working together again! If I couldn't answer all questions during the first "session," I simply kept replaying the recording until all questions were answered.

WALKING MEDITATION

Meditating while walking allowed my inner guidance system to easily take over, and was the foundation of "Success in the Palm of Your Hand."

If sitting meditation doesn't work out as planned on a given day, I've created a Walking Meditation audio recording that allows me to combine meditation and walking for exercise. Once you set up the recording, the audio can be played over and over, making our old friend "repetition" very happy! And it can be used as a "guided" meditation if you can sit quietly, at home.

Before recording, you'll need a music source, and a recorder App that has a "timer," for a total of two Smart devices.

FYI: I've used, with great success, these Apps.

• **Insight Timer**, by Insight Networks, Inc. for music. I selected "music" category. It has no spoken words. I found when recording, I needed to turn Insight Timer volume all the way "up." And I "voice recorded" over the music.

---

* See Principle #2 in *The Success Principles*™ for complete list. Don't forget questions from The Life Purpose Exercise, also in Principle #2.

- **Tap Media**, Ltd, for voice recorder and "timer." Timer allows you to break your meditation into segments.

The idea is to simultaneously play appropriate meditation music for "background" while voice recording your goals or actions, over music.

What follows is an example of a format for a 20-minute Walking Meditation recording. You can expand the time to meet your needs. Or the 20 minutes can be used as a "warm up" for longer or more vigorous walk.

When walking outside, I keep my eyes focused ten to twelve feet ahead of me, on the ground. (Please, remember to walk facing traffic. This enables you to be aware of what's coming towards you.) Because I'm in a very "mindful" state, I'm more aware of what's going on around me than if I were "distracted" – listening to a book or talking on my phone, etc.

When walking on a treadmill, I locate myself away from TV's or other distractions and, if my treadmill has a "personal" TV display, I simply cover it with a towel. Be sure to "hold on" to rails and keep your eyes focused on a "point" straight ahead.

Personal note: You, like me, probably have people you acknowledge while walking. At first I *waved* or said *hello.* However, doing so was an interruption of my meditation; and I had to completely "refocus" after each "greeting." I decided to let friends know why I wasn't saying hello, by beginning to spread the word, within my community, about my Walking Meditations.

Then, while next Walking and Meditating, I "thought" why don't I design tee shirts that have a phrase telling people, on front and back, what I'm doing? With printed tee shirts being so readily available on the internet, I was able that very day to design and order shirts for myself and to sell to others.

I'M
MEDITATING + WALKING
and
SENDING YOU A "SILENT"
HELLO !

MEDITATING + WALKING EXAMPLE

For this example, I've chosen "Goal" to be my focus, based on **Principle #7**, in *The Principles of Success.* I play music while recording the following "prompts," *pausing* between each.

Remember to speak slowly with long pauses between each prompt. (I've indicated pauses with slash marks.) Time passes more quickly when you're "walking" and not just "recording."

Minutes 1 and 2:
- I've chosen *Goal* /// to be our focus today.
- Begin by standing *still* /// and *tall* /// with your weight evenly distributed /// on both legs.
- Hold your head *up*. /// With your shoulders /// *relaxed*.
- Feel yourself *grounded* /// to the earth.
- Closing your eyes, take a few /// slow /// breaths.
- Expand your breath by breathing *in* /// to the count of 4 /// and *out* to the count of 8 /// Repeat 3-4 times.
- Eventually /// let your breath resume its own /// natural /// pace.

Minutes 3 and 4:
- Clearly think *about* /// and *state* /// the goal you've chosen to share /// with your inner self today.
- Set the *exact* date and *exact* time you will *accomplish* this goal.

Minutes 5 and 6:
- Begin walking /// allowing your body to find its own rhythm. /// Speed isn't important.

Minutes 7 and 8:
- Remind yourself to focus on the *in* /// and *out* motion /// and the *sound* of your breath.

Minutes 9 and 10:
- Physically /// and mentally /// allow your body to *experience* /// how you'll *feel* /// once your goal is accomplished.

Minutes 11 and 12:
- *Visualize* /// how you'll *look* /// after accomplishing your goal.

Minutes 13 and 14:
- Think about /// how your environment will *sound* after accomplishing your goal.

Minutes 15 and 16:
- Mentally /// and physically /// allow yourself to bask /// in the *glow* of your accomplishment.

Minutes 17 and 18:
- Next /// offer *gratitude* to your inner-self /// for *accomplishment* of your goal.

Minutes 19 and 20:
Finally /// end your Walking Meditation /// by shaking-out your hands /// and continuing to walk /// at your normal pace /// until your walk in completed.

YOU CAN NOW USE THESE THREE "SYSTEMS" TO IMPROVE *ANY* AREA OF YOUR LIFE:

1. Smart Phone Calendar Reminder
2. Write, Audio Record, Listen and Write Answers
3. Walking Meditation

The process of creating these "systems" reaffirms to me the importance of exponential thinking. Through technology, we have the opportunity to learn in new and exciting ways that are totally "in step" in today's world.

BY USING THESE "SYSTEMS," OR CREATING YOUR OWN, YOU'RE NOW ON AN EXCITING PATH TO "MASTERING," WHATEVER "SUCCESS" IS FOR YOU!

In conclusion, I hope you've enjoyed reading this chapter, as much as I've enjoyed writing it, and that you'll find these ideas help you achieve your life goals, whatever they may be.

I write with a great sense of pride! This is the first time, in my 68 years, I've shared my thoughts and ideas with so many. Where will doing so take me? I don't yet know. However, I do know, with great certainty, I'm on my way . . . somewhere!

"Ready....Fire...Aim..."

EPILOG

Because I wrote the preceding chapter, and committed to taking "relentless action", much has happened in my life! I'm currently partnering on an App that helps students of The Success Principles™ more quickly, effectively and efficiently reach their goals and dreams. (You can learn more by contacting her using her contact info. on the following page.)

About Deb

Deb Shapiro is a *lifelong* entrepreneur who has created many businesses.

She graduated from Ball State University, with a degree in fine arts. Her artistry, creativity and attention to detail, have shaped her many achievements, beginning with a successful jewelry business, in 1976.

In 1980, she increased the "bottom line" of Quiescence Diving, in the Florida Keys, by adding *retail* sales to a shop that, until that time, only sold scuba diving trips. Quiescence Diving, because of her vision, is still thriving today.

Deb co-founded Dockside Mart in 1982. This successful retail business operated for 34 years, until it was recently sold. This kind of longevity is rare in the world of small retail businesses! She is currently working with the new owner in order to assure her success.

During its long history, other businesses were "spun-off" from Dockside Mart.

- "A Taste of the Keys" Key Lime Cake
  In 1991, she received "Top Honor" for Specialty Food Packaging and "Honors" for her Miniature Gift Basket Cakes, from the International Fancy Food Show, in New York City.
  Her Key Lime Cake was featured in "Flour" magazine and in the "National Association for the Specialty Food" trade magazine, January 1994.

- "Dockside Cakes"
  She expanded the product line, and sold it, 1998. You can still purchase the cakes at docksidemarket.com and through "QVC" before Christmas each year.

- "Deb Shapiro Interiors"
  For 15 years, she has successfully worked with homeowners, architects and builders, creating beautiful and highly functional interior designs. She continues to expand and grow this business.

Additionally, Deb has also been instrumental in helping others achieve their dreams. Eric Kessler, a trained chef and his wife Stephanie, a national "natural" body builder champion now work with clients in their homes throughout the United States, and in their Personal Training Center, and Healthy Eating Cafe.

Through Deb's encouragement, persistent efforts and guidance, Mead Mechanical,

LLC is now one of the top HVAC companies in the Florida Keys. Their client list includes a national telephone company.

In 2005, Deb served as co-chairman on the building committee for The Art League in Key Largo, FL. This three-year project resulted in a facility that is not only beautiful and creative in its design, it is highly functional *and* home to over 600 members.

Deb was invited to exhibit her collection of oil paintings, "Los Colores del Paraiso" (The Colors of Paradise), at the above-mentioned Art League, in February of 2011.

Deb's newest projects revolve around using *technology* to help others achieve their goals and dreams, about which you can read in her chapter titled "Success in the Palm of Your Hand."

You can connect with Deb at:

- Deb@successbydeb.com

CHAPTER 36

MASTER YOUR INNER CRITIC
—HOW TO ELIMINATE SELF-DOUBT AND PROCRASTINATION SO YOU CAN GET MORE DONE IN LESS TIME

BY CHRIS SALEM

Over nineteen years ago, I was working relentlessly building wealth, but emotionally, spiritually, and physically, I was bankrupt. This was tied to an unresolved root cause associated with my father and with feelings of anger stemming from my childhood. The destructive habits and behaviors I carried to early adulthood nearly killed me twice and were destroying me.

Though remaining conflicted, I conveyed an image to others and was perceived as a happy and financially successful man. In reality, the money meant nothing if my emotional, physical, and spiritual well-being were not synchronized. It took hitting rock bottom nineteen years ago to have that "aha" moment – realizing the solution to my problem starts with looking within, taking my moral inventory, and learning to be in the moment for clarity. It took nearly two years from that time to come full circle with my true self. I have been able to experience true success living in the solution by resolving the root cause and having balance.

What is balance? Balance is being true to your purpose and not being distracted by shiny objects, surrounding yourself with family and loved ones, nurturing your spirituality, maintaining a healthy balance between

343

emotional and physical health, and being present in the moment. Since completing this process, I now have the awareness of unblocking emotional barriers and achieving sustainable success at the next level – through speaking engagements to organizations and working with business leaders, entrepreneurs, and others as a Change Strategist and Wellness Advocate.

Have you asked yourself from time to time why your life has not unfolded the way you have envisioned? Have you asked what holds you back from getting things accomplished and being successful? The answer lies with past events from early childhood through the teen years, which is the *Cause* that leads to the *Effects* that most people live with, and that keeps them trapped in self-doubt which leads to procrastination. Your unconscious habits and behaviors in adulthood are tied back to trigger events that have molded you into a pattern of self-doubt or success. It is your inner critic that has a choice of tapping into the positive or negative that dictates your habits and behaviors that either serve you or not . . . long term.

For example, you see a man who has never been able to live up to his full potential with his career. He may have had a father who was overbearing and always badgering him to improve his performance or skills. He may have also felt neglected because his father was never there for important events or did not acknowledge him for his childhood successes. These are trigger events that develop the *Causes* that lead to the *Effects*, that in adulthood, will mold habits and behaviors that may be detrimental to his success due to self-doubt. Living in the effect will not change his current situation if operating from self-doubt. The inner critic defaults to the negative and unconsciously feeds off the *Cause*, which creates habits and behaviors that do not serve him. He has lived his entire life not being his authentic-self – always looking to be someone else his dad or other authoritative figures wanted him to be in life.

Another example is a man who struggles with being overweight and cannot seem to gain respect from women in his life. He had a relatively decent upbringing with no traumatic events. However, his mother, who was slightly domineering, would often comment during his growing years to eat everything on his plate because good food is expensive and others were not as fortunate as he was. His mother, while not malicious with intent, planted a seed of guilt in this man as a boy. In addition to struggling with being overweight without long-term success – despite using several weight-release programs – he also gravitated to women more dominant than he. See the pattern here. He was not conscious of this during his adult years, and during coaching did not recognize this at first. It was only through consistent questions were we able to uncover that this was his *Cause*. Once he acknowledged this as his *Cause* and truly forgave his mother, and most importantly himself, he was then able to fully release it and adopt healthier habits. This new mindset and healthier habits allowed him to make better food choices to keep the weight off and wisely choose a woman who was neither dominant nor submissive.

Can someone who is stuck in life change and move toward success operating from a place of peace without anxiety? The answer is YES, but only when you start with addressing the *Cause(s)* and not the *Effect(s)* in your life. Your life is an evolving story and can change when you choose to change for the better. Your life is not confined by past events that negatively affected you. They can be used to strengthen you to evolve in a more positive way. The start to eliminate self-doubt begins with addressing the *Cause(s)*. Go back and write down what they are, even if you perceive they do not really bother you. Often, people do not realize that certain events that happened long ago have affected their lives and play out every day in what they do, in ways that do not serve them. Confront the *Cause* by looking at yourself in the mirror. Accept responsibility and appreciate this negative experience if you created it. Acknowledge the *Cause* even if you did not create it but were a victim of circumstance. Forgive the people that hurt you. You do not have to forget, but just forgive. Let go either way as the story of your life is always evolving and is not defined by these *Causes* from trigger events. This can be frightening for many people, but it's the only way to release the *Cause* that creates the *Effects* that no longer serve you. You can also do that with a therapist, coach, or trusted friend. Use them to build your strength in a positive way and continue to develop a story that operates from a place of joy, happiness, and peace – rather than from negative emotions such as anger, shame, and guilt.

When you release the *Cause(s)* and truly let go, it will unlock the feeling of true peace and joy. You will know your life is about choices, and when you come from your authentic self, your story will only lead you to success over time. Coming from joy and peace, your decisions to act promptly rather than procrastinate will be easier, and the fear of failure less. You will have more confidence in your abilities coming from your authentic-self and know the universe will play its part if you play yours with 100% commitment and action. You will know fear is just fear itself, not tied to any actual objective or goal you have planned. Know success is a journey not a destination, and the only true failures in life are not to start, confront, or follow through to something you fear. Always know that fear is an illusion. It is not real, but only appears so when you focus and give energy to it.

Fear can manifest itself in many forms and often stems from your current emotional state. Anger is a manifestation of fear that is directed outwardly at someone else, while guilt and shame are forms of fear directed inwardly at ourselves. These faces of fear can sometimes be difficult to see in our daily lives.

Here is an example when you operate out of fear. In my twenties, I once bought a car through a salesman who was referred by a friend of mine. My friend told me this salesman was having some personal financial issues but was a genuinely good person who helped his friends. The reason I decided to buy from him was because I held my friend's recommendation in high regard, and I always liked to help out people who helped others without expectations. I figured if he earned a commission from me for purchasing a car, this would be a win-win situation.

I wrote a check for $1,000.00 to hold the car I selected, and handed over photocopies of my driver's license and three recent months' bank statements. That same night after dinner, it dawned on me that I had handed over confidential documents to him without a second thought – documents that a conman could reuse. I've read of conmen who used another person's documents to apply for loans and then disappeared, leaving the unsuspecting victim to settle the loan with the bank.

When I thought about it, I realized that I did not really know this person at all, other than being referred by my friend. Who knew what kind of a person he was? Perhaps he might be in such deep debt that he could be desperate enough to cheat.

My train of thought just continued to move on from one fear to another, each thought making the fear bigger and more terrible than the one before. By the time I realized what I was doing to myself, I was about ready to panic. As it turns out, none of what I feared was true. This was an honest person just trying hard to earn a decent living. All the fear that was self-created served only to perpetuate this negative habit.

Most of our fear arises in the same way – subtle and unsuspecting. It starts with one fearful thought and leads to others. Before you know it, it has taken on a life of its own. If we are not careful or have very poor self-awareness, this type of habit can literally create panic in us.

This fear tendency is actually very common, and we can see it in ourselves almost every day. When we are not aware of it, this tendency tends to perpetuate itself each time we allow it to manifest in us. The good news is that we can change this tendency simply by increasing our self-awareness through mindfulness. The sooner we see this pattern, the easier it is to stop it or replace it with something more positive. When we do this repeatedly, we eventually release the power that fear has over us.

The key is to focus energy toward your goal or dream, and not waste it on fear, that in reality, truly does not exist. It is a choice like anything in life. Growth and fulfilling your dreams only comes when you operate out of your comfort zone and do things that you initially fear. You can begin to change your life living for your "Why" and knowing fear is just a loss of your oneness with your true essence. Here are ten steps to minimize self-doubt.

TEN STEPS TO ELIMINATE, REDUCE, OR MINIMIZE SELF-DOUBT TO ACHIEVE SUCCESS

1. Address and confront the *Cause(s)* that lead to the *Effects* that create self-doubt and to let them go through forgiveness.
2. Make the conscious choice to change toward success by looking at it as a journey and growth process, not a destination.
3. Incorporate a daily schedule of meditation, personal development, healthy eating and exercise to create balance and overall well-being. Important life decisions are best made when grounded and coming from a sense of peace, joy, happiness, and feelings of confidence.
4. Always be grateful where you are now and where you are going forward.
5. Be in the present moment always and know fear manifests itself

when you dwell too much on the past and project too much into the future.

6. Come out of your comfort zone early and be willing to be consistent, but never strive for perfection when it comes to adopting new habits that best serve you toward the journey of success. Never become complacent as greatest growth comes from outside your comfort zone.

7. Write down short-term and long-term goals and set up attainable goals over time. Reward yourself in a positive way for each goal met along the way.

8. Recognize your fear and know it is fear itself, and never label it as a feeling of nervousness or anxiety.

9. Always know failure is only when you do not start or follow through. If something does not work during this journey, always look at it as a learning experience and part of the process to achieve something better. The universe will test you, and when you make the choice to really go for it through belief and action, then the universe will untimely do its part.

10. Know and commit to action consistently with your "Why". Know your strengths and weaknesses. However, always focus on your strengths to be better, not perfect, and leverage your weaknesses to those that can address them for you.

We are all worthy of success. It is a choice and process that comes from an internal place of peace and joy inside of you. The choice to listen to your inner critic will be either positive or negative. You will find success when you truly let go of the *Cause(s)* that create the negative effects that hold you back. Adopt healthier habits over time through the steps depicted above, so more positive energy and greater motivation can lead you toward a better life.

The choice again starts with you.

About Chris

Chris Salem is an accomplished international keynote speaker, change strategist, best-selling author, and wellness advocate focused on resolving the root cause to emotional and physical barriers so entrepreneurs and business leaders can have sustainable success at the next level. He has a special passion for empowering them to take their business and life to another level by operating in the solution rather than the problem.

Chris shares from experience what has worked successfully for him through understanding the root cause behind the effects of limiting patterns in our lives. He is the originator of the term: *Prosperneur*™ – an individual whose health and wealth are in alignment in a way that leads to true prosperity. His book, *Master Your Inner Critic / Resolve the Root Cause – Create Prosperity,* addresses this and went to international best seller status in November 2016.

CHAPTER 37

MASTERING SUCCESS AND LIVING LIFE ON (YOUR) PURPOSE

BY LORI A. WAGNER

Life is a series of individual, yet connected stages. Each stage has its own lessons, yet these lessons, although individual, collectively build us toward becoming a successful human being. At the very moment of conception, the world began to teach us. We learn, instinctively, how to breathe, eat, and focus our efforts toward a respective goal attainment. The goal may vary: getting the attention of our maternal host, later making that same mother proud by our accomplishments, or something different, but our objective must be reached. As we live life, and experience each day anew, the world brings us new challenges, and new lessons with the dawn of each day. Just by living, life teaches us a mainstream formula for success. We learn in order to receive, there are certain things we must achieve. **The Ultimate Goal – Survival** – is unfortunately the life motivator for most people.

It is vitally important to earn enough money to meet immediate needs. As a result, one will never find a mainstream societal formula in which the world stands by us and advises us to go out and look for a career that is meaningful—a purpose—which is a **service to humanity.**

The fact that the mainstream formula is flawed is no lie. Experts have long touted the importance of following this "formula for success", but seldom address how living a life *sans* a defined purpose can be

351

counter-productive to any fiscal success a person may enjoy. A person that may have fiscal success and no true-life purpose, will expend their fortune in a fruitless search for their individual life purpose. A person that lives their life's purpose is fulfilled and satiated, but seldom emotionally exhausted. This is because **living your purpose** will provide you with a life that immediately positively affects others and grants you the greatest opportunity for making a focused positive impact on the lives of others. A feeling of satisfaction and contentment is experienced on a daily basis. Success is routinely ebullient – complete with the knowledge your efforts are the substance of history; giving the world a legacy to remember you by, while concurrently giving you the serenity to have total peace, even while facing imminent death. Your life is "forever" changed when you live your life purpose.

The following reasons will undoubtedly inspire the pursuit of a career that motivates the intrinsic and innate abilities to serve others, as the best and most vital crucial decision you would ever make!

HOW LIVING YOUR PURPOSE WILL MAKE YOU SUCCESSFUL

1. Making a meaningful impact on others.

You are wasting your time if you are not making someone else's life better. By making other lives better, your life will become better.
~ Will Smith.

Living your purpose is the positive impact you have on others around you through interaction, whether by design or happenstance. Living your purpose is about putting a smile on someone else's face. Living your purpose encompasses using your life to motivate others to succeed, lift their spirits, enhance their business growth and improve their life's quality, their life's worth, in a meaningful manner.

There are no disqualifiers. There are no socio-economic, educational, gender or ethnic requirements to live your purpose. There is a direct connection and correlation to how your life changes for the better, when you shift your intention from working to **assist yourself** to working to **help others**. You will achieve a meteoric level of success that you never thought was obtainable. You will be amazed by how you grow into the role of a leader in your community.

2. Living a fulfilled Life.

The pursuit of happiness is a key impetus for people to change. People are willing to switch careers, hire therapists, spend thousands of dollars, attend seminars and flip their entire lives upside down in hopes of connecting with true happiness. These endeavors to "connect" with happiness often appear to resolve the issue, but connecting with real fulfillment, which is imperative to true happiness, is quite elusive. For many of us, especially with all the demands of just existing in this world, let alone what living in this world requires, achieving even a modicum of true happiness is a big struggle.

One of the most powerful ways to feel true fulfillment in life, on a daily basis, is to pursue a career that seeks to contribute, rather than to earn. Pursue a career that motivates you. Pursue a career where going to work feels like living a dream versus dreading a nightmare. This is the only way you can become truly successful.

There is no magic formula, set of procedures or secret initiation if your heart's desire is to connect with true happiness. A proven way to feel real happiness in life is finding a career that contributes to others in a positive way. A career that ignites your passion does not make you sad in any form, even when presentism sets in. The hours spent may exceed those required, yet you continue since your enthusiastic desire rekindles the strength in you.

Lock yourself to a career that you are fervent about. Use your natural abilities and talents to move people to success, fill people up with life and encourage them to feel happier. A vital ingredient for success is to commit yourself to embracing that career—your purpose—for as long as you live.

3. Your Purpose will drive you to Achieve an Exuberant Success.

To live a life of purpose, you just have to be **purpose-driven**. The most successful people in the world today are not driven by fame, power or more, they are driven by a purpose. This contradicts the belief of most people. Most claim to be driven by their desire to gain wealth, fame or fortune, but it all comes back to the purpose which ignites the flame.

The purpose to improve their socio-economic status could be the result of an impoverished childhood, or a litany of reasons, but the fact remains, purpose is by far a greater motivator than fame, status and wealth.

You don't believe me? Just try this thought process—have reflections on the following goals and try to pick out which of these ambitions would push you harder to achieving success than others:

- The pursuit of making sure that no child goes hungry or the desire to earn six figures?
- The drive to save the world from poverty and corruption or the ambition to be the most powerful person in the world?
- The desire to save a million lives or the desire to become a millionaire?

In all likelihood, there is a greater probability that the goals that are purpose-driven—like saving the world from poverty—would endow you with the requisite endurance and strength to push harder to succeed, compared to the goals that are money-driven. This is mainly because when it comes to situations that involves saving or helping others, human beings are naturally more focused . . . more determined.

The fact remains that the individuals who are focused on doing whatever it takes to assist other people – whether it's their communities or even families – always win more often than those that are just in it for themselves. These sorts of people have a proactive mindset in their actions. Their selflessness is enough to make them successful in whatever they lay their hands on. They exude the sort of achievement that can never be compared with people driven by a passion to earn more money.

The entrepreneur, who has the utmost desire to put smiles on the faces of every underprivileged student by providing each of them with laptops, will undoubtedly have more control over being successful than the entrepreneur who has the sole aim of increasing millions to billions. **It takes purpose to master the art and science of becoming successful**. It takes passion to help others, since what goes around sure has its ways of coming around. You wouldn't expect a singer who has the sole purpose of winning awards to sell at a chart-topping rate as compared to a soul singer who sings simply to inspire people across the world, to empathize or sympathize with an action or inaction for the emotions expressed during the given song.

How ambitious your purpose is serves as a prime determinant of how much you will be motivated, and this correlates with how much success you are bound to achieve.

4. Creating a Legacy that the World will never forget.

All of the world's greatest breakthroughs, artworks, contributions, innovations, achievements, accomplishments and legacies were born from purpose—invented by innovators who were keen about leaving the world better off than how they met it.

- **Steve Jobs** made it his mission to create technology when he sought purpose—touchscreen Smartphones, portable music players and personal computers—that would transform all of our lives.
- When **Martin Luther King Jr.** was searching for his own purpose, he shared a vision of a world where no one would be judged by the color of their skin, but by the content of their character.
- **Usain Bolt** established himself as the fastest man ever when he was seeking a purpose.
- **Nelson Mandela** was purpose-driven to have served and endured twenty-seven years in a South African prison, only to become the first black man to attain the nation's presidential position after his release. The history books fail to remember people for their material possessions, power, fame or wealth. A focus on leaving a legacy that lasts is more important than leaving material stuff. You will only be remembered for the positive impacts you have had on mankind, the legacies you left behind.

Creating a legacy can only be achieved by living your purpose. A Legacy may be something as simple as: a contribution that your planet, your nation, your community or your family will remember you for.

5. Peace and Serenity In The Face Of Death.

The sense of happiness, peace, success, accomplishment and serenity that you feel when your time on earth moves closer to an end is one of the greatest and most powerful benefits of Living Your Purpose.

When you have mastered success and lived a life of purpose, you can only smile back at the lives you have touched positively—the less-privileged boy for whom you paid school fees who later became a medical doctor, the crippled child you gave a second chance to live through the wheel chair you got for her, that little blind girl for whom you rekindled hope when you paid for her successful surgery, and lots more.

As people move deeper into their old age, there are some common emotions of regret that glosses over them. Many realize they have lived their whole life like a rat in an empty box, or a hamster on a wheel – following the same routine every day, till they die. So many regrets that they don't even know what they accomplished in a single life. These regrets may range from the contributions they could have added to the world (which they failed to do), about how fulfilled they could have enjoyed life but decided to taste the other side of life instead, or regrets about the lives they could have changed positively and about the places they could have gone. Maybe they even have regrets about the endless dreams they could have accomplished.

Once you fully utilize your abilities, talents and passions to serve the world, you will never grow into one of those people; and this is one of the greatest joys of living your purpose. As you lay on your deathbed, which we all will do one day, the only emotions you will feel are gratitude, peace, serenity, and happiness.

You will be able to look straight into the face of death without any form of regret whatsoever, about how you spent your life and what accomplishments you bagged, once you truly live your purpose. That alone should be a great motivation for you to stand on your feet, go out and begin to do what you were born to do.

About Lori

Lori Wagner helps her clients to birth success to the outside of what has already been gestating on the inside. Lori, a child of the 70s, and the beginning of the self-discovery movement, naturally gravitated toward not only living life abundantly but purposeful living toward her dreams, goals and aspirations. Lori began her personal journey of self-discovery as a child when her childhood comfort zone was shattered. Lori began to look within herself for strength, no longer being changed by her situation, but to change her situation in her favor. She refused to be confined by societal norms and began to seriously pursue the limits of what she could accomplish. Lori started with private research, which honed her desire for formal education in her various endeavors.

Lori is a 22-year Air Force Military Police veteran who received numerous service awards and accolades; accolades focused not only on her personal accomplishments but her infectious drive which motivated others. During this time, Lori took on one of the toughest jobs an active duty service member can do; as an enlisted accessions recruiter, she was responsible for recruiting others, during a time when war was on the horizon and our armed forces members were serving on several battlefronts. Lori's motivational abilities ensured her personal contribution was vital to the safety of our nation. Lori took her skills from the military and currently works in the private sector, helping to elevate a competitive security firm to the level of an elite working force.

Lori is the founder and driving force of Expect Success Today and Coach Lori Wagner – a motivational charter specializing in helping others live a life of purpose on purpose. Lori is also a partner of a fitness line, which helps her client's fitness dreams become a reality. Lori is an avid student of the world. Lori's travel pursuits have enabled her to better understand her clients. Lori's initial foray started as just a motivational approach to Expecting Success, and later blossomed into a holistic full spectrum approach to living a purposeful life for her clients: for financial, physical, emotional and spiritual health. She believes two of the most powerful words for self-actualization are "I AM". Lori's gift is that Lori believes if she can change the mindset of one person at a time, the contagious process will be infinitely duplicated. Lori believes a person that expects success will have thoughts, practices and procedures to be successful. Lori is a certified personal success coach, national speaker and has shared the stage with many successful speakers. Her services are sought and provided nationally and internationally. Her clients range from the common person to CEOs in the business industry. Lori is a multi-best-selling author.

Lori studied Criminal Justice at Columbia Southern University, Business Management at the University of Phoenix and holds an Associate's degree in Criminal Justice and Human Resources Management through the Community College of the Air Force. Lori enhanced her personal skills and refined her mantra of "inspiring as many as possible before expiring" by attending and becoming certified to teach Napoleon Hill's *Success Principles* and the *Law of Success*.

You can connect with Lori at:

- www.expectsuccesstoday.com
- http://facebook.com/LoriAWagner

CHAPTER 38

YOU ARE ENOUGH

BY GAGANDEEP BHATTI

For self is a sea boundless and measureless.
~ Kahlil Gibran

I am glad that we have found each other on this page, through this book, and the very fact that you are reading this is creating a personal experience that would serve you in your own special way.

I am all here with you! Applauding for everything you are today, everything you have achieved so far, every obstacle you overcame, every opinion you proved wrong, every inner-battle you won, every time you reminded yourself "just a little more" and made it so far! I APPLAUD YOU with deep respect in my heart for everything you are today in this very moment.

I believe the reason you held this book in the first place was to find something for yourself which would propel your own success. Amid the chaos of doubts, decisions, experiences, ideals, expectations, growth and learning, you are looking for what would assure you and help you reach where you want to go – to find that ultimate answer, the key, the system, the fool-proof plan, the formula that would end your maze-chasing-run to finally reach a point that you define as your success.

And I am sure you will find what you are looking for and reach your point of success. How do I know this? I know this because for a school-going girl who saved pennies from her pocket money to buy her first ever book – *A 3rd Serving of Chicken Soup for the Soul* – is today a co-author with Jack Canfield. Not only you find your point of success, but also your dreams become a reality.

Being raised in an environment where girls are treated as secondary and partial, I grew up believing the same, and that made it my experience that I am less a person as a girl and I would be better if I did everything like "boys" did. I denied my true-self, hated the fact that I was a girl, feminine and sensitive, and looked down on myself with guilt and shame. I started becoming everything that I was not. But soon I realised that everything I was doing was only taking me farther from myself and putting more power on the external elements making me helpless, rather than focusing on what I had and what I could do.

There came a moment in time where I faced everything I was hiding. It was when I was being operated for Arrhythmia under RF-Ablation (so-called small procedure. Yeah! tell that to an aspiring, ambitious 16-year-old girl who wanted to be a pilot) and I remember it like yesterday. While I was on that table and witnessing the process being carried out, I am thinking, "What if something goes wrong and I die right here? What if there is something incurable and it kills me before I ever find out? What if I walk out alive but die tomorrow in an accident? What have I done in my life? What if my plans to become a pilot, save enough money, author a book. . . never works out? When will I give my dreams a chance? What am I doing to leave this place different other than for my presence? What have I done to be making any difference, even to single life? And what if the curtain falls and I haven't even played my role as yet? Am I taking my life for granted? Am I going to create something worthwhile and play my role the best I can?"

This thought pierced my heart and a tear rolled down my cheek, and I promised myself when I walked out of this procedure, I would do SOMETHING so people would understand how precious their lives are – so that they would play their best and brightest roles in life. That's when I decided to pursue my dream of writing and speaking, serving people with my drive to motivate and empower them to live their fullest potential, and to create the life they were designed for.

In the process of doing this, I stopped being what I was not and started being what I am. It took some time to fully accept my femininity, to accept that I am ENOUGH in every way. I completely, absolutely, unapologetically fell in love with myself – just the way it was supposed to be from the beginning.

I did not become the pilot I was aspiring to be. Instead, I became a therapist, coach, speaker and an author that I intended to be. I found myself, my truest being, empowered with purpose to fulfil that I could no longer hold inside, to share my learning and raise awareness about the power of a true being filled with love and aligned with my own purpose. On this journey to find myself, I discovered my potential hidden under layers of conditioning of my belief-system. I reconnected with my inner-light, rekindled my self-love with an unconditional acceptance of my graceful powers. I found freedom! Today, I am living the dream I always dreamt of with abundance, love, and most of all, being myself—truly and unapologetically. That is what my success is, to live a contented life knowing I am fulfilling my purpose and mission daily.

And you can do the same! You too can claim your success, turn your dreams into reality and live a life that you keep waiting for. When you would know what you are made of, you would never spend a moment doubting the majesty you can create! With my learning and realisation – through my journey of self-love and personal success – I have framed a simple routine that you can model to create ever-lasting success in whatever you choose.

By integrating studies from different fields, I conclude that LIFE is basically comprised of three spheres centring around YOU.

1. *You as Within...*
2. *You as Interpretation...*
3. *You as Expression...*

These three spheres combined become the whole YOU. After all, Success without You [U] is a bunch of s'ccess. Utterly meaningless. Each of these spheres make your life what it is today. All the experiences that come to you are all part of this. Once you master the art of utilizing these spheres in accordance, success will manifest itself like magic.

1. <u>*You as Within*</u> – Is the You who exists even without your name or your identity. This part of you is that part which knows that you

are you and none other – like a truth. Regardless of your looks, gender, colour of your skin, place where you come from or language you speak, this part of you asserts the talent, gifts, skill, ability, the expertise and the unique way for you to be of service to the world. This part of you knows what your purpose is, what you are here for, what you have to do, what role you play and what feels right. This is the part of you which shows up in times of need and takes you by surprise – as you never knew this part ever existed within you – in the moments when you say, "Was that me?" or, "How did I pull it off?" or, "It's unbelievable how I could endure all this." or, "Something inside kept me telling to do so." and many more that are part of you within.

This is you, powered with purpose and a force of unlimited resources, infinite in nature. This is You as Within – Infinite and Limitless! Infinite and Limitless in Love, Wisdom, Power, Strength, Courage, Confidence and everything that you would ever require. You have all the resources within. Period.

When you know this as a fact and believe in yourself – like an undeniable occurrence of your existence in the present moment is beyond knowing and faith. This is accepting and honouring who you truly are – *Self-Love*, mounting from an unconditional acceptance of yourself. For *Self-Love* is the virtue of the Courageous. And that, my friend, is an unfathomable element needed to succeed in life.

2. *You as Interpretation* – Is everything and anything that you have defined, classified, comprehended, learnt and accepted into your own mind with your own set of explanations, and given them their own meaning with the intensity of the emotions they carried for you in the precise moment when it occurred, and that you registered as your own interpretation of happening. Interpretation about yourself, world and life.

This also comprises the beliefs you have incorporated in your growing-up, in your experiences so far, from your parents, grandparents or any authority figure, from your religious community, friends, society and environment, and from everything that you have been ever subjected to so far!

This interpretation in your head is derived from your thinking pattern, and in return is generating the parallel-thinking pattern for the new endeavours you step into. The reality you are living is a cause-effect of your thoughts and how you channel it and its head-hitting alarming truth that, "THOUGHTS CREATE REALITIES."

If you want to change your reality, start changing your thoughts about it. Start questioning every belief you believe in, if it resonates with your present truth, keep it. If it does not, change it.
Check every definition you gave to each episode of emotion in your life. Does it serve true for your growth? If needed, create new beliefs for yourself, for your growth. These beliefs do not have to pass any test other than, "Is it serving your highest good?" and is not deliberately harming others. This "interpretation" part of you is steering the vehicle of your life. The clearer, sharper and simpler the interpretation, the smother your ride would be.

3. *You as Expression* – Every or any act that you do or do not do is the You as expressing yourself in that present moment. Your behaviour is direct expression of what you are doing and not doing. This counts every decision you are making based on your "interpretations". Every moment in life, you are expressing through your actions, behaviour, physical body, your health even while you are thinking or sleeping you are expressing a part of you – creating a ripple effect in your life. Every action you take or do not take is based on calculated thoughts coming from your interpretation and you are "acting" it out through your behaviour, choices, decisions, doing, not doing, etc.

The audacity of every action that you take decides your results. Expressing fully, doing what you are inspired to, taking action and responsibility in creating as you desire, is your true nature as the *You* in *Expression*.

When you recognize these three spheres of life and set and execute your goals in accordance, your goals will manifest naturally, easily and joyfully.

To summarize:

1. Set your Intention behind Goals – from a place of knowing that you are powered by limitless and infinite resources and anything is possible. This automatically activates your resourcefulness, keeping you fuelled.
2. Write down the list of your "interpretations" and beliefs with respect to the above Goals. Keep the ones which serve you, chalk out the ones which do not serve you, and make new ones to support you.
3. Take Action. Attain *Inspired Expression* in your behaviour for your goals – creative visualisations, vision boards, goal planners, etc. Even a small step in the direction of your goals is significant.

And, when you want something, all the universe conspires
in helping you to achieve it.
~ Paulo Coelho

When you align your true self with your purpose and set goals with it, the right things will show-up, you will come across the right people, the opportunities will come your way, you will find an unstoppable energy pulling you towards your goal and soon you will realise your goals. Your dreams will become your reality!

You are beyond any doubt, situation or experience. None of these ever define who you truly are. Your true being is the one that is Unconditional Love – Infinite and Limitless in resources and wisdom.

You are enough to make that call, take that decision, accept that promotion, ask him/her on date, to dress like that, be successful, become a legend, become author or speaker, be a dancer, teacher, painter, musician or even for a noble prize. You are enough even when you make mistakes, you are enough to learn more, grow and be better.

You are Capable enough, Strong enough, Intelligent enough, Wise enough, Loved enough, Creative enough, Smart enough, Kind enough and Powerful enough.

You are Enough the way you are.

You are more than enough for your dreams. Your dreams are waiting for you.

You are ENOUGH. Let's Begin. NOW!

About Gagandeep

Gagandeep Bhatti empowers her clients to *live to their fullest potential to lead an abundance-filled life.* She believes that every individual has all the resources within, the wisdom to resolve any problem, and the power to make any desire into reality.

Being the firstborn to her parents and the eldest of three sisters, she calls herself fortunate and most loved. She describes her sisters as life-support and her parents as a power-house. She claims receiving the strong traits of entrepreneurship from her father, dedication and humility from her mother, both of whom stood against all odds to support their daughters – proving there is no force stronger than love.

Gagandeep works with a basic philosophy of understanding "Why we do what we do." and "How can we do better?" She emphasizes raising self-awareness that help people identify their truth which is liberating and the solution to many problems in life. She believes all of us have a reservoir of limitless resources within, and she helps her clients to find a clear map to channel these resources appropriately to achieve what they desire.

She naturally connects and understands her clients uncovering their deepest issues, recognizing the underlying cause of the surface problems, and assisting them to break through those hidden patterns to step into their own resourcefulness. She helps rekindle the touch of their own excellence, for everybody is equally special in their unique truth.

She coaches people to realize their fullest potential, to re-ignite their light within, to add meaning to their lives, to bring them closer to their true being – of limitless power, infinite resources and unconditional acceptance with love – so that they can create the life they dream of. In her words, "There is an ultimate high when one experiences their true potential. And even if only once, anyone who tastes this ecstasy of their own inner-excellence cannot go back unchanged."

She loves to work with people who want to fall in love with life doing what they love and to create a healthy balance between every dimension of life.

Gagandeep Bhatti is a National Speaker, Licensed NLP Practitioner, Life Coach, Hypnotherapist and Past-life Regression Therapist. She holds a Master's Degree in Counselling Psychology. She has integrated experience of seven-plus years serving clients – from students and youngsters to executive managers and elite personalities from different walks of life. Gagandeep has addressed thousands in her workshops. She has been interviewed and featured in a national educational magazine. Gagandeep is also an elite member of The National Association of Experts, Writers & Speakers.

She has a passion for reading, travelling, meeting strangers and chatting over a cup of tea. She loves to share insights and experiences about life, meta-physics, and spirituality. All in all, she has an undying quest for learning and growing.

You can connect with Gagandeep at:

- contact@gagandeepbhatti.com
- www.facebook.com/authorGagandeepBhatti
- Instagram Id: @thesoulbearer

CHAPTER 39

FOLLOW YOUR SOUL'S BLUEPRINT TO SUCCESS

BY ZOË

Your soul's blueprint will guide you to live a successful life. We all have a particular palette of colors and flavors of source energy, in a perfect composition of the expression of the Divine. You have a unique energy specific for you and your soul's vibration. In business, you can create your energy brand by finding your soul's vibration, which complies with your blueprint to success. Use your soul's vibration as a marketing tool and it will lead you to untouchable success. By using the energy techniques of Soul Vibration Marketing and Be an Attractive Magnet™, you will emanate a strong signal of your soul's vibration to the world. Magical results will be created in your business and in your life in general.

Your blueprint to success

Your soul's vibration contains all the contracts you have signed up for before you incarnated. It is the blueprint for this lifetime. It helps you to stay on the right track in accordance with the agreements you made with yourself before coming here.

The blueprint is your roadmap to success using the soul's vibration in your heart as your compass. Walking on your soul's true path will automatically give you a successful life, because you are following what you came here to achieve. My definition of success is a joyful feeling of wellbeing. It can never be measured in the amount of money or things, although a high living standard is very often the result of following the soul's true path.

The strongest indication that you are living in accordance with your blueprint, is when your heart is singing with joy. You will always be successful when you stick to the blueprint of your soul. Following your heart's biggest excitement is the easiest way to bring you in alignment with your soul's vibration.

Soul Vibration Marketing – People buy the experience of your soul

Traditional marketing strategies tell you to investigate the market for your products and services, and to adjust to the demand of it. Let me just re-wire your brain for a second.

The world needs you and your unique palette of vibrations. The world needs a version of you that is your fullest you. You, with your unique soul's vibration, are here for a reason, and your piece fits perfectly into the puzzle of the Creation.

Using your magical soul's vibration as a powerful strategic marketing tool is a completely new way of selling. What people are buying is the experience of your soul's vibration and what that energy will contribute to in their lives. It is through your soul's vibration that people will be drawn to your services and products. To spread your message on a larger scale and to attract more customers and clients to your business, you want to emanate a strong signal of your soul's vibration. The right people, clients, customers, circumstances, colleagues, business partners and situations will then come to you with ease.

Your soul's vibration is your strongest marketing tool. It is by using your own energy that you master the art of success. The beauty of Soul Vibration Marketing is that there is no competition. Your cosmic facet of perfection cannot be intruded into by anyone else's facet. We all play an equally important and unique role in the whole of Creation.

The purpose of your soul

Realizing that there is a meaning to your life, a purpose for your soul, is the first step to success. A life plan, with so-called soul contracts, is set up before incarnation and acts as a perfect guideline on your life's journey.

Your life plan is a rough outline of the experiences you want to develop, the karma you want to solve, the lessons to learn and your greater purpose.

The starting point of my success was the epiphany of remembering that my soul had a purpose, and it threw me right to the core of my success. In a session, I was guided to a state of consciousness where I remembered the moment just before I incarnated. I saw myself in a meeting with the High Council and my Spirit guide, discussing this life. They assisted me in making my life plan – my soul contracts – for this incarnation.

In 2011, my soul called upon me to fully step into my purpose, and listen to my deepest calling. I took a leap of faith, quit my day job and pursued a spiritual career. The red carpet rolled out for me when I finally started listening to the unique energy of my own soul. My whole life changed. TV started calling, magazines published articles about me and a huge number of clients and customers signed up for sessions and classes.

The misled sensitive soul

We are all affected by our environment, and your soul's purpose can be suppressed if you adjust too much to your surroundings instead of following your heart's calling. It happened to me.

I was born with the gift to read other people's energies, to see through the facade and look in to their souls. Before my gift became my job, it was more like a curse, and at the same time the biggest lesson for my soul in this lifetime. I felt the feelings of other people and the situation became extreme when I started making their anger, sadness and fear into my own feelings. As a child, I frequently acted out other people's emotions in my numerous tantrums. My sensitivity made me an expert in adjusting to my surroundings, and my social chameleon skills transformed my powerful unique soul into a transparent pale copy. As a young girl, I had lost contact with my own soul.

Being disconnected from my soul and not following the song of my heart, got me into trouble. Once, I almost lost my life because of my disconnection. I followed a friend's advice, even though my whole body screamed "No!" and I ended up in a very dangerous situation. That was a wake-up call for me.

I got sick of playing the marionette of a victim, placing my power in the hands of others. I had been walking further and further away from my soul's truth – I was misled, moving down the road of non-success.

In retrospect, I can clearly see how perfectly this was lined up for me to learn my greatest lesson in this incarnation: To come home to self-empowerment.

Incarnate fully to feel your soul's purpose

To be able to live your true purpose, your soul needs to fully incarnate in your body. If your soul is hovering around you, your body can feel disconnected and not in harmony with the world. There are many reasons to why this can happen. One reason can be that the body is vibrating at a low frequency, due to pollution, food additives or feelings of anger, fear and depression. If the soul vibrates with a much higher frequency than the body, they cannot fuse. You are not fully incarnated and you feel disconnected.

The soul can disconnect itself from the body if trauma occurs, for example, in the event of death of a family member or a car accident. When the body is under stress, the soul will have a problem to incarnate fully, and thereby the fulfillment of the purpose of the soul is prevented.

Even though I had listened to my deepest calling, and I knew that my soul had signed up for different missions in this lifetime which I was here to complete, there was a slight problem: my soul wasn't fully incarnated in my body. My soul and my body were not connected and not collaborating in the same realm.

The main reason my soul wasn't fully incarnated was because I did not like to be on this harsh planet. The energies were too rough for my sensitive soul. My heart's delicate openness picked up the violent energies. To save myself, my soul checked out and disconnected from my body.

The urge of my soul to fuse with my body, to be able to fulfill its purpose, became very strong. I was thrown right into a process of acceptance. I had to accept that I was born on earth to prepare for the soul to incarnate fully. I remember the moment when I called upon my soul to come down and fully merge with my physical body. I felt the energy of my soul fully present in me. It was such a strong feeling, a totally new experience for me.

To stay in alignment with your soul's vibration can be challenging when your environment, friends, family and society, is not in vibrational coherence with your soul. My old habit of adjusting tempted me to live my life according to other people's opinions instead of following my own. Luckily my inner knowing always pointed towards my heart and reminded me to stick to my unique soul's path.

The power of a strong heart connection

The vastness of your divine soul resides in your heart. The easiest way to cultivate the contact with your soul, and to feel its vibration, is to be in total connection with your heart. This made me develop the Heart Meditation. By holding your hands on your heart and dwelling in the deepest place within you, your holy temple in your heart, you can feel your soul's unique vibration. The holy temple where the soul resides is placed deep within the heart. This is the place, the holy space, where the song of the soul is the strongest.

The Heart Meditation helps you to stay in conscious connection with your soul's vibration in your everyday life. Feel the vibration of your soul through the contact with your hands on your heart.

Once the contact with your soul through your heart has been established, the only thing you can do is to follow your soul's purpose. Every time you try to go in a different direction than your highest good, you can feel a hurtful squeeze in your core. It becomes impossible to deviate from your soul's path and to fulfill your soul's purpose, once you have a strong connection with your soul's vibration.

When you know how your own soul feels like, you can easily distinguish it from other energies. If the energies of other people, circumstances and situations differ from yours, it is an indication of misalignment with your soul's path.

Be an Attractive Magnet™ – Energy techniques to quantum leap your success

Be an Attractive Magnet™ is a set of energy techniques that will amplify your attractive energy, to boost your success with the Law of Attraction to levels you never thought possible. I developed the concept of Be an Attractive Magnet™ in collaboration with my Spirit guide and other entities in the higher spiritual realms. The super-efficient energy techniques are easy and quick ways to boost your attractive energies and to accelerate your success.

As the Law of Attraction states, like attracts like, your aim is to vibrate with the frequency corresponding to the energy of what you would like to attract into your life. It might be the frequency of money. To become a totally vibrating magnet, as Be an Attractive Magnet™ implies, your whole being needs to vibrate with the specific frequency of your choice.

When working with Be an Attractive Magnet™ you follow these simple steps to boost your attractive energy:

1. Find the frequency of what you would like to attract

The first step is to find the specific vibration of the object, the situation or the event you would like to attract. You find the specific vibration through visualizing that you have already reached your goal. If you want to attract money, you visualize that you have a lot of money and feel that feeling, you will find the frequency of money and this is the vibration you want to continue working with in the next step.

2. Amplify the attractive frequency

You now use the frequency, the feeling you found in the first step and apply different energy techniques. In this way, you will amplify this attractive energy to the maximum, so that you will become a totally vibrating magnet. In one of the techniques you place the frequency of your choice in the area between your heart and your solar plexus. Then you create a swirl of that energy around that area. By continuing to rotate the energy, you make it bigger and bigger, until your whole body and your electric magnetic field will be totally soaked with your preferred frequency. You will be a totally vibrating magnet!

Soul Vibration Marketing – Marinate your business with your soul's vibration

When working with Soul Vibration Marketing, you focus on the frequency of your soul – your soul's unique vibration. When you amplify your soul's vibration you are sending out a super-strong signal of your blueprint, and everything that is in alignment with your soul's purpose will magically come to you and lead you to your success.

There are many ways that you can continue to work consciously with your soul's vibration, in your business and in your life in general.

When I was starting my business, I became overwhelmed with the amount of work it took to market my products and services. This experience led me to develop my energy brand using my soul's vibration. Even today, I magically use the energy of my soul to increase the spreading of my work and my message to the world. I charge all my products and services with my soul's vibration. I marinate my flyers, Facebook events and posters with my energy brand. I attract clients and participants to my workshops and events, as well as co-workers and business partners. These energy techniques boosted my career to the maximum.

Five steps to your Soul's Super Successful Business:

1. Incarnate your soul fully
2. Find your soul's vibration within your heart
3. Use powerful energy techniques to amplify your soul's vibration
4. Marinate your business with your energy brand
5. Follow your heart´s excitement

Do what you came here to do, be who you came here to be.

Follow Your Soul's Blueprint to Success!

About Zoë

Zoë, known from the Swedish successful TV-show, *Life on the Other Side*, is one of Scandinavia's most active spiritual teachers. She is a very sought after healer, psychic coach, yoga teacher and workshop leader. Zoë gives classes and sessions all over the world.

Zoë has a M.Sc. in Neurochemistry from the University of Stockholm and the Medical University – Karolinska Institute, and she has worked within the field of research of DNA vaccines and Alzheimer's disease at Karolinska Hospital and AstraZeneca.

Zoë runs her successful company, Zoëland, aiming to support her clients in finding the superpower within themselves, using her own magical tools and techniques.

Zoë is constantly developing new workshops and modalities. She has created the unique concept *Be an Attractive Magnet*™ together with her Spirit guide and other entities in 2009. *Be an Attractive Magnet*™ is a deep and powerful energy work that makes the users quantum leap their success with the Law of Attraction to a level of super-manifestation. It contains energy clearings to remove blocks to avoid unwanted results, and many energy techniques to amplify the attractive energy to the maximum. She helps entrepreneurs boost their businesses with the magical energy techniques of *Soul Vibration Marketing*.

As a Psychic Coach, she supports her clients through guidance from higher spiritual realms, reading their soul's vibration and helping them to connect with their Star families.

During the years of working as a healer, Zoë has developed her own healing modality – Nordic Light Healing, containing extremely high frequencies. She performs extraordinary powerful healing and achieves great results, using her X-ray sight which reveals injuries and imbalances on physical, emotional, spiritual and mental levels. With her knowledge about the body's energy field, Zoë can move, repair, clear and re-create the energy field – which can then manifest in physical form.

Thousands of people have taken part in her DNA activations and are using her crystal pendant programmed with The Golden Frequency, to upgrade their DNA. In *Atlantean Crystal Technology*, Zoë uses the same advanced crystal programming techniques as she did in Atlantis.

Zoë has her own educational program to develop the psychic abilities in "Zoë's Psychic School in the New Era", and the classes called "Light Gatherings" aim to support people in the Ascension process.

For many years, Zoë worked as a professional singer and songwriter performing in the Swedish version of the Eurovision Song Contest with her song, "Hollywood-Do" and has toured with Andrea Bocelli. Zoë studied music at the music schools Adolf Fredrik and Kungsholmens Gymnasium in Stockholm and Berklee College of Music in Boston.

Zoë spreads unconditional love and work with very high frequencies, which makes her a unique experience. She sees the potential of total self-empowerment and the expression of the Divine Power within everyone she meets.

Connect with Zoë and her team:

- www.zoeland.org (English)
- www.zoeland.se (Swedish)
- www.facebook.com/ZoeLightworkerENG (English)
- www.facebook.com/ZoeLightworker (Swedish)
- www.instagram.com/zoelightworker

CHAPTER 40

SHATTERED! THE MARATHON I NEVER SIGNED UP TO RUN

BY JENNIFER KAUFFMAN

What is success anyway? I used to believe success meant achieving your greatest dreams and goals in life, but sometimes life throws you an unexpected – even horrific – curve ball. After being hit by that so-called curve ball, I now see that even the smallest win can be a huge victory on the path to success.

April 15, 2013 was a day I would never have expected in a million years and is now a day I will never forget! My dear friend, Muriel, asked me to join her watch her son, Dan, run Boston for the first time. Despite being an athlete and living in the Boston area my entire life, I'd never had the desire to be anywhere near the Marathon.

Little did I know how inspiring the Boston Marathon would be or that I would need tissues. Tears of amazement and joy streamed down my face as I watched these brave men and women tackle the course. From the military in uniform with 50 lb. packs strapped on their backs to the elite (*blink and you'd miss them*) to the disabled with prosthetics and even some blind runners; nearly 7,000 runners whooshed right by us in waves about every 18 minutes.

We saw Dan in one of those waves through the sea of people, and we decided to venture into Boston to see him cross the finish line. We settled in front of Marathon Sports near the finish line. We could tell he was approximately a 1/2 mile out. I remember music playing in the background, the announcer calling out names as runners were crossing, and the crowd was electrifying. It was such an awe-inspiring experience. Then all of a sudden out of nowhere, I heard an extremely loud boom, which was followed by a moment of complete silence. In fact, you could hear the shattered glass behind us hitting the ground. I heard a woman yell "That must have been a canon," but the announcer was no longer announcing and the music stopped. The cheers of joy turned into screams for help, kids screaming—crying at the top of their lungs. I began to realize that I smelled something awful and there was smoke all around us. As I lifted myself off the ground, I turned to my left and saw people lying on the ground in a pool of blood. I continued to look around and noticed the windows were blown out of the building directly behind me! My left ear was in excruciating pain. I turned back towards Muriel and said, "We need to get out of here." She said, "I can't leave without Dan." By this time the second explosion had gone off and that's when I knew it was a terrorist attack. I grabbed Muriel's shirt and said we must go now! She was frozen!

We made it a few blocks away when I realized I didn't have my cell phone. I lost it! The thoughts racing through my head were, "How are we going to get out of here alive?" "How can I get a hold of my family when I don't remember their phone numbers off the top of my head?" At this point, Muriel was frantically trying to contact her son, but there was no answer. She didn't want to leave for fear her son might need her help. I couldn't comfort her and I struggled to convince her we had to find safety and to trust her son would be able to find safety for himself. I asked if I could use her phone. I paused for a moment to see if I could recall anyone's phone number. Then I realized my sisters' cell phone number resembles our childhood landline number. I called and she didn't answer so I left a voicemail message. Then I frantically called 411 (information) to get my mom's home phone number. I got her voicemail too! I was heartbroken that I could not reach my family. At this point, we were approximately a half mile from the finish line and all you could hear were sirens and people screaming. It was horrendous! Knowing I wouldn't be able to

Success Tip

TRUST your own instincts even when everyone around you may have different opinions.

get to my car – which was parked on the other side of the finish line – I thought to myself, "What do we do now?"

Growing up, my mom worked as an emergency management director and she was responsible for managing evacuation plans if anything ever happened to the Pilgrim Nuclear Power Station, approximately 15 miles from where I grew up. She used to go over our own evacuation plan often, and I would habitually brush it off as not that important. I had no idea that her periodically going over these plans would help me get out of this horrific situation.

We walked for approximately 45-minutes. During our walk, my sister called back and was able to give me my aunt's phone number so I could call her for help as she worked in Cambridge. I called my aunt and then I began to realize something was seriously wrong. I started to feel light-headed and nauseous and my abdominal area started to swell like a balloon. We were near the Museum of Science in Cambridge. She said it would take too long to get an ambulance, so to get into a cab and go to Cambridge Hospital ASAP. We got to the hospital and I immediately went to the bathroom and got sick. I managed to get myself out of the bathroom, and one of the ER greeters asked me for my name and why I was there. When I told her we were at the finish line when a bomb went off, she immediately rushed me into the ER. I barely made it to a room when a flood of nurses and doctors came rushing in. I was shaking so bad several of them were holding me down so I wouldn't fall off the bed.

Shortly after arriving at the hospital, my aunt, a nurse practitioner, met us. By now I had my first of a battery of tests and they were closely monitoring my heart rate which was off the charts. I remember one of the nurses saying, "She could be having a heart attack." I was terrified! I had no idea what was wrong with me and I had no idea if I was going to live to see another day.

> **Success Tip**
>
> **_LET GO!_** Simply walk away peacefully from anything that does not feel right or is not supportive, uplifting and loving.

Unfortunately, my experience at the hospital ended up being traumatic too! Looking back, I realize the doctors and nurses were scared too! The truth was they were doing the best they could for me. Yet the more time I was in the ER the more my anxiety soared. I remembered hearing a quiet voice in my head that said, "You must learn how to heal naturally." I had no idea why I was hearing this message and I certainly had no idea how to heal naturally. I wasn't sure what was going on, let alone if I would even make it.

As I was lying in the bed waiting for the test results to come back, I realized I was in excruciating pain. I felt shattered, literally! I felt like a hole was blown through my stomach, my body was shaking profusely from the neck down yet the doctors couldn't figure out what was wrong with me. The doctors wanted me to get admitted and I refused. I wanted out! I begged my aunt to let me go home with her, knowing I would be in good hands and if I needed I could get rushed back to the hospital.

As the days and sleepless nights progressed, I was filled with tremendous FEAR! I feared for my life. I feared for our country. I had what they call survivor's guilt. It's where you silently wish you had died that day. I was in so much pain and had no idea how I would ever recover, let alone naturally. Then, one by one, God sent me signs and messages of hope. It started with my psychologist from years past agreeing to work with me again when she wasn't taking new patients. Within a day of the bombing, I was in Immersion therapy. Then a friend put me in touch with her chiropractor who had a pro-adjuster device – a gentle tapping device to help treat my neck and back injuries so I could walk normally again.

Success Tips

FEAR Face Everything And Rise!

ASK for what you need and watch how the Universe responds!

GRATITUDE Foster an attitude of gratitude.

I have been blessed to work with many amazing men and women whom I didn't know prior to the bombings. Each one of them has been extraordinary in teaching me how to heal 100% naturally. I am tremendously grateful these people were put onto my path to help me. I literally owe them my life! I can honestly say I have found a natural way to heal my physical, emotional and spiritual injuries. . .everything from Chiropractic, Acupuncture, whole-food nutrition, Brain Integration therapy, Sound therapy, Pranic healing and Neuro- Emotional Technique to EMDR, just to name a few.

Two years into my healing journey, I was faced with a choice. . .to prepare a Victim Impact Statement and read it in front of the court. I knew I had to write it and yet I didn't feel ready to face the entire impact. . .the financial impact, the emotional impact on me and my family and the physical impact. As I began to write my statement I was flooded with rage and profound sadness. In those dark moments I was faced with a choice to forgive the terrorists or not. Forgive the terrorists? I thought initially, "No way!" but then I began to understand what it really means to "forgive." Forgiveness is not about the other person(s), it is about YOU letting go and no longer being a "victim." Forgiveness allows you to move forward. It is the key ingredient to creating peace within oneself. It took all the courage I had to look the surviving terrorist in the eye while in court and genuinely forgive him. It was a major turning point in my healing. For the first time in two years, I began to feel more at peace and I felt better!

Success Tips

FORGIVE those that hurt you so YOU can move forward in peace!

SET BOUNDARIES Just because you forgive someone doesn't mean you let them back into your life!

After 3-1/2 years I am finally strong enough to break my silence. I am in the process of writing my first book about my journey to bring awareness of healing naturally. Since I began to write about my journey, it has become very clear that in order to come full circle I must participate in the Boston Marathon. Let's be clear that I am not a runner and yet it weighs heavily on my heart that in order to finish my healing process, I must cross that finish line—I am now training to do the April 17, 2017, Boston Marathon. The training is grueling and I am reminded every day as I venture out for a workout that I

Success Tip

MINDSET The power of belief. For me it was believing I would find a way to heal 100% naturally.

am still recovering from the copious amounts of injuries I suffered as a result of the bombings, but this too will make me healthier and stronger!

After being smacked in the face by that proverbial curve ball, I now see even the smallest win can be a huge victory on the path to success like being able to walk again. Celebrate all wins - big or small! It is also important to notice the "gifts" or the good in every situation…even a terrorist attack in my case. Sounds outrageous, right? – but it is like digging for gold. You've got to sift through lots of dirt and rock to find it, but when you do, it is just as valuable as gold. It takes patience and persistence, but never give up until you can find the "gifts." I am all about having fun, so for me it helped to think of it like an adventure or treasure hunt. Achieving success requires a lot of hard work and determination. The bottom line is:

Never Give Up!

About Jennifer

On April 15, 2013, Jennifer Kauffman was standing approximately 15 feet from the finish line bombing at the 117th Boston Marathon. Three people died suddenly that day, while two others lost their lives tragically in days and months later. At least 264 people were seriously injured from the bombings. She was one of those people. Jennifer was hospitalized, but despite the Dr.'s advice to stay, she refused. Why you ask? The doctors were struggling to figure out all that was happening with Jennifer. Her stay at the hospital was also traumatic, so she chose to leave to be with her family and to find a way to heal her "invisible" physical and emotional injuries alternatively.

Jennifer was at the height of her career...she had just come off her best year in business – recently signed a publishing deal with Balboa Press to launch her first book when life threw her an unexpected and horrific curve ball. She literally felt shattered as a result of the bombings. She suffered from ear, neck, back and internal injuries. None of her major systems (cardiovascular, circulatory, respiratory, digestive, nervous, endocrine, skeletal, muscle and immune) were working properly or in sync with one another. She has battled chronic pain for nearly three years. Jennifer has been on a quest to find a way to heal naturally and to share her experience with others.

Anyone who knows Jennifer knows that she is an unstoppable woman who seeks to create breakthroughs for herself and others to achieve a life that is filled with health, wealth, happiness and love. She is passionate about teaching others how to create breakthroughs for themselves.

Jennifer's career includes owning and operating her own business, a consulting and coaching firm called **The Results Group** since 2007, as well as leadership roles at Scudder Investments, DST Output and State Street Bank. At Hobbs|Maddison, she worked as a management/technology consultant with Bank of America and The Hartford Group where she led complex business process redesign initiatives for high-net worth and brokerage clients, merger and conversion projects, as well as technology strategy and development projects.

In 2011, Jennifer was awarded the Stars 40 Under 40 award as an emerging leader in her community. She became a member of the John Maxwell Founders Circle in June 2011. Jennifer holds a Master's degree in Innovation and Technology in Business from Boston University; a Bachelor of Science degree in Economics with a minor in Accounting from the University of Massachusetts, Boston; certifications in Pension & Employee Benefits from Bentley College and Business Process Improvement. She is currently writing her first book about her journey of healing naturally from the Boston Marathon bombings, which is expected to be published in 2017.

Jennifer enjoys spending quality time with family and friends, traveling the world, outdoor activities, attending transformational seminars and workshops, reading and writing, as well as giving back to charitable organizations that make a profound difference in the lives of others.

CHAPTER 41

THE POWER OF SELF-AWARENESS

BY SZILARD KOOS

We all want to live fully, and enjoy a productive life; but many times, we just do not know where to begin.

- I clinically died very young at the age of four.
- Playing any kind of sport was forbidden when I was a child.
- My first love relationship ended due to infidelity.
- The love of my life did not even notice me and chose my best friend.
- My first business went bankrupt after two years.
- At the age of 30, I was working 10-12 hour shifts, 28 days a month, after which I also cleaned the place for extra income.

Train wreck, right? I can imagine you going back to check the title of the book to ascertain you are still reading something about *Mastering the Art of Success*. How do these jumbles add up, you ask? Now, let me disclose to you some other details from another perspective:

I received a wonderful second chance at life when I was miraculously brought back to life after a clinical death. My health condition deprived me of being physically active, so I was resigned to always play the goalkeeper and I did 'a hell of a job' winning multiple trophies as one. Then one year, my best friend broke up with his girlfriend. This girlfriend happened to be my love interest. By means of a very effective romantic approach, she initiated a relationship between us. We got married and still live a wonderful, peaceful and loving life with our son and dog.

When faced with a financial crisis in 2008, we moved to Austria and started everything anew. I eventually became the CEO of a company I previously cleaned for extra cash and started several other new businesses, some of which generate 7-figure revenues.

In a nutshell, I was transformed from that dead, health-impaired, failed businessman, insecure lover, and struggling breadwinner to a multiple-trophy holder, thriving businessman, and a happily-married man. I experienced a shift 'from rags to riches.'

How did this happen?

THE PROBLEM WAS. . .

Circumstances do not change by just willing it away. Something must have led to my positive transition. This "something" could only have come from me, and not from my surroundings. While I do not intend to sound cliché, I still must add that a larger percentage of any changes you desire are under your control. I wanted to be successful very badly. I wanted to experience success with the associated feelings of happiness and satisfaction.

In my quest to unlock the mysteries of success, I had my head bent over several personal development books. One of the books I picked up suggested spending 10% of my time reading any spiritual book. I was pointed to Eckhart Tolle's – *The Power of Now*. This book laid bare the problem to me – perception.

You could see life from many perspectives, but the perspective you choose redefines the way you view the world. This worldview informs your attitude, which in turn influences your attitude in life. Until the age of 33, I only **focused on my intelligence** and was **only interested in materialistic visions and goals**. Now, these boldly-highlighted texts are the two success-unfriendly perceptions very much present, and played definite roles in the low life that characterised my earlier life.

The major problem is the perception of yourself. You think your rational mind (head intelligence) is all that is needed to succeed. Either you are not aware that there is more to you than your logical (mind) and physical (body) entities or you attach so little importance to your third entity. Are you familiar with that feeling of "knowing" without even knowing how you know them? Have you ever experienced that little voice in the back of your mind that says. . . *"Don't take that deal, invest in that stock, don't take this path today."*? These "feelings" come from somewhere – your third entity: the soul. Neglecting this primal entity is causal to many people's tales of woe.

The (lack of) involvement of the third entity reverberates through every area of life. Until I began to make room for my third entity, my idea of success was warped. As with many people, it centered around the achievement of materialistic goals. I wanted to acquire land and properties, own heavy bank accounts, drive the latest cars, and all that. Having these goals are not bad. The problem is that I felt I could not be happy until I achieved these goals. I did not realize that the high point of a truly successful person is finding happiness every step all the way.

There is so much power wrought in our soul, and connecting with it regularly brings the success we crave. Every human's innate desire is to experience satisfaction and happiness. But how we interpret and aim to achieve these desires are areas where many get it wrong. Success is not a destination but a **journey**. So, if your success is set around abundance, earthly goods, cars, etc., you might not truly live (enjoy satisfaction and happiness) because these earthly goods and standards keep changing. To keep up, you will be locked in the 'forever loop' of acquiring more and more. With that new knowledge, I set an extraordinary goal: **To be happy every minute of my life**. This goal is achievable, even for the rational mind. You only need to connect regularly with *your higher self.* Furthermore, this opens exciting new doors which lead to bold and very interesting, "hidden" areas of life such as enlightenment, the law of attraction, the God within and so on.

THE SOLUTION

Every time we feel exposed, weak, fragile and influenced by greater things than ourselves, we tend to look up for a solution. Some actually move their heads up to look to the skies and search or pray to a deity. Others find mentors or masters who have the answers they seek and look up to these persons. One way or another, we get the answer from these beings that the solution lies within ourselves. And then the real exciting journey begins. We still look up for the answer, but this time, we are searching for it in the right place – our **higher selves**.

Many theories see the human being as a trinity of the body, mind and soul; yet a number of us still fail to acknowledge this third layer. How does the body, the mind and the soul come together?

The known theory about body, mind and soul still paints an abstract picture of the soul and spiritualism. One needs a logical explanation acceptable to the mind, otherwise it will dismiss it with contempt or be afraid of it. These are very normal reactions. It is the same as if a two-dimensional being would need to understand a third dimension.

I intend pointing you to your higher being through one of the simpler languages that the intelligent mind understands quite well: math, or in this case, **basic geometry**. I place these three parts of yourself in the realm of **dimensions** rather than side by side or inside one another. I believe it will start making sense automatically as soon as you see yourself this way.

Let us call the body/mind way a 2-dimensional perspective and the body/mind/soul a 3-dimensional perspective.

Your first dimension – the body – moves on the line of **space-time**. The body simply moves on the x-coordinate with a birth date and an expiration date. The origin, point 0 is your birth date and place. The positive side (+x) is your life, and it is finite. I do not want to get into my views about the negative part (-x) of it (the time before you were born) in this chapter – that is another exciting theoretical journey.

**FIRST
DIMENSION**

-X

origin
(birth date and place)

+X

Then, your second dimension – the mind – feels, thinks and decides in the field of intelligence and has a dual sense of this world. The mind moves on the x, y plane – which I call the intelligence plane or the egoic plain; it is always feeling, thinking and choosing between fear (the negative side of the plane) and love (the positive area). It decides and senses the dual world by interpolating and juxtaposing facts and experiences of the present and past.

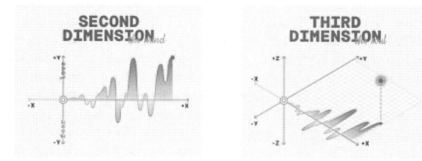

Your third dimension – the soul – is your spiritual faculty. It stands at the core of your existence. The soul by intuition tells you what to do before your mind has it figured out. It is the automatic mindless thought process that does not require analysis or deep thinking. Only with this third dimension are you capable of getting in touch with your higher self. The soul moves in the x, y, z field, being able to move above and beyond our earthly issues either through intuitive creation of solutions or acceptance and faith.

The positive and negative parts of this field are creation and acceptance respectively. The way up is full of intuitive hunches, gut feelings, miraculous ideas - creation. The way down is when we sink down in deep acceptance. Both directions are full of bliss and are divine. This is why I call this third (soul) dimension the God or "presence" dimension.

This field, as described, is the intuitive field. It is much vaster than the intelligence plane and can therefore not be fully comprehended by the mind. You can only **feel** it or **know** it. No logical explanation to back it up. Happenings like: "I have a gut feeling" or "I just know it." This is because the soul sees beyond the past and present to conjure up a likely outcome. It has access to the future.

Geometrically, it means everything that happens in the 3D field, the mind maps it down on its simpler plane to understand it. A beautiful 3D moment or movement might fall on the mind's negative 2D plain where it simply dismisses it out of fear; thus robbing you of your full potential. How often did you come to a decision where the seemingly negative feeling (almost) brought you to a more peaceful form of being?

In the path of success, there are often ground-breaking decisions that come to you by intuition but which fall on the negative side of your feelings. Failure to go by them keep you in a fix. Instances of these decisions in everyday lives are: (a) The need to quit a soul-crushing job in order to start doing what really makes you happy, but that of course would be very frightening. (b) The exigency to have a very honest talk with your partner. And if he or she chooses not to have a common path with you, you need to leave him or her and start a journey either alone or again from the beginning. (c) You want to get healthy but need to start working out which pains you at first.

Intelligence is crucial in attaining success, but don't get me wrong – much more can be achieved effortlessly when you involve your higher self. If you are versed and intelligent, you might be an expert at riding the waves on life's waters. Surfing these troublesome waters, which become even more powerful with society's dynamism and technological advancement, often get people tired pretty quickly. But imagine yourself letting go of the heavy work and strain, closing your eyes and just soaring above the tides into the higher dimension. Can you visualize how magical and peaceful the sail will be? Intelligence achieves success no doubt, but it takes longer and requires vigor to figure things out mostly. Whereas you have a pool of ready-made answers in your soul and you only need to reach within. In his book, *Success Principles*, Jack Canfield gave very useful tips on not only how to surf, but also how to fly. The book crystalizes a practical approach to getting things done through the active participation of all your three layers; try and read it up.

Truly successful decision-making relies on a balance between your deliberate and intuitive voice. Creativity hones on your connectivity to your higher self. Try composing music, writing a poem or creating a painting with the intelligent calculating mind. Or try explaining exactly where that note or swipe of the brush came from. No mathematical equation can produce creation. If you still don't believe me, go check out what Einstein had to say about creation and why he loved his bathtub.

HOW TO BE IN TOUCH WITH THE 3D SELF. . .

Getting in touch with, and leveraging the profound insight of your third dimension is not rocket science. It is and has always been a part of you.

You probably have just been oblivious to the supreme importance of that gentle nudge in the attainment of success.

A few simple ways to connect are: presence/mindfulness practices, meditation, sleep, hypnosis. Eckhart Tolle says presence can be achieved if you concentrate on your inner body (inner self). This means a state where your mind and body are still, and you are free to move up into creation or down into acceptance with much more ease.

A practical example - used by many as an informal meditation:
  (i) Stop the body: sit or lay down
  (ii) Quiet the mind: only concentrate on breathing

After some 20 minutes, you will feel the 3rd dimension. It is quiet and peaceful. It is the space where your inner voice will start communing with you. This voice belongs to your higher self. Use it for solving issues, accepting outcomes, etc. or just simply to be in it.

Other more natural, instant ways of achieving presence are listening to music, being out in nature, and every other "activity" that can put your mind in a still state while still in the body. After a while there will be no need to stop the body or the mind. One is able to be in his/her fullest dimensions no matter the circumstance.

The more in tune we are with our spiritual side, the more intuitively intelligent we become, and the better our chances at unleashing our full potentials.

CONCLUSION

Infusing my knowledge of the business game with the knowledge of presence has been a real game changer for me. I have very often seen "Aha!" moments in the lives of my family, friends, work colleagues and business partners whilst we analyze situations, happenings this way. I believe everyone should experience these moments too. Regularly returning to the inner body or simply inquiring within returns answers that are often surprising and without exception lead to wonderful changes in lives.

Imagine how fluid life would be if we each had an advisor who provided a clear objective and decisive guidance with our best interests at heart.

When we trust our intuition, we do! This is no revolutionary means to living your full potential. Except that before now, it was a fictional concept placed somewhere in space and time; but now you have realized it is something real and already within you. It makes you understand what others mean by presence and spiritualism; and why it plays such an important role in success.

Be yourself and be happy every minute of your life! It is fun!

About Szilard

Szilard Koos is a business man and coach that seeks out creative partnerships that make the world a better place. His insights into growth and development are linked to the progression that people must experience on a personal level, as well. This holistic approach goes beyond viewing what is easily seen and into the third dimension, a place where your soul and inspiration fuse.

It was through Szilard's own journey of growth that he came to realize the importance of the individual role in this world—both in business and in humanity, itself. He's experienced firsthand what happens when a goal is not aligned with something more meaningful. It usually doesn't work, despite intention and effort. However, with some insight into what goes beyond the surface, he has been able to connect with like-minded individuals and entrepreneurs who are defined as successful or struggling to help them tap into this meaningful, more sustainable method of personal and professional growth. This includes focusing on more than business plans and extends to the business's contributions to the communities they serve. The results have been exciting. Because of this unique approach, numerous flailing businesses found the success they wanted but were disconnected from. They learned what was missing! This is inclusive of the businesses that Szilard owns and has partnered in with, too. According to Szilard, "When thoughts of money no longer come first and growth is viewed through a third dimension, people grow and succeed, as do their businesses. The money follows."

Many rewarding opportunities have come Szilard's way once he changed his philosophy on how to grow on a personal and professional level. Since then every day is filled with potential for amazing things. He is honoured to be a co-author and chapter contributor to the bestselling book *Mastering the Art of Success* with Jack Canfield. In addition, he finds inspiration through men such as Elon Musk when it comes to his commitment to growing a business that creates a better world. This motivates him profoundly, as well as inspires him to offer his time coaching people with blockades - such as anxiety or limiting beliefs - based on Barry McDonaugh's DARE book, which he also sponsors in German-speaking countries, as well as Hungary. This work with individuals seeking different results is fulfilling and he's grateful to contribute in this manner.

Szilard resides in Vienna, Austria along with his wife, Bianka, and their young son. Spending time with Bianka is special to him and the adventures they have are always a reminder of their genuine connection to each other. Szilard also loves to travel and engage with people from across the globe, which makes his opportunities to speak with audiences about his passions for personal and professional growth even more exciting. With each rewarding experience that comes to him, Szilard is able to give back, and that feels great.

Also, feel free to visit: **www.MAXXBusinessGroup.com** to learn more about Szilard's visions for sustainable business growth.

You can contact Szilard Koos about his services at:
- koos@maxxbusinessgroup.com.

CHAPTER 42

THE POWER OF A PROVEN PROCESS

BY AHMED ABDULBAQI

In 2009, I was faced with a major life-changing situation. It is this kind of situation that requires a major **DECISION**. I know that once I make an assertive decision, my life will never be the same. At the time, I was an Airline pilot for Saudi Arabian Airlines – a First Officer on the B-747. The decision was either to continue my career or move on to build a new **Dream**. Moving on to a new dream means starting all over from scratch. It means sacrificing the good salary, the life style, the safety net I was living within. Let alone letting go of the prestige that came with it. That was hard at the moment. When you are single, things are far easier than being a family man.

When I started to build my first dream, I was by myself, taking care of my own life, building myself to achieve my first dream of being an airline pilot. But this time, I was not a single man, I was the husband of a gorgeous wife and a father to a two-year-old daughter. I know what it takes to build a dream. I was afraid; I did not want them to go through the journey with me; I felt that I was at a cross roads; I did not know what to do; I did not know what I was going to do or how I would support my family, or myself for that matter. The only thing I was certain of was: I would make it... no matter what I faced, I believed I would pass through and just make it, I didn't know how. But I still believe... **I Believe!**

In March of 2009, I resigned from a 9-year career with Saudia and started a new journey to reach new heights. I went to attend and study with the best mentors in business and personal finance in the U.S. I came back home to Jeddah, Saudi Arabia and raised capital for my first business to be launched in Dubai. The business was a U.S.-based franchise specializing in small business development. I started the business in the mid-summer of 2010. A year later I closed the company and recorded my first loss. It was a painful experience. I had discovered how weak my skills were – how much I did not know. But from that loss came great life lessons I would not have learned otherwise. That loss was the beginning of my greatest success.

After that painful experience, I knew I had to build myself again. A choice of going back to my old career was still possible, but I decided not to quit. I revisited my commitment to my new dream of being a big business owner. I decided to continue the journey with hope. So, the first thing I did was to build myself up physically and emotionally. I joined a fitness retreat for two months to get away from everyone and stay alone. At the time, I lost my identity, so I had to gain it back. I was not a pilot and I was not a business owner, so who am I? Why did I lose my first battle? All those soul-searching questions I had to answer. I am glad I took that time off and rejuvenated. I came out of that two months later with new awareness and insights, and most importantly, a new plan.

The hardest element of my new dream I believe was the transition from an employee mindset to a business owner mindset. The second hardest was moving from a mindset of a middle-class individual to the mindset of a rich person. My new dream required my new being. To be successful I had to reemerge in a new form – a financially intelligent, successful businessman form.

In 2013, I signed a contract with another business development franchise called "The Growth Coach." This time I started out literally from home. I started selling our "strategic business owner mindset program" – a 2-year business coaching program designed for small business owners, and started building my business one step at a time. As I am writing this chapter I am transitioning from the Stability stage to the Abundance stage, where I am expanding to Dubai serving the Middle East region.

Before we move on and dive into the importance of following a proven process, let me stop for a moment and acknowledge all the blessings in my life including the loss of my first business. This loss had taught me what it feels like to lose something you worked so hard for, and how it is possible to rebuild and succeed from that experience. I extend my love, passion and support to all the warriors out there who are making a difference through their products and services, and I am here for your support in any form you need. I salute you. . .

FIRST THINGS, FIRST

Congratulations for having a dream! Most people don't. I am not talking about a goal, but a dream. A goal is a check point toward something bigger. But a dream is a new reality. A reality that exists beyond your surroundings. . . Beyond your imagination. . . Beyond your possibilities. It has to be more about who you will become in the future rather than what you will do or what you will have. A dream is the starting point. A dream is what will pull you in. Your Dream is what will make you face all your fears, hardships, and losses yet pick yourself up and move forward. It is the Dream. It is the MAGNET. With a dream, no more pushing is required, because the law of attraction is on your side as it always has been.

Once your dream is set, goals become your checkpoints for reaching to this dream. Goals are set in a specific way to align your subconscious mind and make it work for you. By now, you have two things working for you before you even took your first step of action. The law of attraction and your subconscious mind. Congratulations! Now what? What steps forward should I take? . . . right or left, this choice or that choice, maybe this will work – if that works, it will be great and then I can do this and that—speculation over speculation over more and more speculation. . .

Don't get me wrong. I know you are smart. I know you might pull it off by yourself. But I don't know about you, I wouldn't risk my dream, my life over 'maybe' solutions. As any intelligent business owner and/or investor, managing risks is extremely important. Minimizing the risk is a must to succeed in life. One strategy is learning from other people who have preceded us successfully in what we want to achieve – people who have left a trail for us to follow. Once we reach there we can add our own. However, in the beginning, it is not just wiser but it is less risky to follow the trail to. . . **A Proven Process**.

A PROVEN PROCESS

To have a proven process in your hands is a blessing in, and of, itself. However proper education and searching is necessary to find it. We will discuss how to find such a process later in this chapter. It might take you days, weeks, months, or even years on rare occasions, but in the end, you will find it.

It is important to note that there is no one-size-fits-all process. Nor will there be one process that, if followed every time in every situation, will fulfill all your goals, hopes and dreams. There are many processes out there have been proven for various areas of your career and life, and I will not be able to outline all of them for you here. However, based on my experience, I can speak to the important guidelines in determining which processes will work best for you and what to look for when choosing them. The following criteria I lay out in this chapter will help you build the platform required to achieve a higher level of success, and it begins with prioritizing your achievements and goals, so you can work on learning and applying one proven process at a time.

So, what is a proven process? A process is set of steps to follow. Most proven processes have the following ingredients:*

- **Sequence**
- **Time**
- **Timing**
- **Lag**

These are specific steps to be taken in order. This can be annoying to follow in the beginning because our minds are not used to it yet. It is not a habit as yet. But with a little persistence you will see immediate huge value. It is annoying because our mind wants to question every step and we end up in a condition called analysis paralysis. A condition where we waste valuable time trying to understand why the steps are organized in this manner instead of just following the process and learning as we go along by experience.

---

* N.B. "Proven Process" components are attributed to Kelly Ritchie, Sales Partners.

One very important point to remember while following the sequence of the process is that the person who created the process has spent thousands of hours of experience to get there. It is PROVEN. So just follow it and you will get everything you need along the way. And once you master it, you will be an expert yourself who can add your own juice to it and continue teaching it to the next generation. It is that simple.

Most of us are familiar with the concept of Time and Timing. A note on Time:

• What can be timed can be measured.
• What can be measured can be improved.

So, your time is your development tool when using a process. Let us take, for example, a Sales Process. Most sales processes include relating to the prospect in their first stage. Someone who can achieve relating in the first meeting or first 45 minutes with a prospect is far better off than someone who takes a couple of meetings before moving to the next step of presenting to the client. The less time taken in each step indicates efficiency. I remember when I started selling our 2-year coaching program, I was following the steps and doing every step in 45 minutes. Now I still follow the process, but it seems more natural now and I notice I am achieving each step in about 25 minutes. That's a 44% improvement over a 2-year period of practice. That is just the sales process. How about if we add the marketing process, Human resources process, customer service and so on. The collective improvement will be in significant percentages and this will be reflected in the bottom line. Most importantly, you will see it in the available time you have to spend with your loved ones or investing in other areas of your valuable life.

Learning by following a new process is like anything else. It will take time. So, do yourself a favor and don't rush – things are not meant to be rushed. In life, any result worth having takes some time. Time is perceptional as well. It is how we look at it that determines what we feel. Relax and give yourself the luxury of time. One major element in learning is going through plateaus. In the process we call it LAG. Lag is a stage where you hit boredom and feel stagnant. It is a common feeling associated with plateaus. We may *feel* like we are not moving forward, but in fact we are. This is a necessary stage in moving from a basic or even mature understanding to a professional understanding. When you feel this lag, just relax and focus on controlling your emotions. The other side of the plateau awaits your success.

TRUST THE PROCESS

As we mentioned earlier, a proven process is created by people who have been there and done that. So the major factor that makes it PROVEN is credibility. Success leaves clues. A good example for credibility is best-selling books and authors. Best sellers carry with them an initial set of credibility. Credibility is shown in many ways, portfolios, years of experience, history of team members involved and back grounds. Credibility depends on previous work done, not work of the future. Once credibility is established, start following the trail. From a book to website to free services to low price products and services to more and more.... Education never stops!!!!

Once a proven process is found and you decided to follow it. . . Believe! . . . Never ever quit! I remember when I first started The Growth Coach, I had no idea what some things meant and why things exist, but remember each step one at a time. You will get there. What you don't understand today, you will tomorrow or the day after. . . an investment of energy is required from your part. Energy of time, money and effort. A little bit of each as you move on. Nothing major or too much. What starts small grows. So Have Fun.

Does following a process guarantee results? Everything involves a risk – which means nothing is 100% guaranteed. But what we are saying here is that the process takes you through your journey with minimal loss, or a better word, investment. Your intuition is required. Common sense is used with a process. A bit of personalization is ok. But no matter what you do, never lose FOCUS. A proven process always works once it is understood. Your flexibility and awareness is never underestimated. Your personal experiences are of extreme importance when applying the process. *So feel free to personalize the application, but not the method.*

Can I learn more than one process at a time? Well. I learned once, "If everything is important, nothing is." I prefer learning the most important skill I need to get to my most important goal. I would rather focus and get to my goal rather than spread my efforts and get nowhere. I learned that:

F.O.C.U.S. is an acronym for: Follow One Course until Success.
~ Robert Kiyosaki

Success is an art in itself. Success requires energy. The best process I found useful to me when it comes to Success is *The Success Principles* by Jack Canfield. It is a proven process to get you from where you are to where you want to be. I recommend it wholeheartedly.

SUCCESS IS A TEAM SPORT

I don't believe I got to this point in my life alone. Numerous people have guided me, helped me, supported me, and extended their generosity and compassion to me. The first and foremost is my mother who tolerated my nonsense for 38 years. My wife for her continuous belief and support, especially when everybody seemed confused on how to judge me or my decisions. Also, for Rich Dad company, Sales Partners organization, The Growth Coach and Jack Canfield for teaching me what I know along the way. Even now, people are showing up in my life who I believe will be a cornerstone to future successes.

Stay tuned. . .

About Ahmed

Ann Arbor, MI – Ahmed Abdulbaqi always wanted to be a leader. From his early dreams of being a ship captain to a 13-year career as a pilot and experience as a business owner, Ahmed found himself striving for a career that would allow him to be part of a team while taking the initiative toward success.

Now Ahmed is taking the next step: helping others to become great leaders by launching his own franchise business – The Growth Coach of Ann Arbor.

The Growth Coach is the only pure business and sales coaching franchise dedicated to helping business owners, managers, management teams, sales professionals and others to find success in business and balance in life.

Ahmed Abdulbaqi says:
"Coaching allows me to express my natural talents to motivate and inspire people to do what they want to do and to achieve their goals and dreams. Coaching is my passion. It connects me with people in a way that is constructive to both of us. My mission is to partner with winners throughout their journey in achieving success and fulfillment."

Before becoming a Growth Coach, Ahmed led a flight crew as pilot, studied finance and investing, and owned his own business consulting firm in Saudi Arabia. When he moved back to the States, he decided he wanted to launch his own coaching franchise with a priority on helping business leaders find more time for life.

Ghid Abolohom, who Ahmed has coached, said his approach is a provoking and motivating one. "Ahmed connected deeply with me. He focused on who I am as an individual and, from there, he worked with me on figuring out what I wanted," Abolohom said. "By raising that awareness, I found my own solutions and made my own steps to making the shifts I needed. Ahmed is a good coach who listens beyond the words and responds in a supportive manner."

In addition to traditional one-on-one coaching services, The Growth Coach offers group workshops, professional recertification credits, strategic manager programs, sales mastery classes and much more, with the goal of helping clients gain greater focus to work less, earn more and enjoy more fulfilling lives by implementing strategies to overcome obstacles.

Ahmed Abdulbaqi's Growth Coach franchises area includes Ann Arbor and Washtenaw County. The Growth Coach is active in more than 140 markets in the United States and abroad and is always looking to expand.

For more information about the company or the process for opening a business coaching franchise, visit:

- Website: www.TheGrowthCoach.com
- Email: AABDULBAQI@THEGROWTHCOACH.COM
- Email: AHMEDABDULBAQI@YMAIL.COM

CHAPTER 43

LIVING THE THREE L'S OF TRUE LEADERSHIP

BY GEORGE RITCHESKE

My exploration of true leadership began early in my career. After working for my best boss, who was a true mentor for me, I then worked for his successor, my worst boss by far. My best boss and mentor accelerated my professional growth and actively shared his values-based leadership principles. My worst boss motivated others through fear and intimidation. Under the former, my competence, confidence, and character strengthened. I approached my responsibilities with positive energy and a can-do attitude. Under the latter, I was discouraged, demotivated, and drained of my energy. I faced each day with apprehension and anxiety.

While I possessed the same talents under the two leaders, with my mentor—a true leader—I flourished. Under the leader who wielded his positional power to keep people off-balance and beholden to him, I was depressed. My experience with the drastically different leadership approaches ignited my career passion. What makes a true leader? What makes someone a leader people want to follow, a leader who strengthens others? From my experience, there are three key areas in which true leaders excel:

- **Listening:** True leaders listen in a generous way to enable others to take action.
- **Language:** True leaders choose the right words to engage and inspire others.

• **Leverage:** True leaders leverage the talents of others to create strong teams.

After launching my fledgling HR consulting business in 1993, I had to make an abrupt shift. Friday, January 21, 1994, was the lowest day of my career and the day I experienced my first independent interaction with a true leader. I got kicked out of one organization in the morning and was asked to help the true leader's company that very afternoon. The morning meeting stunned me. The afternoon meeting changed the trajectory of my career and demonstrated the kind of impact that true leaders can have on the people around them. How did I arrive at that fateful Friday? After 18 years working in human resource development for two large international public accounting firms, I started my consulting business under the umbrella of an outplacement firm I had engaged to help several of our senior managers. The outplacement managing partner utilized independent contractors to provide outplacement services while each of them was building their own consulting business, and he invited me to be a part of his team.

About seven months after I joined the group, the managing partner and his operating partner informed me I was no longer part of their organization. My consulting business was incompatible with another business being built under their umbrella, and they had decided to back this other contractor. The managing partner offered to buy my business name—I gave him an immediate "no" and left, not sure what I would do next. Now I was on my own.

I had a follow-up meeting previously scheduled for that afternoon with the president of a small company for which I had delivered a special career development workshop. After some small talk, the president told me he wanted my advice about how to respond to some major changes happening in his business. Since we were talking about changes, I told him I was no longer associated with the outplacement firm. His response? "That is great. Now you can do exactly what you want to do!" With those words, he created an immediate shift in my thinking. I had been freed from the constraints of that organization and could pursue my business based on my own gifts and talents.

He asked me several thought-provoking questions, and I realized I had been building my business to fit the talents of the other HR professionals in the group. He told me he was impressed with the approach I took to the career development project. While others he had worked with asked him questions to figure out how he had gotten to be who he was, I did not care about that. What I cared about were the steps he was willing to take to become a better leader. Within a week, I was on retainer. He encouraged me to submit proposals on training workshops over and above the retainer work. He guided me in building my business as I helped him and his leadership team navigate the significant changes that came with rapid growth. He recommended me to a local professor to create and deliver a presentation on building long-term relationships in organizational development projects. Although I was not sure I could offer the class what they needed (after all, this engagement was only a year and a half old), my client was sure, as he intended to continue our relationship!

The presentation went so well that the professor gave my name to an executive recruiter who was conducting a search for a classroom facilitator for a series of three-day advanced leadership workshops being launched worldwide at Texas Instruments. My success as a facilitator led to a series of course development projects and related events to train facilitators in the company to teach the courses. By then, I was wrapping up the three-year engagement with my first client, and my business was growing. My first client's active listening challenged me. His choice of words (language) inspired me. His recognition and reinforcement of my talents (leverage) built my confidence. Working with this true leader had accelerated my professional growth.

LISTENING: During a leadership workshop, I was facilitating a session on active listening. As I watched the participants, I realized that what I was teaching was not the way I listened at home. I tended to do more talking than listening, and my listening was focused on figuring out what I would tell the other person to solve their problem. I told my family that I was going to be a better active listener. Our son came to me a short time later with a problem he wanted to talk with me about. I listened for a little while and then jumped in with my solution. He said, "Dad, you're not listening to me." When I responded that I had been a 15-year-old boy once, he said, "That was a long time ago, and things have changed. If you want to help me, then listen to what I'm experiencing." As he shared his thoughts and concerns, he impressed me with the depth of his thinking. I realized he was much more mature than I had been at that age, and if I was going to be an effective guide, I needed to understand his perspective. I gained a new respect for him, and it was a turning point in our relationship.

LANGUAGE: The power of language is something that true leaders embrace. My mentor became the new CEO of a manufacturing company, and shortly after taking over, he made a visit to a money-losing manufacturing plant (the first CEO to do so). When he asked for questions after addressing the workers, one of them handed him a mask and a spray paint can, and then asked him whether he would feel safe using them together. My mentor responded, "There must be a reason you're asking me." The worker pointed to the can's label and said, "The mask is not effective against this paint's hazardous vapor." This dialogue spurred action, and they created a health and safety committee to identify all the potential health hazards <u>and</u> do something about them. That one incident led to a major corporate health and safety campaign and contributed to a rapid turnaround of the business.

In our leadership coaching, we guide leaders to use action language. I regularly hear leaders say, "Let's try this." 'Try' suggests either a success or a failure, an attempt that might end with: "that didn't work." We coach leaders to use the word 'strive' instead of 'try.' 'Strive' is an action word. Some days, we make good progress, and other days just a little. Yet we can strive daily and learn what will work better. We'll discover the ways that work for us.

Another aspect of a true leader's choice of words is that they acknowledge when they do not know something. They invite others to work together to discover, learn, and apply the new knowledge to strengthen the organization. True leaders are neither "glass is half full" nor "glass is half empty" people. They encourage action to "fill the glass up!" Here are a few shifts to engage others:

<u>From</u>	<u>To</u>
Let me tell you…	What do you think?
I think we should…	How will we benefit if we…?
That's a good idea…	How could we get that idea implemented?

Engaging the best of others through open-ended questions demonstrates respect for them. How do we feel when people are truly listening to us?

My mentor provided me with a great learning experience after he had promoted me to a position before I was ready. After he congratulated me, he said I would make some mistakes. And when that happened, he wanted me to come and tell him about it. Well, I did make a mistake and was getting up the courage to tell him when he called me into his office and relayed what he had been told by the others involved. I started to explain my side of the story, and he put his hand up and said he had just one question: "Did you do it on purpose?" I said no, and he said, "Good. Now, how are you going to fix it?" In truth, I had spent my time figuring out what I was going to tell him and worrying about his reaction. So I told him that and admitted I wasn't sure what I could do to fix the situation. He shared some thoughts from his experience—not telling me what to do, just offering some different approaches he had used in similar situations. As we talked, an approach emerged that I thought I could use, and he encouraged me to take action sooner rather than later. As I stood up to leave, he smiled and asked, "What are you going to do differently so this mistake won't happen again?"

And from this interaction came the learning that has helped me throughout my career: When something goes wrong, fix it twice. First, fix it with the people affected by it. Then change something in your approach or thinking process to prevent it from happening with someone else. While I continue to make mistakes (no one is perfect), I strive to avoid repeating them. Making new mistakes is part of the learning process. New learning, especially in communication skills, is not going to be smooth or comfortable. Yet it is so important. To guide desired behavior change, we use a simple framework:

- Our thoughts lead to behaviors.
- Our behaviors lead to results.
- If we are not satisfied with the results, then we need to:
    - Change our thoughts,
    - Which leads to different behaviors,
    - Which produces better results.

If I think someone is going to be defensive when we talk, then I prepare myself to counter each defense. And guess what happens? My words and behavior trigger the person's defenses, and we end up arguing rather than making progress. Now, say I change my thoughts to "when we talk, we frequently end up arguing; I wonder how we might work together to make progress?" Now I prepare by coming up with ways to demonstrate my intent to make progress together. My words and behaviors are more respectful and convey a positive intent. Such a behavior shift is much more likely to lead to progress.

LEVERAGE: The key to leveraging the talents of the people around you is to understand what talents they possess. While there are many assessment tools available, the StrengthsFinder assessment from the Gallup organization is an excellent framework. When I worked in the corporate world, the primary view of professional development was that performance reviews provided you feedback about your strengths and weaknesses, and then you developed a plan to address those weaknesses. One of my first consulting projects was to design a "Managing Your Own Development" workshop for a division of an international company. The intention was to help people be proactive and take the initiative to develop themselves rather than waiting for someone else to design a development plan for them.

My course designer and I were talking about how it felt to work on an area you were not very good in. As we talked, we remembered such situations from our own development and felt the resulting burden and drain of energy. And then came the shift in thinking—if you focus on your weaknesses, then you will have stronger weaknesses. But they still won't be strengths. However, if you focus on your strengths and strive to leverage them, then you become more masterful. As you make progress, you build up your energy and can begin to work on minimizing the impact of your weaknesses so they do not become career-limiting. Leaders can help people with complementary strengths team up and accomplish so much more together. I have a talent for seeing possibilities. My colleague has a talent for seeing the detailed steps to make the possibility become a reality. Which one is better? Each talent is necessary for progress, but neither is sufficient alone. Other people need my gifts and talents, and I need theirs.

The StrengthsFinder assessment was developed from the field of positive psychology. Traditional psychology is based on the premise that we have problems that need to be fixed. Positive psychology is based on the premise that we have all we need if we embrace our talents and consciously use them in our daily efforts. When we were working with a leadership team in a volunteer organization, the team discovered that when each team member leveraged their own unique talents, the team rapidly became a high-performance team. They divided up responsibilities according to whose talents naturally lent themselves to that area of responsibility.

People were much more likely to volunteer to handle an area because it came naturally to them. The struggles the team had been experiencing mostly went away, and they discovered they had a lot more energy as they made faster progress together.

Listening. Language. Leverage.
Choosing to work together, we can accomplish so much more!

About George

George Ritcheske is founder and President of TrueLeaderCoach, Inc., a business based on the principles in his book, *True Leaders: How Exceptional CEOs and Presidents Make a Difference by Building People and Profits.* George and his co-author interviewed 27 CEOs and presidents from a variety of organizations and shared the results by describing the ten principles of True Leadership. TrueLeaderCoach provides a range of services from strategic planning to leadership team development and individual coaching. George's strength is his ability to translate concepts into practical solutions. His positive coach approach contributes to the success of large and small organizations in these challenging times.

George is an in-demand, accomplished speaker on such topics as "Leading Meaningful Change" and "The Power of Collaboration." He inspires his audiences with stories from his experiences as a father of twins, as a Scoutmaster, and as a spouse for more than forty years. He was a co-host on the radio show, "Waking Up in America" and had his own radio show, "Lessons in Leadership." George also wrote the "Coach's Corner" for several companies' newsletters, aimed at helping managers be more effective with their people, and frequently presented "The Manager as Teacher, Leader, Coach." He also contributed an article for *Executive Excellence* on the principles of True Leadership.

George graduated with an Economics major from Dartmouth College, where he also played football, and earned his MBA in Organizational Behavior at the University of Michigan. When he's not working, George performs regularly in shows at a regional theater. He has been a judge, a bailiff, a minister, and a cop (multiple times), and he has played Bob Cratchit in *A Christmas Carol* and Pa Ingalls in *Little House Christmas*. His favorite role? The White Rabbit in *Alice in Wonderland*.

At various times during his career, George has been active in such professional groups as ASTD (now ATD), SHRM, OD Network, and the National Speakers Association. He led the formation of a new Boy Scout troop and served as troop committee chair and as Scoutmaster. During his Scout leader training, he earned the nickname "Jubilant George." After his son earned his Eagle, George moved into other community service organizations. He served on the boards of the Education Foundation of a local school system and the local YMCA branch, where he served as fundraising chair and then board chair. He is active with Rotary International at the club, district and zone levels, and was awarded recognition as the District Rotarian of the Year.

Connect with George on LinkedIn or at george@trueleadercoach.com.

CHAPTER 44

DON'T DILUTE YOUR GREATNESS

BY JOSHUA ARAGON

A good friend and mentor of mine was asking me recently what I've been up to and as I thought about my reply, I realized just how much I had on my plate. At the time however, I never realized just how much it was holding me back. My response was something like… "I am consulting here, coaching there, working on a book, running two online businesses, just started with a direct sales company, traveling for work, had my sixth child, and oh yeah, I sleep sometimes!"

His response gave me pause:

"Remember you can only be really good at one thing due to the limited hours in a day – don't dilute your greatness if you want to prosper. Find your best play and do many encores!"

Of course! How simple, how did I miss this? As an expert in business and personal agility, I was now feeling a little guilty at how much I had on my plate. Where did I go off into the weeds? And how much further was I going to go before I realized I was moving from tree to tree in the forest, and hacking a little bit here, a little bit there, and then wondering why I could never get a tree to fall?

Looking back, it's pretty clear what had happened. I work with businesses, teams, and executives on a regular basis, and talk about things like limiting WIP (work in process), trimming the fat, focusing on what's really important, and finishing what you start before you move onto something else.

Many of the high-performers and leaders that I work with feel that they are immune to doing too much, and that they can and must handle whatever people throw at them. Under the guise of being a 'really-good-multitasker' we take on project-on-top-of-project, hand out yes-after-yes, and before we know it, there's no time left for the things we really want to accomplish. The things that really matter and that would make a ding in our universe take a back seat to the unimportant and usually non-purposeful tasks.

The requests come in all shapes and sizes, but they generally have the same unintended consequence – they dilute your ability to do any one thing really well, and instead force you to do the bare minimum at just about all of the tasks you undertake. Often in the business world, this translates to late projects that are over budget and unsustainable due to their breakneck pace.

Learning how to say 'no' is one way to combat this. However, when the request comes from a boss, spouse, or best-friend, it's much easier said than done. They can really use someone with your background in the Parent Teacher Association. Your local community board has an opening and you're a perfect fit. A friend is starting a new business and your skill set is what they need to get started if you can spare a few hours a week. There's an important deadline and it has to be met by staying late for a few days, or we could lose that big client.

So what are we to do? What are the really important things that we should focus on? And how do we balance the competing needs, wants, and desires of ourselves and others?

One of the first places to start is the clarification of the overall purpose and direction that you're headed in. If you don't know where you're going, and more importantly, why you're going there, then it's easy to get distracted and bogged down in the day-to-day activities that consume the majority of our time.

Having a clear purpose and knowing why you're doing what you're doing is what allows you to weather the hard times, say "no" to projects that aren't in line with your purpose, and ultimately helps you keep focus on the future while still living in the present.

Once you're clear on your purpose, it's important to lay out the details of your vision and what the future state for you or your business will look like when you arrive. Having a clear picture helps guide your direction and allows you to really feel the emotions, picture the scene, and trigger the catalyst that will jumpstart the creation of a roadmap, the next step in this process.

We know where we're going and why, and we have a clear picture of what the end state looks like. So let's start mapping out the steps to get there. In my work with businesses, when we create their roadmap we usually tend to create a runway for about the next three quarters of work. When I work with individuals it's done in much the same way. Using our vision as the guide, we look out about a year ahead, and estimate the progress we believe is possible for us in that timeframe. We then work backwards from there, highlighting and documenting the key steps we will need to take – in order to keep us on the right path. We will use these milestones as guideposts to measure progress and ensure we keep a laser focus in the midst of all of the changes and challenges we will undoubtedly face.

With a long-term map of the journey in place, we are ready to begin the work of 'chunking down' our year into quarters, weeks, and eventually into days and hours. We start by breaking our year-long goals into smaller items of work that could be completed within a three-month period of time. We then place them into calendar quarters by aligning the larger objectives within the quarter we plan to accomplish them within. However, in order to do this we must introduce some type of ranking system or prioritization on our overall objectives. It's imperative that we have a true number one priority, a number two, ... and so on. Because if everything is important then nothing is, and we may end up starting too much work at one time. Some things to consider when you prioritize your backlog of items are: size, scope, complexity, who we might need help from and their availability, as well as the unknowns or potential risks we may or may not be aware of yet.

One of our goals throughout this process is to complete something valuable when we start doing the work. However, how we each define what that value is may vary. When I work with software teams for example, the valuable thing they deliver is often working software. This is something complete that their customer can use and provide feedback on for improvement and measurement. We focus teams on this, because often they are looking instead at milestones for delivering documents or other tasks when the real value is not delivered until the customer actually has something in their hands. If my client were an author, then the valuable thing would be their completed book, or a chapter, or a section. As an individual without a product to deliver, the valuable thing could be a subset of the overall goal you are working towards.

At this point, it's a good time to introduce some of the guiding principles that we must understand and follow going forward. As mentioned earlier, it's important for us to know that we must maintain an unwavering focus on our end goal or vision. By taking the time up front to do the planning, we can uncover many of the things that might pop up and distract us, and define a plan for what to do when that happens. We will also uncover limitations, dependencies on others, risks, and other impediments we are likely to face. The more of these things that we can identify up front, the better able we will be to maintain an overall state of flow throughout the process. It's often these very things that will cause us to lose our focus when they come up, so it's important to take the time now and work through them.

Another good practice while we are working through these larger quarterly-sized steps is to write them down with more definition, and include the 'why' behind each of them. Understanding this 'why' will help us through the creative process as we begin to implement them in the upcoming steps.

Finally, one of the most important principles we are going to exercise are the time-boxes we are planning against and that we will be working within going forward. We have already identified several of them, including: five or more years with our overall purpose, three to five years with our vision, one year with our roadmap, and three months or quarterly with our near-term plans.

We are now ready to go even further and break our quarterly plan for the nearest quarter into two-week increments, and then identify what we plan to accomplish in that timeframe. In order to do this, we must take a look at the larger items we had planned to accomplish in the quarter, and decide on the best way to split them out so they can be accomplished in a smaller two-week period of time. Breaking these tasks down also allows us to check in and ensure that they're still important, relevant, and in line with our overall purpose and direction.

At this point our path has taken us from a year or more out down to a two-week timeframe, and allowed us to size, scope, prioritize, plan, and define our approach for completing our goals. What it has also done is created a clear focus on the highest priority items and the most purposeful objectives. We connect that back up to our original desire of remaining focused on the things that matter the most, and tie in the creation of this purposeful plan. We are then able to ensure that we truly are working on what matters most to us, and that we aren't saying 'yes' to the things which aren't in line with our overall vision for our future.

I think it's now about time that we begin the execution of our plan. One of the key components of this to keep in mind is that we don't start any new tasks or take on any new commitments until we've completed the most important one on our list and carried it all the way through to completion. Once number one is done, we move onto number two and so on. By completing our tasks in this way we ensure that we are always giving our highest priority items the attention they need, and aren't allowing less important things to jump in line potentially causing us to lose focus, take on too much, and repeat the cycle we started this chapter walking through.

The final step we will take is our daily planning cycle where we take our two-week plans and break them down each day into a prioritized to-do list of sorts in order to keep us on track and moving forward.

There are other principles and activities that will help guide us along the way, however, for now this is a great place to get started and regain control over our time and our future. The cycle described above simply repeats at regular intervals with the addition of a few check-in and retrospective activities to ensure we are always learning, growing, and moving forward. As we are presented with a new project or commitment, we would simply insert it into our process from the top and step it through. It would be sized, scoped, and prioritized along with everything else so that we know where it ranks against things to which we have already committed ourselves.

That's it. It's pretty simple once you've gone through the process a few times. So the key is to get started now… and always remember as my friend and mentor shared with me…

Don't dilute your greatness!

About Josh

As an expert in business and personal performance agility, Joshua Aragon is dedicated to seeing his high-performing clients reach new heights they never thought possible. A father of six amazing children, he balances life as a dedicated father and partner with his professional roles – by applying the lessons and stories he shares with others through his writing, teaching, speaking, and training.

As a professional consultant, he regularly works with and trains clients at all levels in some of the largest and most complex business enterprises in the world, as well as smaller, fast-paced and challenging start-up environments. He was one of only 100 people from around the globe who was personally selected to be trained and mentored by Jack Canfield to teach and lead workshops based on *The Success Principles©* through his inaugural *Train the Trainer* program in 2009.

To learn more about Joshua or contact him directly you can find him on his website at:
- www.JoshuaAragon.com